D0916560

Artists, Intellectuals, and World War II

Les

ENTRETIENS de PONTIGNY

à

Mount Holyoke College
South Hadley, Massachusetts

23 juillet au 19 août 1944

DE LA PART DU

COMITE DES ENTRETIENS DE PONTIGNY

Président d'Honneur: Jacques Maritain

Président: Gustave Cohen

Vice-présidents: Jean Wahl
Miss Helen Patch

Secrétaire générale: Madame de Saussure

Secrétaire-Trésorière: Mademoiselle Bourgoin

Membres du comité:
Mrs. Dorothy Canfield Fisher
Pierre Guédenet
Madame Hadamard
Claude Lévi-Strauss
Madame de Manziarly
Henri Seyrig
Horatio Smith
Charles Sterling
Miss Elizabeth Wallace

Artists, Intellectuals, and World War II

The Pontigny Encounters at
Mount Holyoke College, 1942–1944

Edited by
CHRISTOPHER BENFEY AND
KAREN REMMLER

University of Massachusetts Press   *Amherst and Boston*

Copyright © 2006 by University of Massachusetts Press
All rights reserved
Printed in the United States of America

LC 2006003039
ISBN 1-55849-530-4 (library cloth ed.); 531-2 (paper)

Designed by Dennis Anderson
Set in Adobe Minion with Myriad display by dix!
Printed and bound by The Maple-Vail Book Manufacturing Group

Library of Congress Cataloging-in-Publication Data

Artists, intellectuals, and World War II : the Pontigny encounters at Mount
Holyoke College, 1942–1944 / edited by Christopher Benfey and Karen Remmler.
    p. cm.
  Includes bibliographical references and index.
  ISBN 1-55849-531-2 (pbk. : alk. paper) — ISBN 1-55849-530-4 (library cloth : alk. paper)
1. Décades de Pontigny.   2. Mount Holyoke College—History—20th century.
3. Europe—Intellectual life—20th century.   4. United States—Intellectual life—20th century.
5. Scholars—Europe—History—20th century.   6. Scholars—United States—History—20th
century. 7. Bespaloff, Rachel.   8. Philosophy, Modern—20th century.
9. Art, Modern—20th century.   10. World War, 1939–1945—Underground movements.
I. Benfey, Christopher E. G., 1954–   II. Remmler, Karen.
AS4.D38A75 2006
001.109730904—dc22
                  2006003039

British Library Cataloguing in Publication data are available.

Frontispiece: "Les Entretiens de Pontigny" program, front page. MS 0768, Entretiens de
Pontigny records, 1942–45, Mount Holyoke College Archives and Special Collections.

To the memory of Rachel Bespaloff
1895–1949

Contents

Illustrations

Acknowledgments

THE SPIRIT OF Pontigny arose from a trust in the vitality of human conversation. Conversations with colleagues, students, staff, and alumnae of Mount Holyoke College—some of whom contributed to this volume—inspired us to pursue this exploration of a key moment in the history of the college, and in the history of European and American intellectual exchange. We offer special thanks to President Joanne Creighton and Dean of Faculty Donal O'Shea, as well as to our colleagues in the French Department, the Mount Holyoke College Archives, the Mount Holyoke College Art Museum, and the Mount Holyoke Alumnae Association for their collaborative efforts. Many alumnae shared with us their vivid memories of the war years at the college and their encounters with the participants in the first Pontigny-en-Amérique.

We also thank Harriet and Paul Weissman, whose unflagging support for a commemoration of Pontigny-en-Amérique—held on the Mount Holyoke campus in South Hadley, Massachusetts, in November 2003—made it, quite simply, possible. Carol Hoffman Collins's generous support and intellectual curiosity allowed us to invite major scholars to Mount Holyoke to pursue with us this intellectual quest. And Édith Heurgon of Cerisy-la-Salle in Normandy offered her help and intercontinental support for this project, and made Chris welcome at a symposium in August 2002 that celebrated the almost century-long survival of Pontigny, including its three-year detour at Mount Holyoke. The Florence Gould Foundation of New York, an institution that arose in the hope of better French and American cultural ties, generously helped fund both the symposium and the publication of this volume. We are grateful to the editors of the University of Massachusetts Press for their enthusiasm for the project from its inception.

A few additional words of gratitude. Nancy Gustafson, Mount Holyoke class of 1978, took time off from a busy touring schedule for a dazzling recital of vocal music related to the Pontigny gatherings during World War II. Robert L. Herbert, professor (emeritus) of art at Mount Holyoke, expertly handled our panel on the arts at Pontigny. Abby Ferguson, Asha Strazzero Wild, Vidya Sampath, and Nancy Doherty provided creative and logistical support. Holger Teschke's creative vision helped shape the setting for the conversations of 2003.

Christopher Benfey
Karen Remmler

Artists, Intellectuals, and World War II

The mind has added nothing to human nature. It is a violence from within that protects us from a violence without. It is the imagination pressing back against the pressure of reality. It seems, in the last analysis, to have something to do with our self-preservation; and that, no doubt, is why the expression of it, the sound of its words, helps us to live our lives.

Wallace Stevens, "The Noble Rider and the Sound of Words" (1941)

Introduction

A Violence from Within

CHRISTOPHER BENFEY

If ever the search for a tranquil belief should end,
The future might stop emerging out of the past,
Out of what is full of us; yet the search
And the future emerging out of us seem to be one.

Wallace Stevens, "Like Decorations in a Nigger Cemetery" (1936)

Engagées dans un devenir complexe, réalité et sensibilité se créent et se détruisent réciproque-
ment, sont l'une pour l'autre l'occasion et l'obstacle, le prétexte et la fin. Cette lutte nous épuise;
nous cherchons le repos dans une vérité ultime. Nous cherchons ... mais ici la recherche et le
but se confondent.

[Engaged in a complicated process of becoming, reality and sensibility are created and destroyed reciprocally, and are for one another both occasion and obstacle, pretext and purpose.
This struggle exhausts us; we search for repose in an ultimate truth. We search ... but in this
case the search and the goal blur into one another.]

Rachel Bespaloff (1938)

PONTIGNY BEGAN for me with a faded snapshot, a freeze frame in time. I
stumbled across it among the swatch of photographs in the center of Peter
Brazeau's *Parts of a World,* his fragmentary "oral history" of people who had
known the poet Wallace Stevens. The black and white image, slightly blurred
by bright sunlight, shows Stevens, in his habitual business suit—the uniform
of an insurance executive from Hartford, Connecticut—seated on the lawn by
a brick building beside a diminutive man with wavy hair and glasses. Brazeau's
caption reads: "Jean Wahl and Wallace Stevens at Mount Holyoke College in
August 1943, when Stevens lectured on 'The Figure of the Youth as Virile
Poet.'"[1] Now, I was familiar with the lecture—a difficult meditation on the
task of poetry to lift the spirit "in a leaden time"—and I knew the location,
since I have taught at Mount Holyoke for a dozen years. The Beaux Arts building in the background of the photograph is Porter Hall, where I happen to
have my office. But who was Jean Wahl, and what were these men doing on the
lawn at Mount Holyoke on a summer afternoon in the middle of World War
II? To find answers to those questions, I went first to the Mount Holyoke Ar-

1

chives, then to various books and articles, and finally to a seventeenth-century chateau in the heart of Normandy. Along the way, I came across more and more pieces of a puzzle, but its full dimensions and image long remained a mystery. I had a name, though: "Pontigny." And this turned out to be the key.

Pontigny, I learned, was a Cistercian abbey in the Burgundy region of France. Beginning in the summer of 1910, a full-bearded humanist with medieval tastes named Paul Desjardins—imagine a French William Morris—would convene an international group of writers, thinkers, and artists for ten-day informal conversations, or *décades,* on ambitious themes like "Man and Time" or "The Will to Evil" or "Is Civilization Mortal?" Oddly enough, as the British scholar David Steel has discovered, Desjardins had drawn his idea for these

Jean Wahl and Wallace Stevens at Mount Holyoke College, August 1943. From Peter Brazeau, ed., *Parts of a World: Wallace Stevens Remembered: An Oral Biography* (San Francisco: North Point Press, 1985), 174. Reprinted with permission of Peter R. Hanchak.

summer gatherings from an American model, the famous Chautauqua assemblies, held in an old Indian settlement in southwestern New York since 1874.[2] The Chautauqua model—combining adult education and recreation with visits from intellectual luminaries such as William James, at a rural site remote from formal academic institutions—appealed to Desjardins. Desjardins's specific contribution to the model was his vision of the Latin Middle Ages as a time of international (and generally Christian) humanistic exchange. His *décades* were simultaneously nostalgic—for a time in the distant past more culturally unified—and visionary, proposing and enacting an international community of artists and thinkers. The mood established by Desjardins, as Jacques Derrida remarks in his essay on Pontigny as "counter-institution," was both anti-academic and vigorously intellectual, with philosophy as the reigning discipline even when the subject was ostensibly artistic or scientific.

Desjardins inspired great affection and allegiance from his invited guests. Marcel Proust in his childhood had known and admired Desjardins, and mentions him in his novel *In Search of Lost Time*.[3] French writers dominated at the Pontigny sessions; André Gide and Paul Valéry were regular participants during the early years, lending a classicizing temper to the proceedings. Later, the young Camus and Sartre and Raymond Aron gave the sessions a more political turn. Francophile Bloomsbury figures like Lytton Strachey, Carrington, and Roger Fry came as well—the French critic Charles Mauron was the go-between—along with the occasional American exotic such as Edith Wharton. The conversation was sophisticated but the living arrangements were not. Strachey complained that the sanitary facilities were "crushing and inadequate" and his bedroom, like all the others, was a monk's cell, literally. During the 1930s, Pontigny gatherings took on an added urgency, as the very concept of an international community of scholars, with shared humanistic concerns, seemed increasingly imperiled. The close relationships forged at Pontigny between German and French intellectuals—illuminated by Derrida's essay— were at risk. Gisèle Freund's photograph of Walter Benjamin walking along the river by the abbey in the summer of 1938 and twirling a flower between his fingers has a particular poignancy—a moment of meditative calm about to be exploded.

The Pontigny session of 1939, co-sponsored by the *Times Literary Supplement* in a gesture of Anglo-French solidarity, carried the ominous theme of "Destiny." A Sorbonne philosopher and frequent Pontigny participant named Jean Wahl—my mystery man in the photograph—was to have directed it; when he declined, sensing perhaps that there would soon be more urgent things to deal with, the phenomenologist Gaston Bachelard took over instead. The events of September 1, when Hitler launched the German invasion of

Poland, put a premature end to the 1939 Pontigny—the terminus, so to speak, of destiny. The following year, after breaching the Maginot line, the Nazis took over the old abbey of Pontigny as an arms depot and that was the end of the *décades*—for a while.

The thread resumes during the early spring of 1942, in New York City, as Laurent Jeanpierre explains in his historical overview. After Hitler's forces invaded the so-called "Free Zone" of Vichy, many of the original Pontigny participants had fled into exile and now found themselves in New York, in a loosely knit community who worked wherever they could. Some, including Jacques Maritain and Gustave Cohen, were employed in American academic institutions, while others, such as Rachel Bespaloff, joined the United States propaganda machine. Rockefeller money had helped rescue francophone intellectuals of Jewish descent, and Rockefeller money funded the French wing, called the École Libre des Hautes Études, of the New School for Social Research, where many of the exiles—including Claude Lévi-Strauss, Marc Chagall, and Roman Jakobson—were employed during the war.

It seems to have occurred to several of these exiles that there might be a way to resume those spirited conversations at Pontigny interrupted by the war—on themes that suddenly seemed more urgent then ever. This is where the green lawns and towering oaks of Mount Holyoke College enter the picture. The oldest women's college in the country, founded in 1837, Mount Holyoke had a long tradition of internationalism, from its missionary beginnings under founder Mary Lyon (whose grave stood right beside the Pontigny sessions) to its concern for refugee students during World War II. That the poet Emily Dickinson attended Mount Holyoke during the late 1840s gave a literary luster to the college not lost on the Pontigny participants. And Mount Holyoke had the right combination of rural remove and monastic—or at least single-sex—traditions to remind participants of the abbey at Pontigny.

An enterprising professor of French at Mount Holyoke named Helen Patch had ideas for an advanced summer program, primarily for graduate students, in French civilization. She approached her old Sorbonne mentor, the distinguished medievalist Gustave Cohen, living in New York and teaching at the École Libre and at Yale. Cohen, in turn, shared the idea with two distinguished friends in New York, the philosopher Jacques Maritain and the art historian Henri Focillon, both of whom shared his allegiance to the Middle Ages. At some point—though the exact moment of illumination is lost in time—this group realized that Mount Holyoke might serve as a reasonable facsimile for Desjardins's monastery at Pontigny. Just as Desjardins's *décades* sought to recover a vanished moment of European cultural unity, so the Mount Holyoke sessions would try in turn to recover a vanished moment of prewar international cultural exchange.

Cohen, a flamboyant man of extraordinary complexity—as Helen Solterer and Jeffrey Mehlman make clear in their pioneering essays about him—remained the titular head of the Pontigny sessions at Mount Holyoke, soon marketed as Pontigny-en-Amérique. For Cohen, the gatherings represented the survival of "la France éternelle," his own patriotic notion of an unbroken intellectual and artistic tradition reaching back to the Middle Ages. He playfully compared the president of Mount Holyoke, Roswell Ham, to King Arthur, gathering his knights in the castle keep of the college. Cohen's planning is evident in the 1942 *décade,* with its primary focus on the glories of French civilization. But, as Laurent Jeanpierre points out, it was the vision of another man, Jean Wahl, that transformed the force and meaning of the gatherings at Mount Holyoke and gave them their contemporary significance. Wahl reconceived Pontigny-en-Amérique as not so much a continuation of French traditions but rather a site of intellectual and artistic *encounter,* primarily between France and the United States. Since Wahl, a crucial figure for Pontigny and for French cultural history, receives relatively little attention in this volume (compared, for example, to his close friend and colleague Rachel Bespaloff), I will go more deeply into his achievement here.

Jean Wahl was uniquely positioned, by temperament and training, for his role of cultural intermediary. He was a master of the "in-between," a writer and thinker who instinctively worked the seams between cultures, nations, and languages. Born into an assimilated Jewish family in Marseilles, that Mediterranean port of incessant cultural exchange, Wahl, the son of an English teacher, had grown up fully bilingual, as much at home in *Alice in Wonderland* as in *The Count of Monte Cristo.* He was both a philosopher and a poet, with deep interests in the visual arts, and saw no contradiction among these vocations. His first major book, published in 1922, was a study of American pragmatist philosophy which introduced the ideas of William James and Josiah Royce to a French audience.[4] Wahl was careful to include mention of pragmatist strains in Emerson's essays and Walt Whitman's poems.

During the 1930s, Wahl taught Heidegger and Kierkegaard, both little known in France at the time, at the Sorbonne. Wahl was a pioneering figure in French existentialism; he achieved a certain notoriety for failing Jean-Paul Sartre on his first attempt at his final exam. Wahl's own contribution to philosophy, beyond his role as cultural intermediary, remains uncertain, though Emmanuel Levinas has argued powerfully for Wahl's significance as a philosopher of feeling. "The aspect of feelings that Wahl is interested in," according to

Levinas, "is less their affective warmth than a certain violence and intensity. Feeling is something savage, dense, opaque, dark, 'blind, bare contact.' It is described as a jolt, a shiver, a spasm." Such a view of feeling as (to quote Wallace Stevens) a "violence from within" is opposed to Heidegger's view, Levinas argues. "Feeling does not mark our presence in the world, overcome by its own nothingness, but marks the way in which we descend into, and concentrate ourselves on, ourselves." [5]

It is in poetry rather than philosophy, Wahl suggested, that our "kinship with the universe" is better preserved. During the 1930s, while teaching at the Sorbonne, Wahl also translated American poetry. He was particularly drawn to the work of Wallace Stevens, whose philosophically attuned poetry had far greater appeal for Wahl than T. S. Eliot, whose explicitly Christian and anti-democratic work Wahl detested. Wahl's friend Henry Church, a wealthy American living in France and a close associate of the great French editor, critic, and Resistance figure Jean Paulhan, published these translations in his journal *Mesures*. Claire Paulhan, granddaughter of Jean Paulhan, provides an illuminating overview of this friendship. When Church returned to America during the war, he became a very close friend of Wallace Stevens, who dedicated "An Ordinary Evening in New Haven" to Church. All three friends—Wahl, Church, and Stevens—were united at Mount Holyoke during the summer of 1943.

Jean Wahl seems to have made it his business to know everyone and everything, especially in his chosen fields of philosophy, poetry, and the visual arts. He was a friend of Walter Benjamin, with whom he participated in the Pontigny *décade* of 1938, and of Simone Weil. Wahl was precisely the kind of "cosmopolitan Jew" the Nazis reviled. The Gestapo arrested him immediately following the occupation of Paris and subjected him to weeks of interrogation and torture; during lulls in the horrific routine Wahl read *Moby-Dick* in English and wrote short poems. (The Germans, wrote Henry Church, "were told to mistreat him and being obedient did so.") Wahl was incarcerated at the concentration camp of Drancy, where, with tens of thousands of other French Jews, he awaited the death trains to Auschwitz. Details of his unlikely release, which involved a cholera outbreak at Drancy and an invitation from an American refugee organization, remain obscure. He told a reporter from the *New Yorker* that he escaped to the Free Zone in the back of a butcher's truck, hiding among the carcasses.[6] Scarred and emaciated, Wahl made his way to Marseilles, where his friend and fellow philosopher Rachel Bespaloff helped him secure safe passage to the United States.

During his final months in France, and a few weeks in Casablanca waiting with Bespaloff for a ship to America, Wahl, amazingly, managed to complete a volume of translations from American literature titled *Écrivains et poètes des États-Unis d'Amérique,* first published a year later in Algeria, in two issues of the journal *Fontaine.* This publication proves that Wahl's idea of a French-American cultural alliance preceded his arrival in the United States. The translations of American poetry and prose were meant to constitute, in Wahl's prefatory words, "le signe de l'immense continuité intercontinentale." To demonstrate such continuity, he singles out Wallace Stevens as "de tous les poètes américains de notre époque, peut-être celui qui a su le plus profiter de ses lectures françaises"—he who has benefited most from his reading in French literature. The translations from American poetry—including extracts from Hart Crane, Robert Frost, Langston Hughes, and e. e. cummings—are largely Wahl's own, and show the extraordinary sophistication of both his taste and his feel for the American idiom. His versions of Eliot's "Gerontion" and the opening of "Ash Wednesday" are remarkable, especially given his lack of enthusiasm for Eliot's thought; Rachel Bespaloff's translation of Eliot's essay "The Music of Poetry," also in the volume, is a handsome complement. Wahl's translations of the Amherst poet Frost, including lovely and nuanced versions of "Birches" and "Acquainted with the Night" ("J'ai été de ceux qui ont fait connaissance avec la nuit"), suggest that he was familiar with both the New England landscape and idiom before his arrival in South Hadley.

Wahl and Bespaloff arrived together in New York on August 1, 1942. (For more on Wahl's friendship with Bespaloff, see my essay "A Tale of Two Iliads.") In New York, Wahl was immediately drawn into the planning group for Pontigny-en-Amérique. At the 1942 session, he so impressed the Mount Holyoke professors in attendance that he was asked to join the college faculty, replacing a philosophy professor who had joined the air force; he also took over the organization of Pontigny-en-Amérique. At Wahl's urging, Bespaloff, too, was hired by Mount Holyoke. Bespaloff, as the tributes in this volume make clear, remained somewhat aloof from the college—one might say that she never really *lived* in South Hadley. Wahl, by contrast, enthusiastically embraced the life of the college, throwing himself into college rituals such as "Faculty Show" and attending jazz concerts and Polish dances in nearby Holyoke. But Wahl always kept a packed suitcase in his lodgings; one of his poems, titled "Return to Myself," reads in its entirety:

> It's time to pack your suitcases again:
> Your four ideas, your eight feelings.

Jean Wahl had a double vision for the Mount Holyoke *décades.* They should be, first of all, acts of intellectual resistance, the cultural counterpart of de

Gaulle's Free French in London. But they should also be occasions for French-American dialogue, sealing culturally an alliance crucial to the eventual liberation of France. So, as the Allies prepared to storm the beaches of Normandy, Wahl gathered his intellectual troops in South Hadley. Looking again at that faded photograph of Stevens and Wahl sitting on the lawn by Mary Lyon's grave, I realized that I had thought of Stevens, an hour from his home in Hartford, as host, and Jean Wahl, the French exile, as guest. In fact, Stevens, accompanied by Henry Church, was visiting at Wahl's invitation, and he scrupulously tailored his talk for his francophone audience, peppering it with quotations from Bergson, Maritain, and Paul Valéry.

SURPRISINGLY LITTLE has been written about the French community in exile in the United States during World War II.[7] One reason is that most of the intellectuals and artists returned to liberated France after the war and resumed connections and projects temporarily severed, giving the American years the quality of a brief interlude. This was in marked contrast to so many German exiles—Hannah Arendt, Einstein, Josef and Anni Albers, Gropius, Fritz Lang—who remained in the United States and transformed American intellectual and cultural life in the process. When one looks for documentation on Pontigny-en-Amérique, one finds almost nothing in scholarly works. Pioneering articles by Nadia Margolis and Laurent Jeanpierre, and documentation by the IMEC (Institut mémoires de l'édition contemporaine) archive in Paris, have begun to redress this omission. We have only begun to get a sense of how rich the intellectual and creative ferment was at these sessions, and how many significant works resulted directly from it, including published talks by Stevens, Marianne Moore, Arendt, and Robert Motherwell. A question at the heart of this book is the significance of this early interaction and cross-fertilization between French and American intellectual traditions, anticipating by several years the vogue of Camus, Sartre, and de Beauvoir, and later developments, during the 1970s and 1980s, in structuralism and post-structuralism.

Who, then, were the francophone participants at Pontigny-en-Amérique —or "Pont-Holyoke," as it was re-christened? During the summer of 1942, an agent of the OSS, forerunner of the CIA, was sent to South Hadley to find out. His concerns were primarily political: he was eager to gauge the support among exiles for Charles de Gaulle. What he found was, on the whole, a gathering of tolerant, humanistic, and nonsectarian intellectuals and artists. When he asked the great mathematician Jacques Hadamard whether, after a French victory, ethnic Germans should be evicted from France, Hadamard forcefully responded in the negative. The French in that case, said Hadamard, would be mimicking the crimes of the Nazis. The Pont-Holyoke participants were, for the most part, neither communists nor Catholics—the two intellectual strains most closely associated with postwar French intellectual life. Some, like the painter Marc Chagall, the philosopher Rachel Bespaloff, and the linguist Roman Jakobson, had already experienced totalitarian regimes in Russia and had no wish to see a comparable government established in France. Many of the participants were of Jewish background or married to Jews, but few were practicing Jews. The attitude toward religion was skeptical or ecumenical; Chagall's hybrid conjunctions of Jewish and Christian iconography were typical, as were Bespaloff's efforts to draw parallels between the *Iliad* and the Old Testament prophets. Ideas of "myth" were more discussed than organized religion.

A volume like this is bound to simplify an extraordinarily complex array of participants (some four hundred or so in all) and sessions; some of the significant figures—such as the philosopher Suzanne Langer and the filmmaker Jean Benoît-Lévy—will have to await another occasion. In retrospect, certain relatively well documented sessions of Pontigny-en-Amérique have assumed a certain weight among historians and scholars, and these by and large are the focus of this book. There was, most conspicuously, the session in August 1943 on the nature of poetry, which brought Wallace Stevens together with Marianne Moore (the two poets met for the first time at Mount Holyoke) and Jean Wahl, with Bespaloff, Ruben Brower, and perhaps Edmund Wilson in the audience. The poet John Peale Bishop was also a participant, and he wrote an eloquent memoir of the occasion.

Marianne Moore read from her poetry and spoke on "Feeling and Precision," drawing most of her examples from poets writing in wartime. She quoted early on a passage from a talk Stevens had given at Princeton two years earlier, when he described poetry as "a violence from within that protects us from a violence without." The same sentiment is expressed in a line from her great poem "In Distrust of Merits," written at around the same time: "There never was a war that was not inward." Moore wrote to Elizabeth Bishop of her admiration for the "elfin and most touching exile" Jean Wahl. "An unselfish experiment like that of the Pontigny Committee," she added, "leaves a certain memory of exaltation, and a great desire to be of service to those who have suffered, and fought so well." "You should see the tiny hemlock cones at Holyoke," Moore wrote Bishop, "and hear the bells, which clang sonorously every hour and half hour so you feel as if you were in Europe." Word spread of this remarkable occasion. *Time* magazine sent a reporter, who learned that

Marianne Moore and her mother at Mount Holyoke College, 1943. Photograph provided by Carol Ann Crotty, Mount Holyoke College, class of 1946.

Mount Holyoke students thought Wahl was "cute."[8] Proceedings of the poetry session, including the talks by Moore and Stevens, were published, by Allen Tate, in the prestigious *Sewanee Review* (1944).

Since this *décade* explicitly invokes the claims of poetry over and against the claims of philosophy—an issue at the heart of Jean Wahl's intellectual career—it seemed fitting to ask the philosopher Stanley Cavell to provide a kind of "answer" to the questions Stevens raised in his talk "The Figure of the Youth as Virile Poet." Stevens had aimed to provoke philosophers by arguing that poetry is an "unofficial" use of language whereas philosophy is "official." American philosophers, as Cavell remarks, remained unprovoked—until now. Cavell's exchange with Jeffrey Mehlman draws out the implications of the closing of Stevens's talk, when he invokes a "sister of the Minotaur" as muse.

Related questions with regard to philosophy emerged in another famous exchange a year later, that between artists and art critics in August 1944. Wahl was in close touch with several art historians and critics. He collaborated with Meyer Schapiro (who drew a handsome portrait of Wahl) and Marc Chagall on the extraordinary Chagall Bible. He invited the great Italian art historian Lionello Venturi—whose anti-Fascist career Romy Golan explores in this volume—to direct the sessions on art at Pontigny-en-Amérique. The result was the truly extraordinary conversation among Venturi, the Surrealist artist André Masson, and Masson's protégé Robert Motherwell, along with the printmaker Stanley Hayter and the art historian Robert Goldwater, accompanied by his young wife (a French American already), Louise Bourgeois. All signed the register, an extraordinary document. Jed Perl sorts out the various strands of this convergence, while Mary Ann Caws goes into Motherwell's concerns, circa 1943, as he moved from Surrealism to Abstraction.

An overriding concern in the Pontigny sessions on both art and poetry was the proper relation of creativity and political crisis—in Stevens's terms, the violence from within versus the violence from without. It was not by accident, I think, that during the war the great mathematician Hadamard turned his attention to creativity (or "invention") in mathematical thought. Donal O'Shea's excavation of Hadamard's concerns persuasively argues for the significance of Pontigny-en-Amérique in shifting Hadamard's primary interest from specific problems in mathematics toward theories of creativity. Andrew Lass explores a similar cross-pollination of intellectual and creative thought and "structure" between Claude Lévi-Strauss and Roman Jakobson, who shared the podium at Pontigny at Mount Holyoke.

Already during the art sessions of 1944 it was clear that the war was essentially over, and the end of the war brought to an end the bold experiment of

Pontigny-en-Amérique as well. After D-day and the liberation of Paris, the exiles returned. The old abbey at Pontigny was looted and decimated during the war, but the Desjardins family found a fitting substitute in their seventeenth-century chateau in the Norman village of Cerisy, right in the path of the Allied forces as they swept toward Paris. There the conversations soon resumed, with postwar giants such as Jacques Derrida and Jacques Lacan, Marguerite Duras and Alain Robbe-Grillet, making their way to the lawns of Cerisy. Derrida himself offered, a few months before his death in 2004, a brilliant evocation of these ongoing *décades.*

DURING THE fall of 2003, sixty years after the original Pontigny-en-Amérique, Pontigny returned to the Mount Holyoke campus for an intense round of lectures, panels, recitals, theatrical performances, and exhibitions. Had the memory been preserved during the intervening years? Barely at all. The challenge, for the scholars gathered, was to draw inspiration and provocation from the discussions of the 1940s, and to ask what contemporary resonance might still be audible in them. Many of the essays gathered here had their origins in that extraordinary occasion, witnessed—movingly—by many alumnae who had attended Mount Holyoke during the war years. Our own gathering preserved some of the character of the original *entretiens,* captured here in the back-and-forth between Stanley Cavell and Jeffrey Mehlman; in the extended discussion on violence between Elisabeth Young-Bruehl and Jerome Kohn (two former students of Hannah Arendt); and, finally, in the memory-work of the special discussion on Rachel Bespaloff as teacher, scholar, mother, and friend.

The conference was held during the aftermath of the attacks of September 11, 2001, and during the expansion of American military operations in Iraq. No one needed to be reminded of the vast differences separating the political uncertainties of the 1940s from our own historical moment. And yet audience and participants were just as firmly aware of a certain historical "rhyme" in our circumstances: a gathering of artists and intellectuals in a pastoral setting on one side of the Atlantic while a distant war with still uncertain implications raged on the other. That the American involvement in Iraq threatened friendly relations with France conferred an added piquancy to these Franco-American intellectual exchanges of 2003.

To capture the special temper and mood of gatherings held sixty years ago and more, one must be a believer in magical moments, a connoisseur of recoverable instants. That these wartime gatherings were themselves designed to be somehow outside the ordinary constraints of time and space—hence held in the dog days of late August, hence held in a rural setting removed from urban or institutional claims and responsibilities—should sharpen our attentiveness to moments of special insight or charged encounter. That several key participants were themselves poets or philosophers of the "instant"—including, first and foremost, Wallace Stevens and Rachel Bespaloff—gives us an extra handle, a specialized vocabulary, for this act of historical salvage. The moment reclaimed—whether musical rest or "repose" (Bespaloff) or "tranquil belief" (Stevens)—must be our paradoxical goal in this search. And always, always, with the cacophony of war in the background.

NOTES

I thank Nancy Novogrod and Sheila Glaser of *Travel + Leisure* magazine, who encouraged my fascination with Pontigny-en-Amérique and who published an earlier version of this essay.

1. Peter Brazeau, *Parts of a World: Wallace Stevens Remembered* (San Francisco: North Point, 1985), after 174. Brazeau's book includes a great deal of useful information on Stevens's participation in Pontigny-en-Amérique at Mount Holyoke, and on his friendship with Henry Church and other French intellectuals.

2. David Steel, of the University of Lancaster, is working on a study of the origins of Pontigny. I am grateful to him for sharing some of his preliminary findings.

3. On Proust and Desjardins, see Jean-Yves Tadié, *Proust: A Life,* trans. Euan Cameron (New York: Viking, 2000), 76.

4. Jean Wahl's *Philosophies pluralistes d'angleterre et d'amérique* has recently been re-released in France (Seuil: Les Empecheurs de Penser en Rond, 2005).

5. Emmanuel Levinas, "Jean Wahl and Feeling," in *Proper Names*, trans. Michale B. Smith (Stanford: Stanford University Press, 1996), 114–15.

6. Hamilton Basso's informative profile of Jean Wahl appeared in the *New Yorker* in the issue of May 12, 1945, 27–41.

7. See, however, Colin Nettelbeck, *Forever French: Exile in the United States, 1939–1945* (New York: Berg, 1991); and Jeffrey Mehlman, *Émigré New York: French Intellectuals in Wartime Manhattan, 1940–1945* (Baltimore: Johns Hopkins University Press, 2000).

8. The article appeared August 23, 1943.

I

A Hundred Years of Pontigny

The conferences were made possible by the support of Miss Helen Patch, chairman of the French Department at Mount Holyoke College, who saw that one could not do better in time of war than to provide a place where ideas could be exchanged on the immediate issues of the war, in so far as they are things of the mind, as well as on those permanent concerns of men, who, though driven out of their countries by an enemy whose weakness and strength is that he has always wanted to be either more or less than mankind, are determined to remain within the human domain. Massachusetts has a long recollection of freedom, and it was befitting that these Europeans, despoiled of all else, but still maintaining a free conscience, should be received in the little village of South Hadley. . . . In the late morning, there was the noise of army planes passing overhead, while the nearer calm of the summer air was disturbed by the trucks that came to remove the garbage from Porter Hall. All was, no doubt, as it should be; for in these days discussions of poetry must hold their own against irrelevant sounds. What matter if the speakers were interrupted? They waited until they could be heard again. Young men must be prepared for war; garbage collectors must go their rounds and bang their cans if they are to carry away the day's refuse; and poets must hold discourse on poetry whenever they are minded to make explicit in speech what remains implicit in their art.

John Peale Bishop, "Entretiens de Pontigny: 1943"

There was, however, a dominant concern with deeper things, with manifestations of great human crises in the culture of nations, with the social and moral crisis of the day. Unquestionably, the spirit of Pontigny was one of anxious hope that the cultural individuality of nations would be preserved while the national selfishness to wars and the destruction of culture would be somehow put down. . . . The cosmic exchanges of Pontigny in America, its unforced internationalism, will be missed.

Mary Goodwin in *Hartford Courant Magazine* (August 27, 1944)

For the intellectuals and artists in exile, and also for their American counter-parts, Pontigny-en-Amérique—or the "Yankee Pontigny," as Wallace Stevens called it—was a radical departure from institutional business as usual. This primarily historical section addresses three related questions concerning the "fit" of Pontigny-en-Amérique within different institutional narratives. The sociologist and intellectual historian Laurent Jeanpierre gauges the significance of this American detour within the ongoing and primarily French history of Pontigny, and conceives of Pontigny-en-Amérique as an illuminating test case of what one might call the portability of institutions. Elissa Gelfand, a scholar of French cultural life in the shadow of World War II, asks what Pontigny-en-Amérique signified in the life of its host, Mount Holyoke College, during a period of institutional challenge and redefinition. And Leah Hewitt offers reflections on the visit of an agent of the OSS (forerunner of the CIA) to the Mount Holyoke sessions during the war. Jacques Derrida was the foremost French philosopher of our time, and his death in 2004 marked the end of an epoch in French intellectual life. Among Derrida's final works was an eloquent meditation on the meaning of Pontigny and its later permutations for the life of the mind during the twentieth century. Derrida observed that all the Pontigny-inspired *entretiens* in which he participated, even those in which philosophy was not the explicit subject, were "intensely philosophical adventures." In the closing essay of this section, Derrida takes us inside that conversational history—international, unpredictable, improvisatory, transdisciplinary—discerning in the vivid history of Pontigny through the decades the emergence of a "counter-institution" that challenges the traditional forms of the academy.

For the writers in this section, Pontigny in its various guises was a kind of volcanic eruption, a departure from habitual institutional practices and rituals, opening up new intellectual and creative possibilities.

Pontigny-en-Amérique

LAURENT JEANPIERRE

OF ALL THE eyewitness accounts of the annual Décades de Pontigny, the ten-day *entretiens* or symposia held at Pontigny, France, from 1910 to 1940, there is one that has, in retrospect, a particular resonance. For Walter Benjamin, a keen observer of French and European intellectual life and an occasional, admiring participant at Pontigny, the *entretiens* conducted there in 1939 effectively signaled the decline of what Pontigny had stood for throughout the period between the two world wars: the diffusion of French culture and the spread of a cosmopolitan, pacifist ideal. Benjamin observed in a letter to Max Horkheimer that "Pontigny is visible proof that the French can no longer sell their culture, except to small nations."[1] However disenchanted he may have been in 1939, Benjamin ultimately felt a profound debt of gratitude toward Paul Desjardins, the founder of the Entretiens de Pontigny.[2] The outbreak of the war and the death of Desjardins put an end to Pontigny; moreover, as we know, Desjardins's archives disappeared—stolen, no doubt, by the Gestapo. A few months later, at Port Bou on the Spanish border, Benjamin committed suicide. His death seemed to confirm the validity of his belief that he and Desjardins and Pontigny belonged to a Zeitgeist that was not only about to collapse but also doomed to vanish without a trace. By 1940, after a last, anguished, uneasy *décade* held the previous year and dominated by talk of destiny, events suggested that Pontigny would indeed succumb to the war and the "crisis of civilization" that it embodied.

Pontigny, however, did not die out entirely during World War II.[3] An editorial titled "Pontigny Revives," in the March 6, 1943, issue of the *Times Literary Supplement,* bears forceful witness to Pontigny's ability to endure:

> The ancient Burgundy Abbey itself has not been transferred to the States, stone for stone...but the spirit of the Abbey which M. Paul Desjardins had converted into a modern counterpart of the Aristotelian Lyceum or the Platonic Academy has found sanctuary in more congenial surroundings than contemporary France can offer to seats of free thought.... The revival of Pontigny in the United States surpasses in its symbolic significance the actual debates, however fruitful. The kindling in Massachusetts of a flame extinguished by the powers of darkness in Burgundy proves that the spirit still bloweth where it listeth, however fine the meshes of the Gestapo net.

Pontigny's resurrection on the other side of the Atlantic was one of the consequences following from the exile in the United States of some two hundred
French artists, writers, and academics after 1940.[4] Although Walter Benjamin
made the painful decision to join this exodus, in the end he never managed to
leave Europe. He was discouraged by the "walls of paper"—erected by the

David Heald, façade of the church, Pontigny, gelatin silver print photograph, 1986. Mount Holyoke
College Art Museum, Madeleine Pinsof Plonsker (class of 1962) Fund. Copyright David Heald.

Nazis, the French, the Spanish, and the Americans—that rendered exile in the United States a comparatively rare privilege. So rare, in fact, that the *entretiens* of Pontigny-en-Amérique may justly be considered marginal, minor events, both in American intellectual life and in the historical context of World War II, events whose significance fell far short of what Pontigny had represented for the intellectual elite of France and Europe before the war, and which had little in common with the forms of cultural resistance that sprang up in Europe after 1940. For its part, the Desjardins family seems neither to have alluded to nor to have remembered Pontigny's American incarnation.[5]

If we consider Pontigny-en-Amérique on its own terms, however, it becomes a kind of laboratory wherein we may observe, against the background of global conflict, the nurturing and growth of a certain frame of mind characteristic of the period between the two world wars. Historians, participants, and enlightened observers like Walter Benjamin tried repeatedly to describe or evoke this attitude, which was a paradoxical but nonetheless stable amalgam of rationalism and spiritualism, of republicanism and cosmopolitanism, of scientific internationalism and literary humanism, of social progressivism and political pacifism. Although ephemeral and small-scale, the movement to continue the Entretiens de Pontigny in the United States raises some larger, more general problems of particular interest to those who are interested in what Hans-Magnus Enzensberger has called "The Great Migration," the exile of European intellectuals in the United States during World War II: problems of cultural and political identity, and problems regarding the legitimacy and survival of the critical function among artists, writers, and scientists, especially in time of war. The quest for a new way of being a public intellectual seems to have been the backbone of the three years of *entretiens* held at Mount Holyoke College.

The Origins of Pontigny-en-Amérique

The movement to revive the Pontigny symposia in the United States during World War II was initiated not by one of the French intellectuals who found refuge in America but rather by an American academic named Helen Patch. Between the two world wars she had studied literature in France, attending the Sorbonne and later the University of Grenoble, where she held a teaching assistantship. After her return to America, she headed the French Department at Mount Holyoke College in the 1940s. Early in 1942 she decided to write to Gustave Cohen, her former professor at the Sorbonne, now living in exile in New York, to tell him of her desire to organize a "late summer session of the École Libre des Hautes Études." Her idea was to assemble a gathering of top faculty members, as well as interested students, from several colleges and universities in the Northeast, including Smith College, Amherst College, Wesleyan University, Brown University, Yale, and various campuses in and around Boston and New York City.[6]

Gustave Cohen had participated in the Décades de Pontigny during the 1920s and 1930s and, though never a central figure in the *entretiens,* had worked closely with Paul Desjardins. A specialist in medieval literature, particularly drama, Cohen founded the "Maison Descartes" at the University of Amsterdam in the 1910s, where he promoted the diffusion of French culture, despite his Belgian origins. In the fall of 1940, although he had suffered nine combat wounds in World War I and had been decorated by Marshal Pétain in person after the war, Cohen was dismissed from his position at the Sorbonne, where he was a full professor, in accordance with the anti-Semitic laws of the Vichy government. While living in exile in the United States, Cohen had the idea of creating a francophone institution of higher learning on American soil. He obtained the support of Jacques Maritain and Henri Focillon, who like him had taken up residence in the United States and were resolved to participate in the intellectual resistance to Nazism and to help defend French culture.

Together these three persuaded Alvin Johnson, head of the New School for Social Research in New York City, to welcome the establishment of the future French institution alongside the University in Exile which German refugee intellectuals had founded after 1933.[7] One month after the United States entered the war, President Roosevelt, General de Gaulle, and the American press greeted the birth of the new francophone institution, the École Libre. Through the good offices of René Cassin in London, the Free French government agreed to recognize future diplomas granted by the École Libre, which thus became the first Free French university. The French in London, the Belgian, and the Czechoslovakian governments in exile funded the institution, and Henri Focillon became its first president. During the first semester of its activity, one thousand students attended lectures. The next year ninety-one professors gave courses, which were attended by an average number of fifty auditors.[8] The École remained divided for its whole existence as an instrument of cultural politics until 1947. The political divisions were the first grounds for conflict. But when Cohen presented Helen Patch's proposal to his colleagues at the École, their reaction was quite positive.

The records do not allow us to determine exactly how the summer gatherings of francophone academics in exile in the United States ultimately received their explicit association with the Décades de Pontigny. Here, as in the question of the true origins of the École Libre, the ownership claims are numerous.

In her inaugural speech in the summer of 1942, Helen Patch declared that the idea of invoking Pontigny came from the president of Mount Holyoke College, Roswell Ham. Yet—even though there is no doubt about the *décades'* international reputation within academic circles in the 1930s—it is more likely that the movement to attribute these meetings to the legacy of Paul Desjardins originated among the French exiles themselves. Many of the exiled academics had made the pilgrimage to Burgundy at least once during the period between the wars—so many, in fact, that the spirit of Pontigny seemed to hover over the École Libre in Manhattan. In March 1942, Henri Focillon publicly alluded to a "Franco-American Pontigny,"[9] thus making explicit the connection between the discussions to be held at Mount Holyoke that summer and the Décades de Pontigny. Since 1937, after many years at the Sorbonne, Focillon had been a professor of art history both at Yale University and at the Collège de France and was one of the most prominent mediators in Franco-American intellectual relations. A devoted friend of Desjardins, he had remained equally faithful to the *décades* until the outbreak of the war.

The philosopher Jean Wahl's arrival in the United States in May 1942, followed by his appointment to the faculty at Mount Holyoke during the course of the first American *entretiens,* helped reinforce the fidelity of Helen Patch's initiative to the Pontigny of Paul Desjardins while at the same time highlighting her social and cultural openness, particularly to American intellectuals. The anti-Semitic laws of Vichy France had stripped Wahl of his position as professor at the Sorbonne, and he was subsequently interned at Drancy. Thanks to a sympathetic physician and a dysentery epidemic, he was able to leave the camp and enter the so-called "Free Zone" in time to be one of the last Europeans to obtain a visa for the United States. Wahl had been one of Desjardins's faithful supporters before the latter's death in early 1940 and had even been slated to organize the 1939 *décade,* on the subject of destiny. The son of a professor of English, Wahl was one of the few French specialists in British and American philosophy, which had formed the basis of his dissertation on pluralism in 1920. Having successfully survived the extreme conditions in France, especially the widespread collaboration and anti-Semitism, Wahl played a decisive role in the quality and influence of the American Pontigny after 1942.

The meetings to be held at Mount Holyoke, however, were not at first presented as a reincarnation of the prestigious European intellectual institution that had flourished during the period between the world wars. The initial proposal rather envisioned "an advanced workshop, principally for graduate students, although some carefully selected undergraduates will be admitted as well."[10] Helen Patch's ambitions were modest and pedagogical. She was operating within an American academic context that was largely isolationist and often anti-Semitic, and her immediate task was to convince her administration that convening a gathering of refugee intellectuals was in the best professional interests of Mount Holyoke College. In August 1942 the college issued a press release announcing the upcoming conference, which was referred to as "Pontigny at Mount Holyoke College." This compromise was justified on the French side in that it was at least less "restrictive" than "Pontigny franco-américain." [11]

A Faithful but More Open Form of Debate

For the exiled French academics, the first surprise came when they learned the name of the institution of higher learning that proposed to welcome them; few Frenchmen had ever heard of Mount Holyoke College. The intellectual culture of Mount Holyoke, though of a type very much in the minority in the American academic world of that time, was nonetheless quite close to what the spirit of Pontigny represented in French and European intellectual circles during the period between the world wars. The principal difference between the new Pontigny and the pre–1940 Pontigny was doubtless the number of participants and their intellectual professions or backgrounds. In its first year, Pontigny-en-Amérique welcomed 130 academics as residents for three weeks of activities, in addition to 80 one-week guests in each of the three weeks; [12] the number of participants was thus a little over 200 at any given time. In the following year, 1943, there were between 150 and 200 three-week residents attending the symposia and panel discussions.

Unlike the majority of professors attached to the École Libre, who were French or Belgian, the audiences and participants in the Mount Holyoke *entretiens* included intellectuals from all over Europe, as evidenced by the signatures in the register, among them those of the Italian art historian Lionello Venturi, the Austrian literary critic Frederick Lehner, and representatives of more than ten other nationalities. [13] As in Burgundy, the meetings at Mount Holyoke in the first year brought together a European microcosm that with a few exceptions—most of them professors of French—remained closed to American intellectuals. Even though French continued to be the working language of the *entretiens,* they nevertheless retained more of an international flavor than the École Libre, which suffered from confining itself more and more exclusively to francophones and from a tendency to subordinate its activities to the ideological divisions of metropolitan France.

Although there were far fewer writers in attendance than there had been at Pontigny, their places were taken by a considerable number of literary critics, chiefly academics, from France (Henri Peyre, André Morize, Auguste Viatte,[14] Pierre Guédenet) as well as the United States. Helen Patch also invited several of her colleagues from the French departments of Mount Holyoke and other colleges in the region. More scientists were present than in Desjardins's time, among them the exiled mathematician Jacques Hadamard. Evening musical performances brought together such musicians in exile as the composer Vladimir Golschmann, the violinist Léon Temerson, the Opéra comique singer Jenny Tourel, the cellist Erich Cahn, the German musicologist Curt Sachs, and others. Despite the fact that most of the Surrealist artists living in exile in the United States never attended Pontigny at Mount Holyoke, the meetings after 1942 did include practitioners of the plastic arts, a group traditionally absent from the European *entretiens*. In sum, Pontigny-en-Amérique represented one of the most socially heterogeneous cultural institutions of the French intellectual exile in the United States.

The unexpected success of the first *entretiens* encouraged the French exiles and the administration of the college to repeat the experience. "We hope," Helen Patch wrote in November 1942, "that Pontigny en Amérique may continue as a permanent center of international thought and as a real force in the postwar reconstruction."[15] The French academics associated with the École Libre, who doted on associations, decided to create a "Comité des Entretiens de Pontigny." Jacques Maritain, by now the head of the École Libre des Hautes Études, was appointed honorary president of the new committee; Gustave Cohen became the president; and Raymond de Saussure, who had also been present at Pontigny in 1939, was named secretary general. Practically speaking, however, the École Libre provided the American *entretiens* with little but "patronage,"[16] while the organization of the events remained the responsibility of Mount Holyoke College, that is to say, of Wahl and Patch, both of whom were named vice presidents of the committee, and of Pierre Guédenet, who assumed the duties of treasurer.[17] It was also decided that the "Pontigniens," as they now began to be called in the United States, should hold a monthly meeting in New York City.[18] Starting in 1943, however, Wahl decided virtually alone what topics would be discussed and what invitations would be sent out.[19] In accordance with the wishes of Henri Focillon, who died in 1943, Wahl made the experience of Pontigny-en-Amérique more overtly Franco-American.

Thematic Evolution of the Symposia

The break with the past signaled by Jean Wahl's arrival at Mount Holyoke appears all the more evident when one considers that the four weeks of *entretiens* during the summer of 1942 had been chiefly centered on France. Unlike the proceedings at the original Pontigny, the discussions at Mount Holyoke in 1942 did not revolve around a central, unifying theme. Each week, two essentially distinct groups met and discussed various topics. One dealt with literary and philosophical questions, the other with society and politics. The groups tackled such general themes as "Man and Art," "Tomorrow's Democracy," "Democracy and the Planned Economy," "Society and Organization," and so on. At the end of the week, all the participants gathered for an "Entretien Général" meant to promote both free discussion and interdisciplinary exchange. But after all was said and done, the *entretiens* of 1942 left behind an impression of diffuseness, of dissipated energy.

By 1943 the global political situation had altered to the point where it was possible to see beyond the one-sided opening battles of the war; people could judge the significance of the worldwide conflict more accurately and envision its aftermath more clearly. In the light of these new circumstances, Jean Wahl proposed an overarching theme for the 1943 *entretiens* that reaffirmed their connection with the spirit of prewar Pontigny. The invitations sent out that year made no bones about the tradition to which Pontigny-en-Amérique belonged:

> For a few weeks during the summer every year, at the ancient Cistercian abbey of Pontigny in Burgundy, the critic, historian, and philosopher Paul Desjardins famously brought together an international group of artists, intellectuals, and men of letters. The discussions covered eternal themes as well as current events. Paul Desjardins is no more, France is under occupation, and so today we invite you to Mount Holyoke College, in the Connecticut Valley, to take part in the *entretiens* to be held there. Pontigny has been renewed, but it remains faithful to its tradition. "Permanence of Values, Renewal of Methods": this will be the subject of the discussions at which we request the honor of your presence.[20]

The point of the exercise was to combine the literary questions and classical problems of the humanities with the social and political questions that the contemporary historical context was posing so insistently. More specifically, the point was to understand in what way World War II could represent a historic breakdown in Western civilization. The symposia, scheduled for August 1–28, were to focus on art and philosophy in the first week; poetry and politics in the second; the novel, the individual, and the community in the third; and theater and science in the fourth. The framework of the previous year, which had encompassed very general fields of knowledge and kept the humanities separate from the natural sciences, the social sciences, and economics, was therefore maintained. Literature and literary creation were accorded greater attention than had been the case in the previous year, so that their stature in the 1943 *entretiens* more closely approached what it had been at Pontigny. Julien Green was invited to lead the discussions on the novel, and Jean Wahl, himself a poet as well as a philosopher, conducted the poetry colloquies.

As for the 1944 *entretiens,* their program had been fixed in the spring, and so they found themselves out of step with the march of historical events, especially the Allied invasion of Normandy in June, which was in the forefront of everyone's mind at the Mount Holyoke meetings. Even though Jean Wahl proposed to examine the sense of ongoing crisis that had provided the principal matrix for the *entretiens* at Pontigny in the 1930s, and which the war, whether victorious or not, was doing little to dissipate, the times seemed to demand decisions, not discussions. The stated theme of the 1944 *entretiens,* therefore—"The Crisis and Our Crisis"—called upon the participants to reflect on the correlation between the metaphysical sense of crisis and the historical experience of it, such as, for example, what the exiles themselves had undergone. This year each week was devoted to only one discipline.

The participants in the first week, whose subject was philosophy and crisis, included Wahl, of course, as well as the Italian Giorgio de Santillana (a veteran of prewar Pontigny), Paul Vignaux, Claude Lévi-Strauss, the Germans Hans Kohn and Karl Löwith, and the mathematicians Jacques Hadamard, Michel Magat, and Ervand Kogbetliantz. In the second week, early in August 1944, the focus was on literature; attendees included, among others, Hannah Arendt and Rachel Bespaloff, a philosopher who had joined the Department of French at Mount Holyoke in 1943; Marc Slonim, a Joyce specialist and professor at Sarah Lawrence College who directed the *entretiens;* Herbert Steiner, an Austrian editor and friend of Paul Valéry; and Jacques Schiffrin, a French editor of Russian extraction, the creator of the well-known "La Pléiade" series, whose friend André Gide had assisted his flight from France. The third week of discussions, led by André Masson, dealt with the arts and included as participants the American painter and theoretician Robert Motherwell and the art historian Robert Goldwater, husband of the artist Louise Bourgeois. Also present were the Russian sculptor Ossip Zadkine, the American composer Roger Sessions, and the engraver Stanley William Hayter, whose Atelier 17 at the New School for Social Research had welcomed both the European avant-garde in exile and the future American avant-garde of the New York School. The fourth week was dedicated to music.[21] On the whole, despite the desertion of some of the French exiles—for example, Gustave Cohen had left for Algiers, while others were trying to reenter France—the quality of both the *entretiens* and the participants in this third edition of Pontigny-en-Amérique easily bore comparison with the prewar meetings at Pontigny in Burgundy.

The Search for New Models of the Public Intellectual

Although the Franco-American initiative in Massachusetts was limited by ineluctable circumstances and constraints, it represented for a few external observers a significant activity of the intellectual resistance; among the undertakings of the French exiles, only the foundation of the École Libre might be accorded greater importance. And so in 1942 the OSS, the Office of Strategic Services—out of which the CIA would arise after the war—decided to dispatch a permanent agent to sit in on the debates conducted by the French exiles at Mount Holyoke College. This gentleman noted that the exiled intellectuals were divided into two clearly defined camps: there was a Gaullist majority, and there was a minority that was both anti-Gaullist and anti-Vichy. This split corresponded in part to a generation gap; almost all the younger Frenchmen, particularly those who were the children of refugees, wanted to enlist in the Free French forces and leave for the battlefields.[22] But behind this explicit politicization, which was probably rendered all the more exuberant and dogmatic by the fact that the discussions were taking place far from the main theaters of political operations—London and Algiers—one may discern the outlines of a shared utopian dream: a government run by intellectuals. For many of the exiles, Pontigny represented, both before and after 1940, the ideal laboratory for such an experiment. In reality, what was being sought at Mount Holyoke College was a new way of articulating culture and politics, creative work and criticism.

In 1943, for example, the famous debate between Jean Wahl and Wallace Stevens on the connections between modern poetry and philosophy provided a way to carry on this specific quest.[23] Since the outbreak of the war, Wahl had devoted much of his time to poetry, from the sparse verses he managed to produce during his internment at Drancy to his unpublished "Four Anti-Quartets," written in English during his U.S. sojourn as a reply to T. S. Eliot's *Four Quartets* (1942).[24] In his lecture at Mount Holyoke, "The Essential and the Accidental in Poetry," Wahl reproached Eliot for speaking about time as though he were outside of time and for indulging in questionable nostalgia. For Wahl, by contrast, poetry was a means of situating oneself in the present. Refusing to come down on the side of either fascist irrationality or democratic rationalization, and recapitulating here a set of themes dear to the "College of Sociology" (e.g., Bataille, Leiris, Caillois), of which he had also been a member, Wahl saw poetry as a way of existence that combined non-rational knowledge and countervailing power, "resistance to the degradation of human nature."[25]

Wallace Stevens also thought it imperative to understand poetry as a kind

Jean Wahl speaking at the Entretiens de Pontigny Conference, Mount Holyoke College, 1944. MS 0768, Entretiens de Pontigny records, 1942–45, Mount Holyoke College Archives and Special Collections.

of resistance, but he regarded it rather as a moral reinforcement; he was less interested in its links to the foundations of reason. In support of this viewpoint, Stevens's discourse evoked "The Figure of the Youth as Virile Poet."[26] Like Jean Wahl, the American—who was an executive in an insurance company in nearby Hartford—used poetry to carry out a quest that was spiritual but not religious. For Stevens, poetry aims at expansion, at blossoming, while philosophy elicits despair; in this respect, his conception of poetry is diametrically opposed to Wahl's. In Stevens's view, the poet's function is to construct an object of belief that will give modern man the strength he presently lacks. This object must be abstract, not concrete, it must give pleasure, and it must often change. The poetic imagination thus operates in the world like "a violence from within that protects us from a violence without." This task, despite its aristocratic appearance, is in reality accessible to everyone, to the poor man as well as the insurance underwriter; it brings into play faculties common to all. In the same *entretien,* Marianne Moore's views also tended in this direction. Her speech at Mount Holyoke sought to demystify the act of poetic creation through a pragmatic consideration of her own practice. In "Feeling and Precision," this American modernist examines the technical and moral bedrock that underlies our beliefs. Like Stevens, she ends up by insisting on the centrality of the imagination, not only in contrast to reason, as one would expect, but also vis-à-vis inspiration.[27] Thus both Stevens and Moore contributed to the proposal of a new artistic ethic centered on poetry, the writing of which was not a vocation reserved for an exclusive elite.

In the following year, another controversy took place that solidified the disagreements between the French and American positions on the question of the artist's function during times of historical change. This time the opponents were the French Surrealist André Masson and the American painter Robert Motherwell, who at the time was better known for the theoretical positions he espoused than for his works of art.[28] A former student of the art historian and theoretician Meyer Schapiro at Columbia University, Motherwell had been associated with André Breton and the exiled Surrealists during the late 1930s and early 1940s. He collaborated on their journal, *VVV,* particularly with articles about Giorgio de Chirico and Piet Mondrian. To those attending the 1944 *entretiens,* therefore, Motherwell's address seemed like a veritable manifesto of the new generation of young American artists. His talk aimed at establishing a clean break with the Surrealist conception of art, especially in its relation to society. Titled "The Place of the Spiritual in a World of Property," the piece would be published in Mexico City several months later under the title "The Modern Painter's World." The editor of *Dyn,* the review in which it appeared, was a German Surrealist named Wolfgang Paalen, who had broken with Breton and his circle.[29] It was therefore at the Pontigny-en Amérique held at Mount Holyoke College that perhaps for the first time, and at least symbolically, "New York stole the idea of modern art."[30]

At this point in the evolution of his thinking, Motherwell found Surrealism an inadequate response to the conflict between the artist and bourgeois modernity, a response that has demoralized both art and artists. According to the American painter, even before 1940, Surrealism's strategies of re-enchantment had failed; the victory of fascism in Europe sanctioned this failure, which was further confirmed in the United States by the integration of art and artists into the mainstream of commerce. For Motherwell, these proofs demonstrated that it is no longer the case that art must place itself in the service of the revolution; on the contrary, the revolution must place itself in the service of art. "As long as the artist does not belong, in the most concrete sense of the word, to one of the great historical classes of humanity," Motherwell declared, "he cannot achieve social expression in all its public fullness." [31] Neither the artist nor the intellectual, therefore, is in any way called upon to behave like a hero or a prophet. Masson spoke at Mount Holyoke about a simple "crisis of the imagination" in Surrealism. [32] Motherwell replied that artists, neither committed nor uncommitted to a cause, must understand the practice of their art as a common experience and understand themselves as simple resistance fighters in the midst of other resistance fighters.

The presence of Hannah Arendt at Pontigny-en-Amérique a few days later can be considered as part of the continuum of these Franco-American debates on the "crisis" of European intellectual culture during the period between the world wars. The subject of Arendt's address was Franz Kafka. Contrary to conventional belief, she explains, Kafka was no intellectual prophet, neither of bureaucratic totalitarianism nor of anything else. Publicly espousing for the first time the historical theories that Walter Benjamin had been developing before his death in 1940, Arendt asserted that apocalyptic prophecies are a facile reflex inherent in modernism and its ideology of progress: "In so far as life is decline which ultimately leads to death, it can be foretold." [33] According to Arendt, the rhetorical stance invented by Kafka is exceptional because he is an "unrealist"; that is, he erects models of reality that reveal the structures hidden within. Kafka calls on the reader of his fiction to abandon the passivity that traditionally accompanies identification. Starting from this observation, Arendt reinterpreted the more general theme, borrowed from Jules Romains, of the "man of good will," which provided the matrix for the dominant intellectual culture of Europe, and more particularly of the Pontigny symposia, during the period between the world wars. She introduced a new distribution of intellectual territory, dividing it between the realists, who dominate the cultural life of every period, particularly in America during wartime, and the unrealists.

Running through the discourses given by Stevens, Moore, Motherwell, and even Arendt is a denunciation of a certain kind of European elitism, whether displayed in the utopias of the Republics of Letters and Science or in the various manifestations of avant-gardism. Along these lines, perhaps, some loyal veterans of Pontigny were able to set in motion the beginnings of a process of self-criticism, even though the quest for a secular spirituality remained—in an indirect and distant tribute to Desjardins—an undertaking whose paramount value many of the participants seem to have recognized.

Epilogue

Although the participants did not know it at the time, the discussions at Mount Holyoke in 1944 were the last *entretiens* to be held on American soil. That year only about 120 people were in attendance during the whole four-week period. It was not, however, lack of success that brought about the death of the Entretiens de Pontigny at Mount Holyoke College. Right from the start, these events carried a powerful symbolic impact that went beyond the mere diversity of those who participated in them. The weekly publications of the French exiles devoted many pages to the proceedings at Mount Holyoke, including announcements of programs and summaries of some of the discussions. Echoing their French colleagues, the American and British press identified the symposia with the resistance movement among European intellectuals and noted their contribution to the eventual defeat of Nazism. The *New York Times* reported on the 1942 sessions, and after the *entretiens* in the summer of 1943 the weekly magazine *Time* devoted a page to them, complete with photographs of Gustave Cohen and Jean Wahl.[34] In France, it was only after the return of the exiles, particularly Cohen, that the public learned that the Entretiens de Pontigny had not died out during the war, and that their spirit had served as a rallying point for many European and American intellectuals.[35]

The return of most of the French exiles to France precipitated the end of the *entretiens* in the United States. In January 1945, Helen Patch found herself obliged to resign from the Comité des Entretiens de Pontigny. The committee nevertheless continued to function for some time, under the control of the French embassy's cultural consul, the archaeologist Henri Seyrig, a Gaullist often perceived by his countrymen as dogmatic. The partisan conduct of the French personnel now in charge of French cultural policy in the United States so outraged Patch that she came to regret having used the symbol of Pontigny for the gatherings that she herself had helped to revive three years previously. "Whatever shape new developments or the continuation of 'Pontigny' may take," she wrote in her letter of resignation, "may I request that the name 'Pontigny' and references to the 'Friends of Pontigny' be abandoned? I was partially responsible for the use of this name, and I know that the practice offended many people who love the French abbey."[36] The *entretiens* were never to take place in America again, and the name Pontigny was thus "restored" to France and to Paul Desjardins's family. During the summer of 1945, with the exception of an exhibition of André Masson's work at Mount Holyoke College, there was little that might serve as a reminder of the "American Pontigny," and thereafter the institution and the unique role it had played among refugees during World War II fell into oblivion.[37]

Even before the French intellectuals who had been living in exile in the United States returned to France, the Desjardins family had been made aware of the existence of Pontigny-en-Amérique. In 1943 an American friend of the family, Elisabeth Wallace, informed Anne Heurgon-Desjardins, who was then living in Algiers, of the gatherings at Mount Holyoke. In her reply, written the following November, Heurgon-Desjardins expressed her satisfaction at hearing such news:

> I was moved to read your detailed account of the Décades de Pontigny in America; almost at the same moment, Vichy radio announced that a terrorist attack had gravely damaged the beautiful Abbey of Pontigny in Burgundy. I know very few details, but I suppose that my mother was at Cerisy, and if the library had been destroyed I presume that the newspapers would have said so....All the friends who are now staying with me have come from America—their wives are still there—I can't tell you how much love and gratitude I feel whenever I hear news from the United States, which has been so hospitable and so understanding.[38]

In 1948 the Pontigny tradition was resumed once again, in yet another venue: the abbey at Royaumont. Gustave Cohen and Jean Wahl, the two principal French organizers of Pontigny-en-Amérique, participated in the discussions. Some American academics were invited, among them the Francophile anthropologist Nathan Leites, an associate of Ruth Benedict, and the sociologist Edward Shils.[39] The participation of American intellectuals and scholars who worked in the social sciences marked a significant break with Desjardins's conception of the culture of Pontigny. Thus the institution of Pontigny, revived in yet another new version, tacitly acknowledged that the general upheaval caused by the war had changed the balance of power not only in international relations but also in the intellectual world. Nevertheless, it would take more than twenty years of gradual change before Pontigny became more open to the American intellectual world and more willing to grant the human sciences an equal place alongside literature, criticism, and philosophy, the institution's traditional disciplines. Although Pontigny-en-Amérique may be regarded as a parenthesis today, at the end of the war and for a few years thereafter it would seem like a turning point.

THAT VIEW is certainly not widely held these days, when—both in France and in the United States—the history of the American Pontigny must be wrenched from oblivion. Perhaps the greatest mystery surrounding this small, ephemeral adventure is the improbably successful transatlantic migration of the name of Pontigny. To make the name *stick* in America—where it meant practically nothing—required, first of all, that there should be no claimants to the Pontigny inheritance other than the French intellectuals living in exile in the United States. The *entretiens* at Mount Holyoke were able to claim spiritual descent from Paul Desjardins because after 1940 no one in the intellectual resistance in France or in the Desjardins family imagined doing anything of the sort. A further requirement was that the connections between the exiled French intellectuals and the previous history of Pontigny must be sufficiently solid to allow the conveyance of its symbolic capital to take place without any sort of challenge. Had it not been for the collaboration of many people who had been more or less faithful visitors to the Burgundian abbey—among them Henri Focillon, Alexandre Koyré, Jean Wahl, Gustave Cohen, Raymond de Saussure, Irma de Manziarly, and Giorgio de Santillana—it is certain that Helen Patch's initial idea would not have achieved the international resonance or acquired the legitimate status that it did. Its legitimacy, however, would always remain shaky. This is the reason why Pontigny-en-Amérique expired after the majority of the French exiles returned to France. Those who remained in the United States were not former participants in Pontigny and were therefore unable to lay claim to any symbolic co-ownership of its legacy. No doubt it was also for this reason that the Desjardins family, desirous of recovering its entire estate, had to let the memory of Pontigny's American episode fade into near-total oblivion after the transfer to Royaumont.

If a civic ethos, republican in nature, presided at the foundation of Pontigny-en-Amérique, it was nonetheless soon complemented, thanks to Jean Wahl, by the literary and philosophical culture that had formed Paul Desjardins and his circle. The most significant rupture with the spirit of Desjardins and company was perhaps due to the fact that Pontigny-en-Amérique acknowledged—and, to a degree, mourned—the passing of the old-style French public intellectual, with his republican convictions and his *Dreyfusard* sympathies. There was at least a partial recognition of the public intellectual's plight: his notion of "good will" had failed, his faith in it was in crisis, and that failure had called into question the European—and, above all, French—model of the "universal intellectual." Pontigny-en-Amérique also played a minor role in the history of Franco-American cultural relations, thus participating in the globalization of cultural and intellectual life. But it still served as the theater of a discreet but persistent conflict between two national intellectual cultures with universal pretensions, one of them French, the other American. Pontigny-en-Amérique was, perhaps, only a very marginal episode in the process of opening up the French intellectual world; nevertheless, the Mount Holyoke meetings provided a training ground in cultural reciprocity, and they may even have marked the beginning of the end of the notion that universalism was to be found in one country alone. For as Jean Wahl wrote during this same period in *Fontaine,* "Creating a world today requires nothing less than the world." [40]

Translated by John Cullen

NOTES

1. Walter Benjamin to Max Horkheimer, May 16, 1939, in Benjamin, *Gesammelte Briefe,* vol. 6, *1938–1940,* ed. Christoph Gödde and Henri Lonitz (Frankfurt am Main: Suhrkamp, 2000), 279–82.

2. A few months before his death in March 1940, Desjardins was among the witnesses who testified on Benjamin's behalf and obtained his release from the work camp at Nevers, where Benjamin had been interned as a "foreign national" at the beginning of the war.

3. As of now only one scholarly article has dealt with this "resurrection": Nadia Margolis, "Exiles in Arcadia: Gustave Cohen and the Colloques de 'Pontigny-en-Amérique' (1942–1944)," *French Studies Bulletin* 57 (Winter 1995): 12–14.

4. For a panoramic overview of this exile, see Colin Nettelbeck, *Forever French: Exile in the United States, 1939–1945* (New York: Berg French Studies, 1991); for a more focused literary view, see Jeffrey Mehlman, *Émigré New York: French Intellectuals in Wartime Manhattan, 1940–1944* (Baltimore: Johns Hopkins University Press, 2000).

5. An observation made by Édith Heurgon at Cerisy in August 2002.

6. Helen Patch to "My dear Pr. C.," January 7, 1942, Mount Holyoke College Special Collections (MHCSC), Entretiens de Pontigny Records, folder 1, Correspondence, 1942.

7. For an initial general approach to the history of the École Libre des Hautes Études, one may consult Aristide Zolberg (with the assistance of Agnès Callamard), "The École Libre at the New School, 1941–1946," *Social Research* 65, no. 4 (Winter 1998): 921–51; and François Chaubet and Emmanuelle Loyer, "L'École libre des hautes études de New York: exil et résistance intellectuelle (1942–1946)," *Revue Historique* 302, no. 4 (2000): 939–72.

8. "Chronique de l'École libre des hautes études," *Renaissance* 1, no. 1 (January–June 1943): 168, New School Archives, École Libre, folder 3.

9. MHCSC, folder 2, Programs and Schedules, 1942.

10. Helen Patch to Gustave Cohen, February 21, 1942, MHCSC, folder 1, Correspondence, 1942.

11. MHCSC, folder 3, Articles and Press Releases, 1942.

12. Ibid.

13. MHCSC, folder 13, Register.

14. This Catholic professor left one of the few extant eyewitness accounts (another was written by Gustave Cohen, who invited him) of the proceedings at Pontigny at Mount Holyoke College in 1942. His views concerning the Jewish origins of the majority of the exiled French academics are, to say the least, ambivalent. Auguste Viatte, *D'un monde à l'autre. Journal d'un intellectuel jurassien au Québec (1939–1949),* edited and presented by Claude Hauser, vol. 1, *March 1939–November 1942* (Paris: L'Harmattan, Les Presses de l'Université Laval, Éditions Communication Jurassienne et Européenne, 2001), 453–55.

15. Helen Patch, "Pontigny en Amérique," *Mount Holyoke Alumnae Quarterly* 26, no. 3 (November 1942).

16. Jacques Maritain to Helen Patch, October 16, 1942, MHCSC, folder 1, Correspondence, 1942.

17. MHCSC, folder 2, Programs and Schedules, 1942, Comité Directeur.

18. *Pour la Victoire*, September 19, 1942.

19. For further information on Jean Wahl's sojourn at Mount Holyoke College and his organization of the Entretiens de Pontigny, see Wahl's archives at the IMEC (Institut pour la mémoire de l'édition contemporaine), Paris, particularly the notebook titled "Album Mount Holyoke."

20. MHCSC, folder 5, Programs and Schedules, 1943.

21. MHCSC, folder 11, Programs and Schedules, 1944.

22. Richard Lachmann, OSS Report, FR-529, "Symposium of the French University in New York at Mount Holyoke College," August 17 to September 11, 1942, National Archives and Records Administration, OSS Archives, Washington, Foreign Nationalities Branch.

23. For a consideration of the debate between Jean Wahl and Wallace Stevens, see Anne Luyat-Moore, "Wallace Stevens and Jean Wahl," in *Strategies of Difference in Modern Poetry: Case Studies in Poetic Composition,* ed. Pierre Lagayette (Madison, N.J.: Fairleigh Dickinson University Press, 1998), 74–86.

24. Jean Wahl, "Four Anti-Quartets/Quatre Anti-Quators" (1943), trans. Jacques Darras, *In'Hui* 39 (December 1992): 41–77.

25. Jean Wahl, "La poésie comme union des contraires," in *Poésie, pensée, perception* (Paris: Calmann-Lévy, 1948), 27 .

26. Wallace Stevens, *The Necessary Angel: Essays on Reality and the Imagination* (New York: Knopf, 1951).

27. Marianne Moore, "Feeling and Precision," *Sewanee Review* 52 (Autumn 1944): 499–507.

28. See Mary Ann Caws's contribution in this volume.

29. See Robert Motherwell, "The Modern Painter's World" (1944), in *The Collected Writings of Robert Motherwell,* ed. Stéphanie Terenzio (New York: Oxford University Press, 1962), 26–35.

30. This account provides an element of confirmation for the views expressed in Serge Guilbaut, *Comment New York a volé l'idée d'art moderne?* (Paris: Jacqueline Chambon, 1992).

31. MHCSC, folder 12, Articles and Press Releases, 1944.

32. André Masson, "Une crise de l'imaginaire," *Fontaine* 6, no. 35 (1944), reprinted in André Masson, *Le rebelle du surréalisme,* ed. Françoise Will-Levaillant (Paris: Hermann, 1976), 23–26.

33. Hannah Arendt, "Kafka," *Partisan Review* (1944): 416.

34. "Burgundy in Holyoke," *Time,* August 23, 1944, 84.

35. Gustave Cohen, "Un Pontigny franco-américain?" *L'Âge d'Or* 1 (1945): 49–53.

36. Letter of January 14, 1945, MHCSC, folder 8, Correspondence, 1944.

37. Helen Patch was nonetheless decorated on two different occasions by the French government. She died at the age of sixty-seven in 1959.

38. Anne Heurgon to Elisabeth Wallace, November 23, 1943, MHCSC, folder 4, Correspondence, 1943.

39. The source for this information is an account given by Madame Gilbert Gadoffre, Royaumont, November 9, 2002.

40. Jean Wahl, "Préfaces," *Fontaine,* nos. 27–28 (August 1943): 6.

The Vision of Helen Patch

Elissa Gelfand

I CANNOT think of a more propitious moment than our own to reflect on the extraordinary event that was Pontigny-en-Amérique, a series of three summer retreats held during World War II in which some of Europe's best minds gathered at Mount Holyoke College to talk and argue about nothing less than the future of Western civilization. In light of the frenzy of anti-French sentiment that has swelled in this country in the wake of the war in Iraq—an occurrence I fear I cannot take lightly, "freedom fries" notwithstanding—the words of one of Pontigny's creators, the eminent medieval scholar Gustave Cohen, ring with particular poignancy. In his 1944 essay "The Teaching of French Outside of France," written upon his return to Paris from exile, Cohen says of the United States: "This is a country where [France] enjoys immense intellectual, aesthetic, and emotional respect. This respect is based both on a hundred-and-fifty-year-old alliance that was forged in shared causes and the blood of victories, and on the same passion for liberty and democracy proclaimed in the American and French Declarations of Human Rights." [1] A historical view such as this is, alas, a sorely needed antidote to the current wave of American amnesia. An equally compelling reason for honoring Pontigny is the rise in anti-Semitic incidents that has blighted Europe in recent years. Desecrations of synagogues and Jewish cemeteries, along with the slippery usage of "anti-Zionist" rhetoric in some political circles, remind us that the impulse underlying Vichy's "racial laws" has not entirely disappeared. We remember that Vichy forced French Jews to wear the yellow Star of David on their coats and deported them to Drancy and to German and Polish camps; of the 76,000 Jews sent to camps from France, only 3 percent returned. [2] But we also need to be mindful of the striking instances of generosity on the part of Americans during the Occupation: for example, the Rockefeller Foundation helped prominent Jewish refugees such as Gustave Cohen and the philosopher Jean Wahl establish a university in exile, the École Libre des Hautes Études, in New York, and the Pontigny sessions at Mount Holyoke welcomed European Jewish scholars who had been stripped of their academic and professional functions. Jean Wahl drew on his Pontigny experience when he summarized the wartime United States as "[l']Admirable Amérique de 1942–1943." [3]

My own point of entry into Pontigny-en-Amérique was my predecessor, Helen Patch, chair of the Mount Holyoke French Department during the first half of the 1940s. Previously, all I knew of Professor Patch was the prize that carries her name and that we still award annually for excellence in French. I also knew she had published her doctoral dissertation on the nineteenth-century poet, novelist, and critic Théophile Gautier, whose rejection of bourgeois philistinism might well have resonated with her own intellectual courage.[4] When I learned that Patch had been the impetus for the wartime re-creation on this campus of the original Burgundian Pontigny meetings, I couldn't help wondering what motivated her. Why would a faculty member at a relatively isolated women's college undertake to bring together, during a time of global crisis, some of the finest minds of her generation? Why would her reach be so geographically broad? And why would her vision bridge the humanities, the sciences, and the social sciences, in an era when the disciplines were deeply entrenched in American universities? As for the international profile of Pontigny at Mount Holyoke, Laurent Jeanpierre sees its roots in the "missionary experience [that] was considered a necessary part of the education [the college] offered"; one consequence of that missionary heritage was that "Mount Holyoke students had an international outlook and a greater curiosity about other countries than young people who attended other institutions." Jeanpierre aptly summarizes, "The intellectual culture of Mount Holyoke, though of a type very much in the minority in the American academic world of that time, was nonetheless quite close to what the spirit of [the original Pontigny in Burgundy] represented in French and European intellectual circles during the period between the wars."[5]

To find out more about the interdisciplinary scope of Patch's project, I read her annual chair's reports to the college president, Roswell Ham, an ardent supporter of the Pontigny-en-Amérique initiative. At its inception, this special summer session had a rather limited, practical goal: to provide language courses for the French-speaking exiles teaching at the École Libre des Hautes Études in New York. And yet Pontigny took on much greater symbolic importance: it was the site of tremendous intellectual cross-pollination, some moments of which, in retrospect, are now viewed as turning points in European thought. For that reason, I needed to return to Patch's reports and do what literary scholars call a "strong" reading. While I inevitably impose hindsight on her words, I am struck at once by the restraint with which she evokes the war and by the sense of urgency that underlies that restraint. She writes in May 1943: "French courses have been modified to meet the world emergency. To further training for reconstruction work, emphasis has been placed on French civilization and social institutions as well as upon literature and heavy stress has been put upon oral and written command of the language." She ends with a modest request for resources "so that spoken French may not perish from

Jean Wahl, Gustave Cohen, and Helen Patch at the Entretiens de Pontigny Conference, Mount Holyoke College, 1943. MS 0768, Entretien de Pontigny records, 1942–45, Mount Holyoke College Archives and Special Collections.

the curriculum." As for the first Pontigny meeting of summer 1942, she makes cursory reference to the "intellectual stimulus" provided by the two hundred participants, "most of them French-speaking refugees," and to the "interesting international contacts" that took place. Chairs' reports are notoriously dry and formal. But in Patch's cool descriptions of Pontigny and her passive constructions about the Mount Holyoke French curriculum—"emphasis has been placed" and "stress has been put upon" French civilization and social institutions—I read a fervent statement of the department's mission at a time when that civilization and those institutions were under siege.

Another of my predecessors, Rachel Bespaloff, an eminent critic and philosopher, and also a Jewish refugee hired by the French Department in 1942, evokes the crisis more passionately. She describes the cultural devastation against which European thinkers struggled as "le fond le plus déchiqueté de l'histoire" (the most shredded backdrop in history).[6] To return to Patch's admirable vision: I read her to be arguing that French studies at Mount Holyoke was to do nothing less for its students than to ensure the preservation of the French humanist and republican traditions, and the language from which they are inseparable. The link between Patch's sense of mission for her department and the venerable purpose of the original Burgundian Pontigny *décades* comes into view: both sought to maintain and propagate French culture, and both espoused making compelling connections between the arts, the sciences, and the social sciences. What more urgent moment to reaffirm European civilization than the point where Vichy's anti-intellectualism was transforming French universities into agricultural schools? And what better way to do this than to re-create at Mount Holyoke the Pontigny dialogic model of encounters among Europe's most influential thinkers?

Professor Patch's report to President Ham the following year, 1944, makes the same case for expanding the department's offerings in civilization and language. And with the second, "more brilliant and better organized" Pontigny meeting, as she puts it, now behind her, she speaks of her own efforts that year to maintain "close touch with French groups beyond the campus in order really to teach 'contemporary France.'" Clearly, Pontigny's model of international dialogue remains central to her personal and professional agendas. But particularly striking this time is her claim that Pontigny-en-Amérique "carried the college's name far afield into distinguished intellectual and social groups." Not only had the world come to Mount Holyoke; Mount Holyoke was going out into the world. If the original Burgundian Pontigny had been closed in upon itself—the participants were overwhelmingly French—Pontigny-en-Amérique evinced an openness to national diversity. It was not simply a transplanting of a French institution on American soil; it was its own creature—international, interdisciplinary, interethnic, and ecumenical.

In lingering on what I imagine Helen Patch's intellectual and ethical vision for Pontigny to have been, I by no means wish to slight the absolutely central roles both Cohen and Wahl played in Pontigny's conception and organization. But seeing this remarkable event from Helen Patch's perspective allows me to raise another question: What moved her to provide a haven, albeit temporary, for European Jewish exiles? At a time when elite colleges and universities in the United States imposed quotas on Jewish students, Patch's gesture gives further evidence of the comparative accessibility of Mount Holyoke during the war years. The contrast, for example, with the school experience of Alice Kaplan's mother in the 1940s is striking. In her marvelous memoir, *French Lessons*, Kaplan, now professor of French at Duke University, quotes her mother: "You've got to understand, things were very different then. At the Douglas School they said that Jews smelled like garlic. We Jewish students sat together in grade school, in high school, and at the University of Minnesota. Why, we even had our own table at the library. It was so limiting!"[7] That Mount Holyoke hired Wahl and Bespaloff as full-time faculty members is also notable in this context. The "active engagement with the world" which has long been central to Mount Holyoke's credo was, I believe, richly fulfilled by these actions.

There is one last question about which I would like to share my thoughts: Why is Pontigny-en-Amérique relevant now? I believe that Pontigny puts into focus two issues that are still very much with us today. The first is: What constitutes a cultural identity such as "Frenchness"? Stripped of their French citizenship, many of the refugees who attended Pontigny symbolized one of the tensions at the heart of French history: the conflict between France's democratic tradition of equality and its intolerance for cultural and ethnic pluralism. That same debate is front and center today. It is visible in recent elections, in the strong showing of the extreme-right National Front, whose slogan is "France for the French." It is visible, too, in the widely held fear that the European Union will bring a relinquishing of French national identity. How is "Frenchness" to be defined? Is it belonging to a particular geographic location, the appropriation of a certain cultural patrimony, or the mastery of a specific language? And the question "Who is French?" informs current scholarly divergences between those theorists who embrace universalism and those who embrace particularism. Are what Americans call "identity politics" divisive and self-defeating, or is the claim to universal values on the part of certain French thinkers an erasure of formative differences? If, in the critic Lawrence Kritzman's words, some "lugubrious harbingers of doom [now maintain] that France is undergoing an identity crisis that is symptomatic of a feeling of decline," others—myself included—can only cheer on those who question blind faith in the French republican myth of assimilation.[8]

The other issue that Pontigny's participants wrestled with and that remains contested is the role of the artist or writer in relation to public and political life. The important figures who met here in the 1940s did not just debate the question of literary and artistic engagement; they embodied it. Despite their ideological differences, they all engaged in intellectual resistance to what Jean-Paul Sartre called the "extreme situation" of the Occupation. Pontigny can be seen as a site where, in Laurent Jeanpierre's words, "the intellectual's exteriority in relation to society was put into question."[9] No longer able to remain above the fray, she or he—through the immense ethical potential of art, literature, philosophy, and scientific inquiry—had to take a stand. The same problem finds itself conceptualized somewhat differently in France today. Thanks to the legacy of the political upheavals of May 1968 and the influence of feminist and postcolonial thought, all knowledge is seen as local; the writer, artist, or scientist cannot claim to step outside his or her conceptual framework. And it is precisely as this kind of "specialist" of local knowledge—the sociologist and social critic Pierre Bourdieu is perhaps the best-known example—

that the intellectual now engages with political issues and the public memory that ties the present to the past.

I end by drawing on a study that, in my view, helps illuminate Pontigny's significance. I have recently had the pleasure of reading Christopher Benfey's splendid narrative of nineteenth-century cultural reciprocities between Japan and America, *The Great Wave*. In his epilogue, he brings together the ideas of preeminent writers, artists, and critics from several continents, in the crucial year 1913. These thinkers display powerful intellectual convergences, even some extraordinary revelations—for example, that Shuzo Kuki foreshadowed Sartrean existentialism by several decades, or that Albert Camus, in his *Myth of Sisyphus,* may have come close to plagiarizing Kuki. It was in the early years of Pontigny in Burgundy that some of those convergences emerged. What joined these diverse artists and writers, as *The Great Wave* deftly shows, was their shared "overmastering sense of [the] precariousness and impending peril" of their respective cultures at certain key moments.[10] If we click forward thirty years to Pontigny-en-Amérique, we find similar transnational reciprocities and, once again, a common sense of urgency about cultural extinction. Precisely because both Pontignys embraced that "impending peril," our collective intellectual life is all the richer.

NOTES

1. Gustave Cohen, "L'enseignement français hors de France" in *L'oeuvre de la Troisième République,* ed. Jean Benoît-Lévy (Montreal: Éditions de l'Arbre, 1945), 270.

2. The most authoritative study of France's treatment of Jews during the Occupation remains Michael R. Marrus and Robert O. Paxton, *Vichy France and the Jews* (New York: Basic Books, 1981).

3. Wahl is quoted by Monique Jutrin in her recent edition of Rachel Bespaloff's *Lettres à Jean Wahl, 1937–1947* (Paris: Éditions Claire Paulhan, 2003), 33.

4. Helen E. Patch, "The Dramatic Criticism of Théophile Gautier" (Ph.D. diss., Bryn Mawr College, 1922).

5. See the essay by Laurent Jeanpierre in this volume.

6. This phrase begins an unpublished article by Bespaloff, "La poésie de Jean Wahl," cited in Jutrin, *Lettres,* 12. Jutrin reproduces Bepaloff's article in its entirety, 129–36.

7. Alice Kaplan, *French Lessons: A Memoir* (Chicago: University of Chicago Press, 1993), 7.

8. Lawrence D. Kritzman, "France, Culture, and the Idea of the Nation," in *French Cultural Studies: Criticism at the Crossroads,* ed. Marie-Pierre Le Hir and Dana Strand (Albany: State University of New York Press, 2000), 11.

9. See the essay by Jeanpierre in this volume.

10. Christopher Benfey, *The Great Wave: Gilded Age Misfits, Japanese Eccentrics, and the Opening of Old Japan* (New York: Random House, 2003), xviii.

The OSS Pays a Visit

Leah D. Hewitt

IN RETHINKING FRANCE's identities through the memory of its interactions with its various "others," inside and outside of France, I note that the Mount Holyoke celebration calls attention to the interplay between margin and center, of French intellectuals and artists decentered or marginalized by the war striving to make Mount Holyoke, between 1942 and 1944, a new "marginal center," if you will. I am not sure, however, who is the center and who the margin, the French or the Americans, in this context. I think that while all were discussing emerging trends, new forms of creativity, new forms of art, and new ways of understanding human cultures, they were also reflecting on new ways of thinking about themselves and one another in a global, political context. As we look back on this slice of the past, we may note the Janus-like pose of the French participants: while preparing for the future, debating new possibilities of thought and action as they awaited the end of the war, many of them were also setting about rescuing the traditions of the French Republic before Vichy in order to create a new postwar republican France. In 1945, *L'oeuvre de la Troisième République* (The Work of the Third Republic) came out with essays by many of the Pontigny participants: Boris Mirkine-Guetzevitch on French politics, Paul Vignaux on workers' movements; Jean Benoît-Lévy, the filmmaker, wrote on the social work of the Third Republic; Jacques Hadamard, the mathematician, wrote on education; Gustave Cohen on French teaching outside France, and so on. In 1946 another work, titled *Esquisse de la France* (Sketch of France), also featured Pontigny participants' contributions in defining France. One may well wonder if being outside France in South Hadley provided a fresh context in which to think about what France was and would become. Concurrently we may wonder whether the Americans' interaction with the French offered the former a decentering perspective too.

The celebration of Pontigny-en-Amérique certainly seems to fit Pierre Nora's description of a "lieu de mémoire," or "site of memory." "*Lieux de mémoire,*" Nora says, "are complex things. At once natural and artificial, simple and ambiguous, concrete and abstract, they are *lieux*—places, sites, causes—in three senses: material, symbolic, and functional....*Lieux de mémoire* are created by the interaction between memory and history, an interaction resulting in a mutual overdetermination."[1] And *lieux de mémoire,* Nora adds, are "hybrid places" that "thrive only because of their capacity for change, their ability to resurrect old meanings and generate new ones along with new and unforeseeable connections (that is what make them exciting)."[2] Pontigny-en-Amérique evokes just such a hybrid site, bringing France to the United States with an international cast of characters.

I would like to concentrate for a moment on the material aspect of the *lieu de mémoire* as it resides in its archival traces. The once secret report from the Office of Strategic Services (the forerunner of the CIA) about the original Mount Holyoke gatherings can perhaps provide us with an example of an archival overdetermination in its connections with the present. As I read through this OSS report, I couldn't help but wonder in what guise the OSS agent appeared as he took copious notes on what was said during the Mount Holyoke encounters. Of course, history tells us that the OSS included a substantial number of leftist university teachers and intellectuals (including such notables as Herbert Marcuse), so the political perspective of the agent was probably close to that of many of the intellectuals visiting Mount Holyoke. Nevertheless, I couldn't help but imagine the OSS agent as a trenchcoated figure with dark glasses writing furiously in his black notebook about the theater of the Middle Ages, or creativity in mathematics, sorting through the talks and debates to ascertain who was pro– or anti–de Gaulle, who forgave the Germans, who had had to flee France in the nick of time…The author of the OSS report notes with some surprise that it was the French participants who seemed more like the hosts than their American counterparts, thus confirming our notion that the ambiguous question of center and margins is pertinent to Pontigny-en-Amérique.

The OSS report is candid and thoughtful, sometimes amusing, straightforward and yet puzzling. What kinds of information was the agent trying to glean? Was he a historian, as were many OSS officers in high positions? For us now, the "spy" report has paradoxically become one of the key materials to commemorate the event, especially given the fact that many of the talks and exchanges have been lost. Although we don't know the report's original intent, the result of this secret information-gathering has, with time, become a historical account of Mount Holyoke's Pontigny.

It is also interesting to note that the OSS did not last much longer than the Pontigny-en-Amérique gatherings. The OSS began in June 1942 and was dismantled in 1945, so, like Pontigny-en-Amérique, it did not survive the war. Given our current political context, and the recent French-American tensions, one wonders if some day in the future a secret account of the commemoration of Pontigny-en-Amérique might surface from the Department of Homeland Security, adding another version of our activities.

NOTES

1. Pierre Nora, *Realms of Memory: Rethinking the French Past,* vol. 1, *Conflicts and Divisions,* trans. Arthur Goldhammer (New York: Columbia University Press, 1996), 14.

2. Ibid., 15.

The Philosophical Model of a Counter-Institution

Jacques Derrida

ALTHOUGH THIS SESSION is devoted or restricted to philosophy, to the established and statutory discipline named "philosophy," recognized and designated as such, I believe it legitimate to posit that all the *décades* in which I have participated—even when their title or name gestured in the direction of literature or poetry—were also fully and unreservedly philosophical moments, intensely philosophical adventures that were at times as worthy of "philosophy" as any one of a number of such *décades* that might more legitimately lay claim to the title.[1] This stipulation is important to me, to limit myself to the instances to which I can bear personal witness, in the case of works whose most conventional rubric would be literature, poetry, or theater, such as those of Francis Ponge, Jean Genet, and Hélène Cixous. Those three *décades* (and no doubt still others which are less familiar to me) were also of great richness and great daring in philosophical thought, in the invention of a philosophical language; and beyond my memory, I hope that their publication attests to as much as well. Inversely, regarding those *décades* whose expressly philosophical thematic may be more readily acknowledged (those of which I shall speak here), they were also traversed by interrogations, incursions, excursions, and analogies that were not recognized, according to the legitimate conventions and the institution of academic disciplines, as "philosophical." I insist on that richness and that freedom in the crossing of disciplinary or academic borders because they seem to me to be specific to what I shall call the "counter-institutional experience" of Cerisy.

What, then, is the counter-institutional experience of Cerisy?

"Experience," in this case, will mean, in a word, two or three things:

First, that one has to have undergone the experience in order to understand what is in question here: one has to be here, now, on these premises, in the château, and during the rhythmic progression of a *décade* in order to accede to the unique reality we are discussing. Since Pontigny, ever since Paul Desjardins had decided that there would be no publication of the proceedings of the colloquia, conversations, exchanges, debates (which nonetheless already had the institutional singularity of being neither private nor public, neither secret

nor disseminated by the media), there has been, to be sure, an immense transformation, shifts even in the methods of archiving and publishing the events
of Cerisy (recording—the first time it was granted me to hear Heidegger's
voice carried all the way to the rue de Boulainvilliers, Paris—sound or visual
recording, then publication according to increasingly diversified modes, and
if the IMEC [Institut mémoires de l'édition contemporaine] is intimately associated with these days, it is precisely because of those changes that constitute
the history, the past, and the open future of Cerisy); but never will these shifts
in techniques of archiving and publication have succeeded, nor should they,
in placing in doubt the unique and irreplaceable *experience* (what I am calling, in a first meaning, "experience") that brings together the participants—I
was about to say the actors—in a manner at once prescribed and unpredictable, during ten days in the same place. There has never been and, I hope,
there will never be a teleconference or a *tele-décade* in Cerisy or from Cerisy.
But those who have had the responsibility and the wisdom to orient Cerisy in
this manner, those who have had the experience of this experience, will have
succeeded in implementing, and will continue to do so, the best possible
transaction between the live, risky, and unpredictable experience of an encounter "here and now" and the calculable contexts of programming, archiving, and publishing, in France and in the world, with the help of the most
advanced technologies (e-mail, Internet), without ever abandoning the classic
supports of the book. Naturally that very practice, this strategy of transaction
between the encounter (the *décade* strictly speaking), in its technical minimality (since the language of a communication already entails, to be sure, in
its very grammar, a measure of *technè,* there never being a pure improvisation,
and there is an order in the meetings, which is why I speak of a technical minimality of the *décade*), in this strategy of transaction, then, between the technical minimality of the encounter, between the *décade* itself and the technological
maximum or optimum of all its trajectories, those leading to the *décade* and
those following in its wake (programming, archiving, publication), there is a
whole politics and a whole philosophy, already, and since Pontigny; there is in
it a philosophical history, a transformation that presupposes simultaneously a
faithfulness to the spirit of Pontigny, to its implicit charter, and an equally
controlled unfaithfulness, an unfaithfulness as faithful as possible to the spirit
and to the letter, if it can be said, of the unwritten charter.

I WILL NOT engage on this occasion the great metaphysical problem of presence and the living voice that has concerned me for my whole life; and it is not
in the name of the privilege of presence and the living voice that I am referring here to the irreplaceable *experience* of place and time, of the here-and-

now of the château, from north to south, from the library and granary to the cellar, and of the cadence of ten days, nor even in the name of the gathering and the proximity of dialogue and speech addressed to the other. No, it is because, on the contrary, that unique experience of an encounter in an irreplaceable place and time augments and seals the chances of the incalculable, of improvisation and the unpredictable. Even if one can anticipate many things, one never knows truly, totally, what, in the future, is *going* to happen when one *comes* to Cerisy; one comes, as well, without knowing where one is going and what is going to happen—and that is the experience: when one comes, one doesn't know everything that is going to occur, and when one arrives or when one is going to come, one does not know all that is about to come, nor even *who,* for that matter: one truly knows neither who nor what. This indeterminacy is, to be sure, something that one feels always and everywhere, and in particular each time one goes to a colloquium in a public space, but it is more pronounced when one comes to Cerisy than when one goes to one or another symposium. For here, at Cerisy, one knows that one is going to isolate oneself in a kind of community, comfortably, for a rather long time. (It is already a kind of retreat, an exit from the world, with a vaguely religious or monastic connotation, as if one had taken a kind of vow, and those who, like me, come back often to Cerisy have the vaguely amused, complicitous, and deliciously ironic sense of belonging with total freedom to a secular order, to a congregation that is more philosophical than religious, in which transgression, above all a transgression of the vow of silence, would be the rule, a counter-regulation that I have always taken it to heart to observe for as long as possible. Those religious connotations are not extrinsic and superficial, and at bottom the debate between religion and philosophy remains, from Pontigny to Cerisy; one could demonstrate as much if one were to study it in depth, the heartbeat, the respiration and pulsation, the very pulse of Cerisy.) When one comes to Cerisy, then, one knows that one is going, for a fairly long time, to share the existence of so many others (at times as many as a hundred), in a manner both intimate and distant despite the proximity, in a kind of tension between community and solitude, a tension whose intensity is for me without other example. One is aware, then, that one is going simultaneously to live quite close to and very far from friends one has known well and for a long time, others whom one knows slightly and has met only recently, others whom one has never met, and who, all of them and in any event, are going to say and do unpredictable things that will touch you intimately, incalculably. (Concerning "touching," without subjecting you still again to a philosophical disquisition on touching, I recall what was said to me barely more than a month ago, right here, during the July *décade,* by a Portuguese colleague and friend whom I had never met previously; that remarkable philosopher was sensitive, vulnerable, extremely timid, of uncommon discretion, and even during her presentation, she never raised her voice above a murmur; now at the end of the *décade,* and even as she told me how happy she had been to be part of it, she communicated her surprise at the facility with which people here, she said, "touched one another"—that was her word to describe the familiarity, familial effusions of all those friends embracing one another every morning at breakfast, men and women, sometimes even between men, holding each other by the waist or the neck as they were photographed.) One thus never knows what or whom to expect, because of the tension between a warm, intimate closeness and an abyss of solitude, dispersion; but also, and above all, one does not at all know what is going to be said, and consequently what one will be called on to experience and do, accept or contest in the course of "Cerisy days," in this spot which is at once more open and more closed than any other, where the greatest freedom is promised within the risk of a delectable enclosure. I say "Cerisy days" in order to indicate that if there is a unity to the *décade* (the ten days), there are also the individual days, *les journées,* with everything with which that word can be invested, the rhythmic unity of the time of day, of time in the sense of the time granted and indicated by the tolling of the bell, the variations of the weather *(temps),* of the journey to Cerisy; and each day has its essence, its signature, as does each *décade.* The last time I came here, last July—it was about the tenth time—every morning, between six and seven in the morning, as I walked more or less alone, before the first bell, between the Orangerie and the château, I appealed to my memory, at times without success, at times thanking the gods for the grace they accorded me: I attempted to let myself be infused with the essential flavor, the original and irreplaceable feeling of each *décade,* by the taste or unique essence of each *décade* (the word *décade* itself, moreover, has an aura which it owes entirely to Cerisy; it would have deserted the French language, the idiom would have fallen into disuse were it not for Cerisy—such is one of the numerous services that this international institution will have rendered to the culture and traditions of this country); but I tried to make my memory receptive to something like a philosophical truth of each *décade,* a meaning, a teaching, an adventure of thought at once palpable and intelligible and which could be reduced not to the philosophical content of what was said, the themes and problems debated, but to something more affective, more tenacious, more inward, at once unsayable and even unthinkable, but which would have counted in the experience of thought—and which was inseparable from the specific individuals, the names of those whom we crossed paths with here. I know (we all know) that something is repeated and has not changed at Cerisy, in any event not for me, at least since 1959, the date of my first visit (the walls haven't changed, nor the library, nor so many other places which remain impassively what they were, like certain rituals to be respected and left untouched), and yet no *décade* resembles any other. The unpredictable is always on the agenda of what is to be celebrated. Incalculably. Because one never knows, in the future, what is *going* to happen when one comes to Cerisy; one comes there—in any event, I always come there—with a feeling whose chemistry, or rather whose alchemy, is rather difficult to analyze: the happy and childlike, even jubilatory impatience with which one awaits the celebration is imbued with a certain anxiety, above all as it was on several occasions my fortune, when one occupies a slightly privileged and thus overexposed place in the *décade.* Whereupon one wonders, as before trying a soft or hard philosophical drug: What is going to happen? What more is going to happen to me?

BUT I AM simplifying when I say that one does not know what is *going* to happen in the future. One doesn't know either what *is happening* in the present. For all is not presented, nor does it occur in the assembled presence of the organized sessions, but occasionally as well in the asides, in what might be called the comings and goings, the cross-comings and goings of Cerisy, in the course of private (if not secret) encounters and discussions which are never collected and published. One thus never knows what is going to happen, nor does one know what is happening in the present, which remains in large part unpresentable. But neither does one know, sometimes long afterwards, sometimes never, what *did happen*, what *will have happened*, in the past or in the future anterior. To restrict myself to philosophy, one would have to devote long analyses to the aftereffects, the reinterpretation, years later, decades later, to the relief assumed by one or another Cerisy *décade*, whose philosophical— or philosophico-political, ideological, or historical—import was not fully apparent at the time. It is a matter of certainty, to consider but two examples, that Heidegger's trip to Cerisy will have been adequately assessed and interpreted, in the future, only over the course of a long span of time, considerably exceeding the immediacy of the *décade* and the living presence of those participating in it, including Heidegger himself. As was the case of the encounter at Davos between Heidegger and Cassirer, which was witnessed by Maurice de Gandillac, who told us of it so well in *Le siècle traversé* (Paris: Albin Michel, 1998). That encounter in Davos has never ceased to haunt a certain philosophical Europe, and it continues to represent a landmark, something of an invisible peak, a summit in a mountain range. The encounter with Heidegger in France at Cerisy would represent another one. And perhaps within the same range: between the two, Nazism, a second world war, and the Occupation. That too is part of the experience. There is a "from Pontigny to Cerisy," and a "from Davos to Cerisy" might be imagined as well. For a thesis—and, why not?, a *décade*—might be dedicated to the comparative analysis of those two Franco-German and European events from after each of the world wars, in institutions welcoming, during the summer, a non-academic season, renowned philosophers and academics, both of them dominated by the presence and thought of Heidegger, both of elevated stature and under high philosophical tension, with long-term ethico-political stakes in play. Similarly, if the "Nietzsche Today?" *décade* had its idiosyncratic content in 1972, its composition, motivation, and roots in the state of reading Nietzsche in France (and here too the analysis of the subject would be endless), it will not have ceased, among other effects, being reinterpreted. In Germany, even as we speak, the organization of another colloquium is being envisaged to celebrate the thirtieth anniversary of the memorable Cerisy *décade* and to inquire into what transpired there and what has transpired since, concerning Nietzsche, in Europe and in the world.

The two examples I have just evoked (among so many other possibilities) confirm in any event the singular and eminent role that Cerisy will have played in what might be called, from the philosophical (and more generally the philosophico-political) perspective, the Franco-German annals between and after the two world wars, which were so massively Franco-German wars. Above and beyond so many fronts and confrontations, it was at Pontigny and Cerisy that the French and German paths of thought, literature, and philosophy often came to cross. I have just named Nietzsche and Heidegger. A lecture I was unfortunately unable to attend will have evoked, a few days ago, several great German figures at Pontigny: Curtius, Heinrich Mann, and Groethuysen. Habermas came here not long ago, and I recall having read with great emotion, in the exhibition at Caen, a handwritten letter from Benjamin, who, at the death of Desjardins, expressed all the gratitude of which this tradition was deserving.

But I have said that the word "experience" corresponded to more than one meaning. Experience is also the crossing, the voyage, the ordeal, and the passing of limits. Well, Cerisy, it may be said, is also the name of an institution or a counter-institution (I shall expand on the "counter-" and the "countercontract" in a moment) which will have made of the ordeal and the passing of borders its specific mission. Ever since Pontigny, and in an increasingly pronounced way at Cerisy, limits between disciplines and areas of expertise have been deliberately trespassed in order to grant legitimacy and opportunity to new problematics, but the borders between cultures and countries have also been violated. I will say a word about languages in a moment, but we know that Cerisy's hospitality is broadly international. Cerisy is an institution expressly intent on being regional, national, and international. I can attest to as much for having frequently delighted in that circumstance and as recently as a few weeks ago: the guests of Cerisy come from all countries, at times from between ten and twenty countries, and from all continents for a single *décade*.

IN SPEAKING about the "model" or the "philosophical" model of a counter-institution, I had in mind something else to which I am in a position to bear witness. When, in 1982, I was commissioned by the government at the time, specifically by Jean-Pierre Chevènement, to coordinate a project and prepare a report intended to create a new institution, in proposing at the time to found (something accomplished in 1983 and which is still alive) an International College of Philosophy, I frequently allowed myself to be inspired by the model of Cerisy as I had already known it over the previous twenty years. What are the features that the college, despite obvious differences, shares with Cerisy? First of all, it is an institution, and an institution of nongovernmental origin. It is not a state institution, even if, like Cerisy, the symbolic (and, to a point, financial) support of the public authorities serves to confirm a certain acknowledgment by the state without violating absolute autonomy in the functioning and orientations of the institution. In addition, it is a counter-institution, namely, an institution (with a statute, rules of procedure, a physical site) that, contrary to what might be suggested by the word "counter-institution," is not destined to make war, to counter, to oppose, or choose systematically the counter-position or counter-current, for instance, the one dominating state academic institutions of instruction or research, but rather to balance out or freely question their hegemony, to open up and occupy their margins. For instance, in the college (and I believe this is also true of Cerisy), without at all abandoning the most classic paths, the canonical corpus, the major texts or major questions (Plato or Aristotle, for example, as Cerisy has just dedicated a *décade* to Spinoza), we had nonetheless imposed on ourselves the rule of granting priority either to approaches to those canonical matters that were not common or accorded legitimacy in the university, or to new objects that had not yet received a kind of consensual status in university curricula.

AS FOR "trans-" or "interdisciplinarity"—a word of which we were not particularly fond for reasons into which I will not enter here—in the quest for those new objects, new themes, new fields, new crossings ("intersections" is the word we use in the college), it was our principal imperative, our primordial and constant concern. At this juncture, the place of philosophy requires us to pause an instant, since I believe that there is in it something quite illuminating as well concerning the role played by philosophy at Cerisy. The International College of *Philosophy* was thus intent on granting a large place to philosophy, to be sure, but (as I had attempted to explain and justify in what was called the "Blue Report," that is, the report which preceded the founding of the college and which is currently published by the Presses Universitaires de France), even as it was to be inscribed at every crossroads and intersection, philosophy was not to occupy a preponderant, imperial, and hegemonic place at the vertex of a pyramid, as in classical architectonics (however dead—or of which philosophy died). Philosophy is at home everywhere, just as I suggested a moment ago that it is everywhere at Cerisy, but it is not master in its own home; it retains a relation of non-domination, a horizontal relation with all the other disciplines, the hard and social sciences, literature, and the arts; and as happens at Cerisy as well, we posited as a principle at the college that those arts would issue not only in theoretical or critical studies, but also on occasion in creations or performances in the college itself: exhibitions, concerts, the production and projection of films, writing experiments. In all of this, and even while collaborating, like Cerisy, with numerous other institutions and inviting many (university and *lycée)* professors, we had decided, and have for the most part done so, to invite non-teachers, both French and foreign, among the lecturers and program directors and naturally for the audiences, which were open to whoever opted to enroll. As for internationality, a feature that distinguishes both Cerisy and the college from so many other French institutions, and specifically from the university, it was from the outset inscribed and respected as a sacred principle in the charter and the title of the college. This raised the question of language and translations (which are also a theme treated systematically in the college, above all concerning the languages and translations of philosophy). The solution adopted also resembles, in practice, the one adopted by Cerisy. Since that international institution remains in law and in fact French, inscribed in French law and on French territory, the principal language is French, which we do everything to protect, to be sure, but while welcoming other languages, even in Paris (since certain sessions of the college take place abroad in places that have enacted agreements with the college). And I can recall several occasions on which, at Cerisy, we experimented in a way that seemed fascinating to me (even a few weeks ago, but it was not the first time) with the reading of a presentation in an English whose ingenious investigations and idiomatic inventions resulted in an equally inventive translation, which was simultaneously projected on a screen. On that day, Nick Royle and his exemplary translator (Geoff Bennington, who is also English, but an impeccable francophone) had us participating in a dazzling and unforgettable experience of philosophical thought in the poetics of more than one language.

THE EXPERIENCE is not only the live and incalculable encounter, in the "decadophonic" *viva voce* time of Cerisy-la-Salle itself, and nowhere else; it is not only the counter-institutional trespass of disciplinary and academic frontiers, not only the crossing of one culture to another, one language to another; it is also *expertise* and *experimentation.* Expertise because, if there is an unwritten principle at Cerisy (but also at the Collège international de philosophie), an imperative respected by all, it is that the floor is given only to experienced and competent individuals, whether or not they have academic credentials (whence, on occasion, the reproach, which I have heard again just recently, and which is unjust in my view, of elitism, or even of esotericism). But if I say "expert" and "experienced" individuals, I immediately add that this counter-institution neither requires nor distributes any (academic or professional) credentials, and experienced expertise does not exclude (on the contrary) experimentation, experimental adventure, the risky propositions of a vanguard as yet unacknowledged (or legitimated) by established institutions. The vanguards of the past are on occasion duly studied there, to be sure, but one also puts to the test, in philosophy no less than in the arts, hypotheses or virtual models which have no currency or place in court within existent institutions and in places known for their official powers of legitimation. Of course, let us not pretend we are unaware that because of that experimental daring and as a result of the expertise I have just evoked, by dint of its very successes, Cerisy has also become an envied place of legitimation or consecration, and not only in France. For a number of foreigners, to have been invited to present a paper at Cerisy becomes a privilege and already a kind of university credential.

THUS IT is that an experimental counter-institution can become, through its experience, a model or paradigm. That is how, by virtue or in spite of its irreplaceable uniqueness, that original counter-institution can become exemplary for other institutional experiments, in France or abroad.

Translated by Jeffrey Mehlman

NOTE

1. Jacques Derrida graciously granted permission for the publication of this talk, in a translation by Jeffrey Mehlman. The talk, condensed here, was originally given at Cerisy in August 2002, on the occasion of the fiftieth anniversary of the Centre culturel de Cerisy. Édith Heurgon, co-director of the Centre, also kindly granted permission, as did Christian Bourgois, publisher of the French version, in proceedings of the colloquium: "Pontigny, Cerisy, dans le S.I.E.C.L.E." (Paris: Éditions Christian Bourgois, 2004).

II

Poetry and Philosophy

Poetry is the imagination of life. A poem is a particular of life thought of for so long that one's thought has become an inseparable part of it or a particular of life so intensely felt that the feeling has entered into it. When, therefore, we say that the world is a compact of real things so like the unreal things of the imagination that they are indistinguishable from one another and when, by way of illustration, we cite, say, the blue sky, we can be sure that the thing cited is always something that, whether by thinking or feeling, has become a part of our vital experience of life, even though we are not aware of it. It is easy to suppose that few people realize on that occasion, which comes to all of us, when we look at the blue sky for the first time, that is to say: not merely see it, but look at it and experience it and for the first time have a sense that we live in the center of a physical poetry, a geography that would be intolerable except for the non-geography that exists there—few people realize that they are looking at the world of their own thoughts and the world of their own feelings. On that occasion, the blue sky is a particular of life that we have thought of often, even though unconsciously, and that we have felt intensely in those crystallizations of freshness that we no more remember than we remember this or that gust of wind in spring or autumn.

Wallace Stevens, "The Figure of the Youth as Virile Poet" (1943)

The centuries have a way of being male. Without pretending to say whether they get this character from their good heroes or their bad ones, it is certain that they get it, in part, from their philosophers and poets. It is curious, looking back at them, to see how much of the impression that they leave has been derived from the progress of thought in their time and from the abundance of the arts, including poetry, left behind and how little of it comes from prouder and much noisier things. . . . When we look back at the face of the seventeenth century, it is at the rigorous face of the rigorous thinker and, say, the Miltonic image of a poet, severe and determined. In effect, what we are remembering is the rather haggard background of the incredible, the imagination without intelligence, from which a younger figure is emerging, stepping forward in the company of a muse of its own, still half-beast and somehow more than human, a kind of sister of the Minotaur. This younger figure is the intelligence that endures. It is the imagination of the son still bearing the antique imagination of the father. It is the clear intelligence of the young man still bearing the burden of the obscurities of the intelligence of the old. It is the spirit out of its own self, not out of some surrounding myth, delineating with accurate speech the complications of which it is composed. For this Aeneas, it is the past that is Anchises.

Wallace Stevens, "The Figure of the Youth as Virile Poet" (1943)

Adventurous philosophical thought was always at the center of the Pontigny tradition, especially when the philosopher-poet Jean Wahl assumed the direction of Pontigny-en-Amérique after 1942. Wahl invited his favorite American poets, Wallace Stevens and Marianne Moore, along with John Peale Bishop, to speak at Mount Holyoke during the summer of 1943. The topic was to be the relation of poetry and philosophy. Moore lectured on "Feeling and Precision," carefully choosing her examples of understated eloquence from poetic responses to war. "An unselfish experiment like that of the Pontigny Committee," she wrote in a letter, "leaves a certain memory of exaltation, and a great desire to be of service to those who have suffered, and fought so well." Moore remembered Wahl as "an elfin and most touching exile, escaped from prison…drudging over the executive part of his committee-work and prompt to guide visitors to buildings or to 'see the lake'; and as John Bishop said, 'despite his griefs and losses, almost gay.'" Moore met Wallace Stevens, whose poetry she greatly admired, for the first time at Mount Holyoke.

Among the most impressive talks delivered during the three years of Pontigny-en-Amérique was Wallace Stevens's "Figure of the Youth as Virile Poet," later collected in *The Necessary Angel.* An acolyte of George Santayana in his youth, Stevens was a self-consciously "philosophical poet." (Stanley Cavell comments on Stevens's "zest for the philosophical.") In 1943 Stevens was a fully mature poet, but he had not yet achieved the exalted place among American poets that he now holds. Some of his earlier and shorter poems (such as "The Emperor of Ice Cream" and "The Snow Man") were already anthology pieces, but his longer and more reflective poems met with resistance. Some critics found him too "philosophical"—too enamored of grand abstractions—while others found him too "aesthetic" and insufficiently grounded in contemporary realities. Stevens gained, at this period in his life, a sympathetic hearing among French and Francophile American readers, including Jean Wahl and their mutual friend Henry Church.

For his Pontigny contribution, Stevens carefully contoured the talk for his audience. Apologetic that he could not deliver the lecture in French, he filled out his arguments with quotations from or about French writers. Like the other poets on the panel, Stevens sought to provide a defense of poetry in what he called "a leaden time." He meant to argue that poetry had claims to truths unrevealed by the more abstract strictures of philosophy. To what he called the "official language" of philosophy Stevens contrasted the "unofficial language" of poetry, associating the two languages with reason and the imagination, respectively. In his response, Jean Wahl took issue with this particular point, arguing that philosophers such as Heidegger (and by implication Wahl himself) had often turned to poetry for insights unavailable in philosophical discourse. This point probably would not have satisfied Stevens, however. Stevens was not calling for a philosophical *use* of poetry so much as a reading of poetry *as* philosophy, or as a meaningful challenge to philosophy-as-usual. Stevens, like Derrida, was in search of an "unofficial" mode of thinking.

In the section that follows, the distinguished American philosopher Stanley Cavell, who has all but single-handedly salvaged and celebrated the specifically philosophical achievements of Emerson and Thoreau, sets out to do something kindred for Wallace Stevens. Drawing on the beginnings of his own career in the immediate aftermath of World War II, Cavell evokes those fissures in American and European intellectual life that have made it difficult for poets and philosophers to get a hearing from one another. Stevens's essay, ignored or dismissed by American academic philosophers for sixty years, is finally accorded—in Cavell's eloquent interpretation—a hearing from American philosophy. Jeffrey Mehlman's response and Cavell's counter-response tease out a probable French subtext, Racine's *Phèdre,* for Stevens's invocation of "a sister of the Minotaur" as his muse. It is worth noting in this context that Stevens wrote to a friend during the winter of 1937 that "recently, Racine...has had an immense attraction for me."

Patronage and financial support were key for the artists and poets of Pontigny-en-Amérique. A concluding essay introduces the compelling transatlantic patron of the arts, Henry Church. At Pontigny-en-Amérique in August 1943, Wallace Stevens was accompanied by Church, his close friend and supporter. On that occasion Church wore, according to Marianne Moore, "an astoundingly beautiful Panama hat—a sort of pork-pie with a wide brim, a little like Bernard Berenson's hats." Church's career as patron of the arts in France and the United States is mapped by the scholar Claire Paulhan, granddaughter of Church's friend and publishing colleague Jean Paulhan.

Reflections on Wallace Stevens at Mount Holyoke

STANLEY CAVELL

I COUNTED on the fact that by the time it fell to me to present these remarks, we would have had sketched more of the texture and the details of the event sixty years ago that we are gathered to commemorate than I have learned in the course of my preparation, on and off these past months, for composing them. It went almost without saying in Christopher Benfey's invitation to me, and in our exchanges about how I might think of my contribution, that I would include reflections on what might have been expected in 1943, from the still moving, wonderfully American effort, with the nation absorbed in a total and fateful war, to transport the spirit of a signature institution of French high culture to a setting in a characteristic instance of a fine, small New England college. One might even call the event classy, except that this might slight the democratic willingness of its welcome.

Benfey and I touched especially on the question of what might have been gained or been missed in the philosophical voices that had been part of that original effort at Mount Holyoke. The question was inevitable, given the specific suggestion that I might include some response to the text Wallace Stevens prepared for and read at that event, "The Figure of the Youth as Virile Poet," one of the four principal prose texts from Stevens's hand, each of them directed intensely and explicitly to philosophy, asking from it a response to what he felt himself able and compelled to say about the relation of philosophy and poetry. Benfey and I turned out to share the sense that these texts have still not received a response from philosophers adequate to Stevens's request. The additional suggestion that I might write somewhat autobiographically was, I take it, meant to assure me that I should not suppose I was asked to present myself as a scholar of Wallace Stevens's writing. Indeed, while I have read and in various texts of mine quoted lines of Stevens's poetry, the present occasion is the first on which I have not evaded the impulse actually to attempt something like consecutive responses to reading through the work of this strange, wondrous, often excruciatingly difficult writer.

It is a difficulty rather opposite to that posed in other American writers whom Stevens admired and with whom I have spent considerable stretches in recent years in exhilarating contest, above all Emerson and Thoreau. But in writing about them I have been moved to *insist* on their difficulty, too often finding them quoted as if their sentences are transparent, yielding their signif-

1943

Les entretiens de Pontigny

2ème semaine

du 9 au 15 Août

PROGRAMME.

Poésie: 10 h.30 ; 12 h.30.

Lundi 9 Août : John Peele Bishop : "On Modern Poetry."

Mardi 10 Août : Jean Wahl : "Essence et accidents de la poésie."

Mercredi 11 Août : Wallace Stevens : "The poet and his art."

Jeudi 12 Août : James Rorty : "The ground the poet stands on."

Vendredi 13 Août : Marianne Moore : "Feeling and Precision."

Samedi 14 Août : Discussion générale et conclusions (provisoires).

Politique : 2 h.30 ; 4 h.30

Lundi 9 Août : M. B. Mirkine-Guetzévitch : Introduction à la discussion.
              M. A. Mendizabal : La philosophie politique de la démocratie.
              M. L. Venturi : Le problème Italien d'aujourd'hui.

Mardi 10 Août : M. Pierre Cot   )
                M. Amé-Leroy   ) Organisation internationale après
                Miss Ellen Deborah Ellis)   la guerre.

Mercredi 11 Août : M. H. Gregoire   )
                   M. E. Hamburger   ) L'Avenir de l'Allemagne et de l'Europe
                                            Centrale.

Jeudi 12 Août : M. J. Weiller)
                M. E. Gumbel) Problèmes économiques et sociaux.
                M. Heuertz   )

Vendredi 13 Août : M. Pierre Cot   ) Problème colonial.
                   Pasteur Maynard   )
                   M. B. Mirkine-Guetzévitch : Conclusion.

Conférences :

M. Henri Grégoire : "L'actualité des Classiques" Jeudi - 12

M. Benjamin Abraham : "Ces planificateurs ! Un réquisitoire"

                Samedi 14 Août 10 h.15 à Porter Hall.

M. Emile Buré : "Souvenirs de Paris."
                Vendredi 13
                ~~Dimanche 15 Août~~ 8 h.30 à New York Room

"Les entretiens de Pontigny / 2ème semaine / du 9 au 15 Août," program, 1943. MS 0768, Entretiens de Pontigny records, 1942–45, Mount Holyoke College Archives and Special Collections.

Wallace Stevens (in profile) lecturing at Pontigny-en-Amérique, 1943. Photograph provided by Carol Ann Crotty, Mount Holyoke College, class of 1946.

icance at a glance, without resistance. My idea is that Emerson and Thoreau characteristically conceal their difficulty, as if to make it seem easier than it is to read and to act better than we do, as they ask us to do. While Stevens will posit ease as an eventuality in taking poetry to our lives, he makes inescapably obvious the initial difficulty in preserving, let us say, our intactness. To recognize and to accompany both our possibilities and our obscurities are, I would say, necessary assists for us.

The autobiographical latitude given me also came, I believe, from the knowledge of the publication roughly a decade ago of conversations with the composer Roger Sessions, another of the greatly distinguished American artists who had accepted an invitation to Pontigny at Mount Holyoke in 1943. In those conversations, Sessions tells an anecdote concerning the world premiere of his first opera, *The Trial of Lucullus,* on a text of Bertolt Brecht, at Berkeley in 1946, in which I figure momentarily but rather superbly as the resourceful clarinet player in the small orchestra for which this marvelous piece is scored, who overcame a crisis in the middle of the opening night's performance, transposing an English horn solo on the clarinet when the English horn suddenly broke down. While I would, the year after graduating from Berkeley, recognize the fact that music was no longer my life, namely, that something other that I would eventually learn to call philosophy was what gave my life its drift or gist, the experience of having worked young in the company of an absolutely serious and accomplished artist, whose life-and-death stake in his art is unstinting and unquestionable, leaves impressions whose powers of orientation and inspiration are undying.

Are such reminiscences to be thought of as marked by anything that happened in South Hadley sixty years ago? But that question is among the motivations of my remarks today, namely, the question: What counts as an effect of what happened then and there? Is our commemorative occasion an effect of it? It seems hard to imagine that these events have been *caused* by that earlier event. Yet I know that having in recent months first learned the bare outlines of the life of Rachel Bespaloff has intangibly affected the color and certain emphases of what I have given myself to say here. My image of this gifted intellectual, a Jewish refugee from eastern Europe through Paris to New York and South Hadley, is affected by its general contrast with the difference in the experiences I continue to imagine of my Jewish family's immigration a generation earlier from Bialystok to Atlanta, remembering reports heard and overheard; and affected most specifically by a detail on her itinerary westward that gave her time to stay for two years in Switzerland to study music with Ernest Bloch.

During my years at Berkeley, Bloch visited there from his home on the coast of Oregon to give a summer class whose ecstatic effect on me was to transform what I conceived I was meant to do with my life, specifically enabling me to choose the path of philosophy rather than composition when, a few years later, my gradual withdrawal from the life of music precipitated the major intellectual, or spiritual, crisis of my life. There is no counting the times I have gone over, more recently in writing, my images of those encounters with Bloch—craving to remember every detail of his moods and ways of moving as he thought, or wrote a progression on the blackboard, or read from Stanislavsky's book on acting, or from Schumann's criticism, or played illustrations at the piano, or at a certain moment lapsed into an irreverent but loving imitation of the manner of recitative Debussy had invented for *Pelléas and Mélisande,* as Bloch described himself and his fellow music students improvising such ethereal exchanges throughout entire meals in Paris in 1902, after attending the world premiere of the opera (which because of Bloch's representation seems as close to me now as it did half a century ago in Bloch's animated presence). But now my memory is affected by the question whether anything in this greatly impressionable and expressive man's presentations that summer bore the mark of his experience of the young Rachel Bespaloff— it was not unusual for him to show that his students were on his mind, and who more likely among them than a fellow musician and intellectual and Jew seeking a life in the strangeness of America?—thereby perhaps conveying an effect that may or may not have made an impression on me.

I am speaking not about probabilities now but about the question of what human knowledge is that it is at any time based on such impressions, and the question of what a human life comes to that it is modified by such fitful things. In classical philosophy, as in the writing of Locke and of Hume, impressions are understood as predictable effects of objects upon my senses. I am interested rather, as is Emerson, in the concept of an impression as an experience that a portion of the world unpredictably gives me, in which it captures my interest, matters to me, or fails to—a product of significance, not of causation.

A companion question to that concerning the consequences of the Mount Holyoke Pontigny event is that of its antecedents—meaning not just empirically a question concerning who was invited and who attended, but also meant speculatively as the question concerning who was not invited who might have been. For example, in responding philosophically, according to my lights, to passages of Wallace Stevens's writing, I will be invoking the names of Emerson and of Heidegger (as others have) but also of Wittgenstein, implying that a response cannot match Stevens's zest for the philosophical that is unresponsive to what these philosophers have urged about language and the human inhabitation of the world. And yet, is it imaginable that the philosophical pertinence, even necessity, of these figures could have appropriately been invoked at Mount Holyoke in 1943? If we agree that in some obvious sense they could not have been, but agree that they have become philosophically pertinent, even indispensable, then how are we to think about what a culture is, and what its change is? Are we to think of it as out of synchrony with itself, or as maintaining a polysynchrony? And would we want it otherwise?

Let's imagine briefly how or by whom each of these figures might have been handed around the table then in South Hadley. Stevens himself might of course have invoked Emerson, but evidently he could not have envisaged a response from Emerson as assuring his own philosophical pertinence, or his protection against the mastery of philosophy, since he could not count on Emerson as a philosopher—and neither, still today, can most philosophers. As for Wittgenstein, one of his early pupils, Alice Ambrose, one of the two to whom in the academic year 1934–35 Wittgenstein had dictated what came to be called the "Brown Book" (from which the opening and further extended passages of Wittgenstein's *Philosophical Investigations* ten years later can be seen to be derived), had begun a long lifetime of teaching down the road at Smith College in 1937. But in 1943 that philosophical material was still some ten years away from publication and still quite secure in its state of esotericism. At Mount Holyoke, Jean Wahl already possessed a knowledge of Heidegger's work (Wahl is reported to have joked with students of his at the Sorbonne, before he was arrested and imprisoned by the Gestapo, that the Germans might take kindly to those whom they knew were studying Heidegger), and Rachel Bespaloff had published an early essay on Heidegger, but, except for a stray remark on Heidegger's interest in Hölderlin's poetry, it seems doubtful that they spoke much of Heidegger's thinking on that occasion.

Another philosopher present then at Mount Holyoke was Suzanne Langer, who had been a student of Ernst Cassirer's. Cassirer had left Germany for Scandinavia soon after Hitler's rise to power, moved to Yale in 1940, and died suddenly in New York in 1943. I do not know whether Langer would have been present at a fateful conference in Davos, Switzerland, in 1929, at which a confrontation had been arranged between Cassirer and Heidegger, both offering assessments of the achievement of Kant in the history of philosophy; but she would certainly have known that Heidegger was widely thought to have been victorious in that confrontation (Cassirer himself is said to have had that impression), which can be said to have meant the defeat in Germany of the classical humanistic, scholarly reading of the history of philosophy that Heidegger had contempt for, and to have left Heidegger the most advanced philosophical voice in Germany. (Emmanuel Levinas was one of the students present at this conference. He reported in an interview with the philosopher Arnold Davidson more than sixty years later that at the end of the conference the group of students in attendance composed and performed a skit in which Levinas, because of his shock of light hair, was cast as Cassirer, and in which Cassirer was shown up as the goat of the encounter with Heidegger. Levinas added in the interview that he still felt wrong about having been carried away by the proceedings.)

Another student witness present at that Davos conference was Rudolf Carnap, one of whose most influential polemical papers would take the form of an attack on Heidegger as the very type of the purveyor of metaphysical meaninglessness that the school of logical positivism, of which Carnap became the most fruitful founder, was meant to uproot.[1] With the emigration of Carnap and other key figures of the new movement from Vienna and Berlin to the United States at the beginning of the 1940s, logical positivism became, by the time I entered graduate school to begin the study of philosophy in 1948, the dominant avant-garde of the field, and while it is today no longer seriously uncontested, what we might call its style—call this the part of it that shows—remains dominant in what is known as analytical philosophy, still the dominant mode of philosophizing in most of the major departments of philosophy in the United States. In fact, positivism's influence during the 1950s and 1960s was felt throughout large stretches of the humanities and the social sciences in North American academic life. That it could have achieved this prominence is marked by the well-recognized fact that the migration to North America of intellectuals from central Europe, unlike the rescue and transportation of intellectual refugees from France, began soon after the event of Hitler's ascendance to power and, continuing throughout the years leading up to the outbreak of World War II, took root in American university culture. The only comparably massive effect on that culture in my lifetime was caused by the reception of French thought (so-called poststructuralism) beginning in the late 1960s. But while this later reception served to transform studies in literary and cultural theory, it has had only marginal effects within the professional study of philosophy. We are still working these things out.

Stevens quotes, in his essay "Imagination as Value," from 1948, even pits against each other, passages from both Cassirer's *Essay on Man* and A. J. Ayer's *Language, Truth, and Logic,* the latter the book from which most people learned the version of what they would know as logical positivism (it remains indeed one of the most successful philosophy textbooks ever written, with sales of over a million copies, and continuing). Heartened by Cassirer's praise of the imagination, in its role as illuminating reality metaphysically— explicitly the obsessive topic of Stevens in his prose writings—Stevens wonders whether, in his words, "we [will] escape destruction at the hands of the logical positivists."

How much Stevens knew of the work of Heidegger remains, so far as I am aware, still uncertain. Frank Kermode, in an admiring essay from the early 1980s, in which he quite unqualifiedly locates Heidegger's interpretations of the poetry of Hölderlin as the revelatory site for an understanding of Stevens's achievement, notes that Stevens had tried to obtain a copy of a French translation of Heidegger's Hölderlin essays from his French bookseller—which strikes me as expressing a wish to keep his curiosity about Heidegger a secret, as Stevens seems to have kept, or protected, so many of his curiosities. Without evidence that Stevens knew Heidegger's writing, Kermode has to content himself with saying that Stevens just did somehow know the truths Heidegger elicited from reading Hölderlin.[2] William Flesch tells me that Stevens had discovered in a French journal an essay by Maurice Blanchot on Heidegger's Hölderlin interpretation. Neither Kermode nor Flesch has, to my knowledge, said whether Stevens sought out anyone with whom to discuss Heidegger's work. Here I think of the opening lines of section 22 of Stevens's long poem "An Ordinary Evening in New Haven":

> Professor Eucalyptus said, "The search
> For reality is as momentous as
> The search for god." It is the philosopher's search.

As part of responding to Stevens's appeal to philosophy, I would love to know whether Stevens would have recognized in this quotation from Professor Eucalyptus an allusion to Heidegger, since, with the term "Being" substituted for the term "reality," the assertion could be an epigraph for Heidegger's work, especially the later work, which would I think have interested Stevens more than *Being and Time*. If this were initially plausible, it could get a touch of confirmation on considering that the Greek roots of the term *eu-calyptus* suggest the beneficence of something that is hidden or covered: this is not a bad rendering of what Heidegger finds in the Greek for "truth," *aletheia*, which Heidegger reads, not uncontroversially, as giving the sense of uncovering something concealed. It is not controversial to recognize that Stevens unendingly returns to questions or scrupulosities of truth, and of the truth, and of a truth. There are other reasons for suggesting the presence of Heidegger hereabouts, to which I shall come back. (But unlike Cassirer, Heidegger never taught in New Haven.)

I have heard that it was assumed among students of literature of a certain period at Yale (my informant studied there in the late 1970s) that the name Professor Eucalyptus referred to Professor Paul Weiss, perhaps the most prominent of the few philosophers from the United States to appear at Mount Holyoke in 1943, who was professor of philosophy at Yale from the late 1940s through the 1960s. The assumption of this identification is natural enough concerning a reference apparently to a professor of philosophy in a poem with New Haven in the title, and there would have been scholars of literature at Yale, and specifically of modern poetry, who would have been in a position to verify this. Yet I like what Stevens's New Haven professor is reported to have said about the search for reality and so I hope the attribution is wrong, or unnecessarily exclusive. In the last essay Stevens composed, called "A Collect of Philosophy" (written some years after Stevens's participation in the Pontigny commemoration, and published posthumously), Paul Weiss is cited as among those who had responded to Stevens's question concerning the poetic nature of philosophical concepts, and Weiss is part of the sad story concerning the publication, or non-publication, of that essay. After hearing Stevens read it at Yale, Weiss invited him to publish it in the philosophy journal he edited, the *Review of Metaphysics*, but on receiving it, and after consultation with others, turned it down as more suitable for a literary journal. Weiss is reported—in *Parts of a World: An Oral Biography*, put together in 1985 by Peter Brazeau—

to have said that he wrote a courteous letter of rejection to Stevens and was therefore surprised to learn that Stevens had notwithstanding been hurt by it.[3]

It is quite true that, as Weiss and his colleagues agreed, the piece must be thought by professional philosophers to be in various ways naïve, perhaps above all in the sources Stevens cites for his philosophical examples; one of the sources is a history of philosophy for students. Naturally professors as well as artists have, and are entitled to have, their pride, but one can think of courses of action more imaginative than explaining courteously to Wallace Stevens, having invited his contribution, that what he writes is literature and therefore not appropriate to a philosophical enterprise. But perhaps it was too late for that. When Stevens had written to Weiss asking, as he often asked others (including Jean Wahl), for examples of poetic philosophical concepts, Weiss had obliged him by supplying a list of encapsulated philosophical theories associated with great names in the history of the subject—entries one might imagine are suitable for a student's history of philosophy—quite as if it was obvious what Stevens was asking for, obvious what, we might say after Stevens, would suffice.

But it is no more obvious what Stevens was asking for than it is obvious what Stevens's poetry calls for in coming to terms with it. The search for philosophy can make an alarmingly sophisticated and private person say unclear, naïve things, things he himself may not quite mean. But can that itself not be said? The naïve thing in this encounter was shared, I think, by both sides, namely, the assumption that Stevens's questions about the poetry of philosophy could be answered without speaking either poetically or philosophically.

Alerted by the complexities suggested in these juxtapositions of characters and these fragments of narratives, let me begin proposing some more consecutive, if still initial, responses to episodes in Stevens's search, sometimes in poetry (that is, by example) and sometimes in prose (that is, by theory), for the poetic register of philosophy.[4]

Take a case Stevens offers in that rejected paper of his, where he speaks of the poetic arising within non-poetic circumstances. He says, "According to the traditional views of sensory perception, we do not see the world immediately but only as the result of a process of seeing and after the completion of that process, that is to say, we never see the world except the moment after."[5] Philosophers I grew up with would surely have questioned the formulation "seeing the world only the moment after." For example, it may be asked *what* it is that the moment of seeing comes after. If you answer, "After seeing," then you owe an explanation of the paradox or contradiction in saying that you see only after you see. If, again, you answer, "After the conditions of seeing are satisfied," then you seem to have uttered the banality that you see only when you can see. But suppose, as is not unlikely, that Stevens was speaking poetry. Carnap, in the influential paper of his I alluded to earlier, from 1932, declares his readiness to grant that metaphysics, while scientifically or cognitively meaningless, may be understood and accepted as poetry, which accordingly means, in a form that makes no cognitive claims on the world. Carnap's example is, it happens, a passage of Heidegger's, from his *What Is Metaphysics?* of 1929, the year of the Davos conference. The passage contains the notorious phrase "The Nothing nothings," but Carnap does not go on actually to give a reading of the passage on the basis of the claim that it may be poetry. Whereas it seems clear enough about Stevens's poetry that it makes repeated and tenacious claims for poetry as an understanding of the world, of our lives in the world. To whom are we to listen? Who are we to listen?

In his first book of poems, *Harmonium,* from 1923, in "Thirteen Ways of Looking at a Blackbird," Stevens had said:

> I do not know which to prefer,
> The beauty of inflections
> Or the beauty of innuendoes,
> The blackbird whistling
> Or just after.

This seems to warrant the reaction Stevens expresses to the idea he came upon years later about seeing things the moment after, or say, not at first, or at once. (Philosophers have variously found that we do not see things immediately, by which they have meant roughly that we see them, at best, mediately or indirectly. When my teacher J. L. Austin—more famous now for his invention of the theory of the performativity of language—claimed to have shown that the idea that we are fated to see objects indirectly is an empty idea, he went on to insist this meant that the idea that we are fated to see them directly is equally empty. To understand why philosophers are led to sum up our relation to the world in either of these ways was not something Austin had patience for; it was a principal cause that led him to an impatience altogether with what had come to be called philosophy.) Stevens's late reaction to the perpetual lateness of perception is that the idea "instantly changes the face of the world," and it may strike one that the blackbird's turns had already signaled how easy it is for us to miss the experience of the world's arrivals and of its departures, its inflections and innuendoes, as if the world naturally keeps the face of its beauty partially turned from us.

Modern philosophy has generally attempted, unless it has accepted, or merely dismissed, an irreducible skepticism, to overcome some sense of a gap or barrier between human perception and the world (unless reassured by the perpetual intervention of God, as in Descartes or in Berkeley), by proposing, as Kant did, that the way humankind necessarily organizes its perceptions necessarily reveals what we understand as the world we know, or, as idealists in response to Kant's proposal did, by positing a new form of human intuition or immediacy. What Stevens seems eventually to come to in his poetic idea that perception is not blocked or interrupted but that it comes just after, that it is late, is the thought that the way to overcome the gap in what Professor Eucalyptus calls the search for reality lies in finding how to appear to reality early, earlier than philosophers now imagine to be possible, in what Stevens calls, in "An Ordinary Evening in New Haven" (section 22), an "original earliness"—to get to objects, to get before objects, before they are given to us or dictated to us; or before, we might say, the division hardens between objects and subjects, or between outside and inside.

My invocation of modern philosophical skepticism as an intellectual environment in which to assess Stevens's search for reality is no doubt a function of my own preoccupation with the threat of skepticism as posing the underlying task of Wittgenstein's *Philosophical Investigations,* the twentieth-century text that more than any other has served to convince me that philosophy remains alive to issues of modern life that concern me most. When Stevens writes, again in "An Ordinary Evening," "the theory / Of poetry is the theory of life" (section 28), and implies perpetually that poetry is the imagination of life on earth and that failing to imagine one's life is a failure in living it, I take him to be responding to the threat of skepticism more clearly than, or as the condition of, the loss of metaphysics, although metaphysics more explicitly enters his prose articulations of his position. But I am not here trying to prove an epistemological priority in his work.

Yet to indicate Stevens's seriousness and diligence in, let's say, theorizing about knowledge, I note that the short poem he places at the end of his *Collected Poems,* a poem to which he gives as its title the motto "Not Ideas About the Thing But the Thing Itself," ends with the claim, "It was like /A new knowledge of reality." Here Stevens is not content, as he was in his initial assessment of the lateness of perception, to conclude that we are confined to a knowledge of what is always past. He is now rather occupied with the conviction that what we perceive—instanced by the cry of a bird and the coming of the sun—comes from outside the mind. This poem consists of six three-line stanzas, of which the opening two run as follows:

At the earliest ending of winter,
In March, a scrawny cry from outside
Seemed like a sound in his mind.

He knew that he heard it,
A bird's cry, at daylight or before,
In the early March wind.

I note that half of the poem's stanzas contain the idea of being early or coming before or preceding, and another includes his giving himself assurance that he is not asleep, not dreaming. Stevens names Descartes, and I assume also alludes to him, in his poetry. In "Notes toward a Supreme Fiction" we find: "I have not but I am and as I am, I am," which I understand to say, roughly, "Nothing I possess, including my body, proves that I exist; but I since I can think, or say in my mind 'I am,' it follows that I am." This is substantially one formulation Descartes gives to his *cogito ergo sum* argument. And I take it as uncontroversial that Stevens's citing here the possibility that I am dreaming what is real is meant in this context to invoke a relation to philosophical skepticism concerning the existence of the world.

I do not know whether Stevens knew that in the preface to the second edition of *The Critique of Pure Reason*, Kant characterizes the issue of skepticism as Stevens does here, not as turning on a distinction between subjectivity and objectivity or between the mental and the material or between appearance and reality but on that between being inside or outside the mind. Kant says there: "It still remains a scandal to philosophy and to human reason in general that the existence of things outside us…must be accepted merely on *faith*, and that if anyone thinks good to doubt their existence, we are unable to counter his doubts by any satisfactory proof." I imagine that it would have pleased Stevens to know that Heidegger will respond to Kant's idea of the scandal of skepticism by remarking that the real philosophical scandal is the idea that the answer to skepticism requires a proof. An implication of Heidegger's retort is that seeking a proof merely perpetuates the skeptical attitude, or in any case makes the existence of the world, as surely as it has made God's existence, hostage to the fate of human constructions, inherently open to collapse.

A further implication may be that a permanently valuable response to skepticism will be one that traces the circumstances of human life and thought that make skepticism possible, perhaps necessary, and exemplifies the resources of that life that overcome skepticism, or show it to be a habitable, even welcome, moment of human existence. If so, Stevens to my mind enters a claim to have made, in his body of poetry, a distinctively valuable contribution to that task, most patently perhaps in his encouragement to raise the question why philosophers choose the examples they do, Descartes taking the case of his sitting before the fire, Kant that of a drifting boat, Bishop Berkeley that of a cherry, Heidegger of a tree, G. E. Moore that of a human hand, countless academic epistemologists of the twentieth century taking those of a piece of chalk or of a pen—never anything like, as in Stevens, the scrawny cry of a bird before daylight, and not just the colossal sun but the distant coming on of the sun. Acknowledging that Stevens's promptings here might be consequential philosophically will no doubt require being prompted to a willingness somewhat to re-conceive our received ideas of poetry and of philosophy, a willingness some of my favorite philosophers of the past century and a half have shown, notably—beyond Wittgenstein—Emerson, hence Nietzsche, hence Heidegger.

Stevens's interpretation of human perception as late, as happening the moment after, hence as suggesting a poetic counter-action directed to making something happen the moment before, would link up remarkably with a work Heidegger was preparing the year before the one my remarks principally commemorate today, namely, in 1942 in Freiburg, on a major text of Hölderlin's, the "Hymn on the Ister River."[6] I might not have become impressed by this connection between Stevens and Heidegger had I not several years ago published an essay that works through a continuously surprising web of relations between what Heidegger calls Hölderlin's poetizing of this river and Thoreau's philosophizing, let's call it, of his woodland lake, Walden.[7]

Passing by such matters as Heidegger and Thoreau both requiring of philosophy that it be a matter of awakening, and their both understanding their respective bodies of water as preparing the earth for human habitation, and both emphasizing the construction of a hearth, and both detecting the pervasiveness of mourning (or melancholy) related to the learning of remaining patiently near or next to the origin of life, and their both taking the marking-out of paths as signs of destinies (something Heidegger takes to unify a people, something Thoreau takes as a cue to rebuke himself), let's focus simply on the three-word opening line of the Ister Hymn (a poem of roughly seventy comparably short lines): "Now come, fire," a line to which Heidegger devotes the opening pages of his text on the poem. He says of the line, addressed to the rising of the sun, that it is a call (the concept of calling is also thematic in *Walden*) and, Heidegger continues, "The call says: we, the ones thus calling, are ready. And something else is also concealed in such calling out: we are ready and are so only because we are called by the coming fire itself." That is, we are there before the sun arrives; awakening must happen thus earlier.

Thoreau is still more explicit. Early in the first chapter of *Walden*, in introducing himself by "attempting to tell" how he has "desired to spend" his life (one attempt he describes as "trying to hear what was in the wind"), he lists the work of "[anticipating] not the sunrise and the dawn merely, but, if possible Nature herself!" Later in that paragraph Thoreau concedes, "It is true, I never assisted the sun materially in his rising, but, doubt not, it was of the last importance only to be present at it." To "assist" at a social event—for example, a theater performance—is precisely an old-fashioned term for making oneself present, or attending. An importance of Thoreau's observation, as elsewhere, is his demonstrating that he can make sunrise a communal event even when what is called religion has forgotten how. This kind of remembrance is something Wallace Stevens requires of poetry, as he names the very idea of God to be the responsibility of poetry. Thoreau's work of anticipating is something he thematizes as being early, and earlier, and earliest.

So *Walden* is a source from which Stevens may be thought to have acquired truths characteristic of Heidegger's work, ones indeed outstripping that work on Hölderlin. I do not know whether it is materially provable that Stevens read Thoreau, but it is enough that there is no doubt of his having read Emerson, which would have sufficed in this region. A favorite quotation of Nietzsche's from Emerson's essay "Circles" speaks of "another dawn risen on mid-noon," which, however, was derived from Milton and is to be found also in Wordsworth's *Prelude.* The difference here is that Emerson is not picturing awakening as an anticipation, but the basic affinity is the perception that an inner dawn is not given to us by the bare fact of the rising sun. More specific to Emerson is the idea of closing the skeptical distance between mind and reality through the concept of what is *near.* (Thoreau's variation is to speak of what is happening at all times *next* to us.)

In Emerson's great essay "Experience" he says, "I cannot get it nearer to me," having identified his experience of the being of the world with his grief over the death of his young son. I have argued in other contexts that Emerson's implication is that, through mourning, and patience, we can reverse skepticism and let the world come nearer to us. This is figured in what happens in Stevens's late poem "The World as Meditation," where Penelope, wondering whether it is Ulysses or the sun lifting over the eastern horizon, notes that "the warmth of the sun / On her pillow" means that it is only one more material day; hence,

> She would talk a little to herself as she combed her hair,
> Repeating his name with its patient syllables,
> Never forgetting him that kept coming constantly so near.

In accepting this account of keeping near reality, living with it, as opposed to claiming coincidence or immediacy with it, of the patience the human creature has to learn in its relation to the world it cares for, accepting the active patience that philosophical skepticism construes as an intellectual puzzle to be solved, be put to rest, I accept the poem as a successful celebration of a happy marriage, which understands it to be an epic event. It may then be taken as an answer to Kant's taunting philosophy with leaving the existence of things outside of us at the mercy of faith rather than settled by a proof.

The knack of the answer is to render faith as faithfulness, as daily as the coming of the sun, obscured or not. Stevens refers to such an accomplishment in his conjecture, near the end of "Notes toward a Supreme Fiction," which runs: "Perhaps, / The man-hero is not the exceptional monster, / But he that of repetition is most master," precisely the mastery that faithfulness requires. There is a prominent interpretation of "The World as Meditation" that takes it to be Stevens's confession of a failed marriage, in which case the implication of the "barbarous strength" the poem attributes to faithfulness would become a recipe for spiritual torture, hopeless distance, the dully tantalized world as hell. It is a thought not beyond Stevens, but not, I think, in this poem.

In the concluding paragraph of "Experience," Emerson announces what will become one of Wallace Stevens's most repetitive motives or motifs, namely, to "realize his world," and two paragraphs earlier Emerson provides instruction in this process that has various echoes for us. Emerson says, "I am and I have; but I do not get, and when I have fancied I had gotten anything, I found I did not." "To find the real" is how Stevens comparably puts things in "Notes toward a Supreme Fiction," in the section preceding that from which I earlier cited the line "I have not but I am and as I am, I am." The contradiction between Emerson's "I am and I have" and Stevens's "I have not but I am" is canceled as it turns out that what Stevens says he has is "No need, am happy, forget needs' golden hand, / Am satisfied" (what he has is respite). And when in that same essay of Emerson's we find the claim "Thus inevitably does the universe wear our color," I must hear this as asserting jointly both sides of Stevens's perpetual oscillation between claiming for poetry that it is, and that it is not, the construction, or abstraction, of the individual poet. Of course, Emerson draws the implication of his observation by seeing "every object fall into the subject itself"; but what his words actually say is that the universe jousts for our attention and approval. This double sense of "our color," as idiosyncratically or (as Stevens just might have said) idiotically ours and at the same time worn publicly, seems to me a useful way to think of Stevens's punctual signature bursts of color adjectives across his surfaces, from early blackbirds flying in a green light and a rose rabbi and a dream of red weather to a blue guitar and the azury center of time.

Before looking for a place to stop, remembering that one of the incitements to these beads of philosophy I have strung along was the name and the saying of Professor Eucalyptus that measures the search for reality by the search for God, I pause to voice my sense that so particular a name as eucalyptus (other trees are content with names such as elm, pine, maple, cedar, oak, fir, spruce, beech, birch) is too particular to be confined to a given professor. I take the name, referring to a tree some of whose species bear a leaf that is aromatic and yields an oil used medicinally, as being used by Stevens to refer, somewhat ruefully, not necessarily exclusively, to himself. That the eucalyptus leaf's properties are here held in check by the title "Professor" is an effect equally pertinent to a streak in Stevens, who likes to include pronouncements in his poetry (he collects them separately under the term "Adagia," adages), such as "We seek / Nothing beyond reality" ("An Ordinary Evening," section 9). Is this fact of isolated pronouncement less important than that what goes on to happen in this poem is not what we would expect to happen in a treatise of philosophical puzzlement? Noting that "eucalyptus" is related to the term "apocalypse," meaning the uncovering or revelation of what is hidden, and letting this send us back to the connection with Heidegger's conception of truth as *a-letheia*, I cite again Emerson's "Experience," which opens by depicting us as finding ourselves waking on a stair, stairs below and above us, where, as we reenter existence, "the Genius stands at the door and gives us the lethe to drink [but] mixed the cup too strongly, and we cannot shake off the lethargy now at noonday" (the term "lethargy" making explicit the state induced by drinking from the river Lethe).

And Emerson's essay "Experience" explicitly challenges the philosopher's idea of experience to be found in Kant and in the classical empiricists (Emerson characterizes the idea as a "paltry empiricism," an impoverishment of experience), implicitly resisting Kant's metaphysical, fixed separation of the two worlds Kant perceives humankind to live in, the world of sense and the world of intellect, and Emerson explicitly rejects the despair of what Kant had already called "realizing his world" (a formulation critical for both Emerson and Stevens), a despair fated by a paltry empiricism. Stevens is surely moving similarly when he speaks, in the "Figure of the Youth" essay, of poetry as "destroy[ing] the false imagination." A parallel I cannot doubt was in Stevens's ear when he thus speaks of the poet's destructiveness I find in a passage from Emerson's essay "Fate," in his saying: "We should be crushed by the atmosphere, but for the reaction of the air within the body. . . . If there be omnipotence in the stroke, there is omnipotence of recoil." Stevens casts this thought slightly differently, within his own philosophical palette, when at the end of the essay written the year earlier than "Figure of the Youth," namely, "The Noble Rider and the Sound of Words," he says: "It is a violence from within that protects us from a violence without. It is the imagination pressing back against the pressure of reality." But Stevens speaks for himself, or rather for poetry, as Emerson had spoken for his prose, when he claims for this violence, with modest exorbitance, that it "helps us to live our lives."

I must try, before having done, some brief answer to the most obvious two cruxes posed in the essay "The Figure of the Youth as Virile Poet": first, the title insistence on the poet as a young male; second, the repeatedly invoked "sister of the Minotaur," to whom, as a new muse, Stevens early confides that he no longer believes "that there is a mystic muse," which is only, he goes on to say, "another of the monsters I had for nurse, whom I have wasted." He declares to her that he is part of the real and hears only the strength of his own speech. Then at the close he again asks this apparently non-mystical and monstrous muse to hear him, who knows that he is part of the real, but beyond this to recognize him as part of the unreal—that is, as part of what is still to be realized, hence to be fictionalized—and to guide him to the truth of the imagination, which he cannot reach by the strength of his speech alone, but which requires "exchanges of speech in which your words are mine, mine yours."

About the first crux, the young male, I note only what is clear on the surface, that he needs to be violent in a male way (virile) because the burden of the past, from which he needs liberation (poetry is always of the present), has been an affair of males; and also because he needs to attract and withstand the indispensable recognition and guidance of a female monster. (The old poet Stevens figures as a tramp, having, I imagine, given away all the intelligence he had to give; no match for a Minotaur's sister.) To say more then depends on following the second crux, concerning who or what this monster/muse is. I shall just try looking at the idea that she is monstrous because, as Stevens puts it earlier, this "muse of [the young poet's] own" is "still half-beast and somehow more than human." (I will assume, though it is not certain, that this rules out her being one of the Minotaur's well-known half-sisters, Ariadne or Phaedra. I am here following the thought that Stevens is conjuring an unheard-of female Minotaur, a domesticator of the maze, the world, and its words, not a rescuer from it.)

I find Emerson a further help here, in his articulation of the intersection of the subjective and the objective, or perhaps of their collusion, where he observes, "We but half express ourselves," which I understand, however else, to imply that the other half of our expression is in the hands of language, which is never wholly ours. I hear a version of this in Stevens where, instead of, as in Emerson, a Genius is standing at the door, Stevens places an Angel "seen for a moment standing in the door" who announces that "in my sight, you see earth again, cleared of its . . . man-locked set, / And, in my hearing, you hear its tragic drone." The figure who announces this (in the poem "Angel Surrounded by Paysans," which concludes *The Auroras of Autumn*) identifies himself as "a man of the mind," and as "The necessary angel of earth," describing himself as "only half a figure of a sort, / A figure half seen" who offers "meanings said / By repetitions of half-meanings." So whereas the sister of the Minotaur—another half-figure of a sort, a figure of halves—can be invoked and asked to make her words ours and ours hers, the Angel who offers to make his sight and his hearing ours can only be awaited and glimpsed, like all that goes unseen, unheard, unimagined, unrealized, unsaid. The poet is the one who knows how to invoke and to await these appearances.

There is no question now of pursuing how Stevens's location of the human as moving between Minotaur and angel compares with Aristotle's location of us as neither beasts nor gods, or with Pascal's location of us as between beasts and angels, or with Kant's somewhat different location of us as neither beasts nor angels. I have been led to emphasize the figures in Stevens as representing moments in which, primarily in my efforts to come to terms with Wittgenstein's *Philosophical Investigations,* I have recurred to the idea that in philosophizing we wish to escape our humanity—our finitude—from above or from below, a wish I have also expressed as the all but inescapable wish of the human to become inhuman, as if to accept monstrousness would be to escape the perpetual knowledge of our disappointments, the maze of infinite desires in finite circumstances.

In each of the appeals Stevens addresses to philosophy there is, to my mind, a false step that helps ensure he will emerge unsatisfied. The error comes out in the opening sentence of his preface to the prose texts in the volume *The Necessary Angel.* In that preface he says, "One function of the poet at any time is to discover by his own thought and feeling what seems to him to be poetry at that time." What Stevens will not conceive is that the philosopher may have a comparable function of discovery, as if for Stevens philosophy, in its otherness, is a fixed, oracular structure and those who speak for it are in possession of an authority that goes beyond what they are able to articulate out of their own experience and practice and wit on each occasion of being stopped to think.

I end with one more link between Stevens and Emerson, glancing at a moment in each at which the right to speak is staked against the mortal dangers and the injustices of their times. Emerson, with shocking intent, deflects imagined charges against his neglect of the poor by claiming in effect that he means his writing to serve the poor in the way he is best fit to serve. And Stevens, in the ambience of World War II, appends to his manifesto "Notes toward a Supreme Fiction" stanzas addressed to a soldier in which he claims the poet is joined in a war of the mind that never ends and that depends on his, on the soldier's, war. These stanzas include the words "The soldier is poor without the poet's lines." So Emerson and Stevens thus each subjects his work to an extreme test—call it the test of maintaining the truth of the nation even when the nation is mobilized in maintaining its existence. Presumably they do this to alert us, their readers, that in taking up their words, we subject ourselves to judging their survival of this test, hence to the test's reflected judgment of us; we judge that we be judged. This was true in 1943, as it was in Emerson's 1843 and the years after, as it is in 2003.

NOTES

1. Rudolf Carnap, "The Elimination of Metaphysics through Logical Analysis of Language," in *Logical Positivism,* ed. A. J. Ayer (Glencoe, Ill.: Free Press, 1959).

2. Frank Kermode, "Dwelling Poetically in Connecticut," in *Pieces of My Mind* (New York: Farrar, Straus and Giroux, 2003).

3. Peter Brazeau, *Parts of a World: Wallace Stevens Remembered* (San Francisco: North Point, 1985), 214.

4. I am conscious of having been helped by the literary-critical writing of Helen Vendler, and of Laura Quinney, and by a late essay of Randall Jarrell: Helen Vendler, "Stevens' Secrecies," in *Wallace Stevens: Words Chosen Out of Desire* (Nashville: University of Tennessee Press, 1984), 44–60; Laura Quinney, *Poetics of Disappointment* (Charlottesville: University Press of Virginia, 1999); Randall Jarrell, "Reflections on Wallace Stevens," in *No Other Book: Selected Essays,* ed. Brad Leithauser (New York: HarperCollins, 1999), 112–22.

5. Wallace Stevens, *Opus Posthumous,* ed. Samuel French Morse (New York: Knopf, 1957), 190.

6. Martin Heidegger, *Hölderlin's Hymn "The Ister,"* trans. William McNeill and Julia Davis (Bloomington: Indiana University Press, 1996).

7. Stanley Cavell, "Thoreau Thinks of Ponds, Heidegger of Rivers," in *Philosophy the Day after Tomorrow* (Cambridge: Harvard University Press, 2005), 213–35. An earlier version appeared in *Appropriating Heidegger,* ed. James E. Faulconer and Mark A. Wrathhall (Cambridge: Cambridge University Press, 2000), 30–49.

Thoughts on Wallace Stevens's Contribution at Pontigny-en-Amérique

Response to Cavell

JEFFREY MEHLMAN

"The Figure of the Youth as Virile Poet" is a confusing text, but it does have a recognizable armature of sorts, pertaining to the three references to a muse said to be "a kind of sister of the Minotaur." The mythographer immediately thinks of Ariadne and Phaedra, but because she first appears in relation to a "younger figure," a "son still bearing the antique imagination of the father," Phaedra-and-Hippolytus (rather than Ariadne-and-Theseus) seems the more apt allusion. This impression is reinforced by a number of additional elements. First, there is the somewhat jarring insistence on the "virility" of the poet-youth, for virility (which, in the Greek, went hand in hand with misogyny) was the signature hang-up of Hippolytus. Indeed, for anyone surprised by Stevens's decision to come to the women's college Mount Holyoke to announce (a bit offensively?) that "the centuries have a way of being male," it is almost as though Stevens were entertaining an identification with the Euripidean hero.

Pontigny, however, was a gala French occasion, and Stevens, as Christopher Benfey has noted, seems to have been particularly eager to lace his texts with French references (Bergson, Valéry, Mallarmé, Cézanne, etc.), so that there is a good chance that the subliminal reference was less to Euripides than to Racine. The suspicion is sustained by the fact that the initial reference to the sister of the Minotaur is *directly* preceded by two invocations of the seventeenth century ("When we think of the seventeenth century...," "When we look back at the face of the seventeenth century...").

At this point it may be helpful to review the fundamental way in which Racine modified Euripides' plot. In the Greek, the tragedy tells of the punishment of Hippolytus, devotee of the goddess of the hunt (and virility) Diana Artemis, for failing to make offering at the altar of Aphrodite. In contemporary parlance, Hippolytus doesn't date: he has no interest in women, is proud of it, and is about to suffer for it. Racine, who may have suspected that a gay hero would have been laughed off the French stage, gives Hippolytus a girl-friend, Aricie, about whom he feels terribly conflicted, but to whom he declares his love (in a scene directly echoing Phèdre's declaration of love to

Hippolyte). The subject of Racine's play, in sum, is Hippolytus' emergence from the closet as a straight male.

Whereas Euripides posits a diametric opposition between Phaedra and Hippolytus (who are stand-ins for the warring goddesses Aphrodite and Diana Artemis), Racine serves up a Hippolytus who, in his guilty love for Aricie, is a pale reflection of Phaedra and whose struggle, ultimately unsuccessful, is to work his way free of her clutches. This is a quintessentially Racinian posture: Néron, in Racine's *Britannicus,* spends a good part of the play fending off his incestuous mother, Agrippine.

But this brings us back to the Stevens essay, for it recounts the unsuccessful struggle of the "virile" poet-youth to free himself from his muse, the sister-of-the-Minotaur. At a key juncture he announces: "No longer do I believe that there is a mystic muse, sister of the Minotaur. This is another of the monsters I had for nurse, whom I have wasted. I am myself a part of what is real, and it is my own speech and the strength of it, this only, that I hear or ever shall." May we say that poetry here is imagined as an exercise in de-mythologization, the "incandescence" of its "intelligence" marking a "triumph over the incredible"? If so, it would be part and parcel of the Enlightenment project: "washing the imagination clean," Hippolytus will have laid waste "monstrous" Phaedra.

Yet whatever the validity of that project, it would appear that for Stevens, it is destined to fail, and that the success of poetry may lie in its failure. Whence the last lines of the essay, attributed to the virile poet-youth: "Inexplicable sister of the Minotaur, enigma and mask, although I am part of what is real, hear me and recognize me as part of the unreal. I am the truth but the truth of that imagination of life in which with unfamiliar motion and manner you guide me in those exchanges of speech in which your words are mine, mine yours." In terms of what I take to be the Racine intertext, Hippolytus ends up the defeated mirror image of the monstrous maternal superego he no longer has the force to resist. It is quite un-Euripidean, but deeply Racinian.

And then there is the fact that a meandering version of the quintessential Racinian alexandrine, spoken by Hippolyte—"Le ciel n'est pas plus pur que le fond de mon coeur"—just happens to work its way into Stevens's argument: "When we look at the blue sky for the first time, that is to say: not merely see it, but look at it and experience it and for the first time have a sense that we live in the center of a physical poetry, a geography that would be intolerable except for the non-geography that exists there—few people realize that they are looking at the world of their own thoughts and the world of their own feelings." The lines may cry out for interpretation (or refutation), but what seems unassailable is their coherence with the genealogy I am constructing.

But why would Stevens have laced his apparently philosophical (or anti-philosophical) argument with fragments of a Racinian genealogy? Perhaps our best answer lies in the definition of the poet Stevens offers early in his Pontigny excursus: what is a young poet, he asks, if not "the voluble convert or the person looking in a mirror who sees suddenly the traces of an unexpected genealogy." It is a proposition that is enacted by the fragments of Racine's masterwork strewn through the body of Stevens's essay.

An unexpected genealogy...About fifteen years after Pontigny-en-Amérique, Charles Mauron, who was nowhere near there, but who makes a significant appearance elsewhere in *The Necessary Angel*, wrote his master-work, *L'inconscient dans l'oeuvre et la vie de Racine*, a work whose decisive influence on me I have explored elsewhere.[1] One of the principal points registered by Mauron is that the monstrous maternal superego against which the author—the would-be virile poet—in Racine was constantly struggling was a figure for the heretical religious community, the Jansenists of Port-Royal, who had raised him in his childhood. Port-Royal was violently opposed to all "spectacles," and Racine's career effectively meant a break with the community that had raised him. Stevens at Pontigny: "Summed up, our position at the moment is that the poet must get rid of the hieratic in everything that concerns him and must move constantly in the direction of the credible." The hieratic (or sacerdotal) in this context would appear to refer to the world of Port-Royal. Might Stevens have picked this stroke up from Mauron? Probably not. Mauron makes a handsome appearance in *The Necessary Angel*, but in a context bereft of the sacerdotal. The artist according to Mauron, we are told, "transforms us into epicures." His is a loving engagement with the real world, of which he is the *amoureux perpétuel*. No sign of the struggle against the sacerdotal—be it Racinian or Stevensian—here. Might Mauron, in that case, have picked it up from Stevens? There is even less empirical probability of that. What one is left with is the enigma of the final lines of the Pontigny excursus: "those exchanges of speech in which your words are mine, mine yours." And the hope of finding one's own words within them.

I WOULD not have undertaken a reading of the Stevens essay had I not heard that Stanley Cavell was scheduled to offer a reading of the Stevens contribution at Pontigny at the colloquium we were both scheduled to address. As it happened, the Cavell address was far-reaching, subtle, characteristically engaging—of everything except the supposition that the sister of the Minotaur might at some level be Phaedra (and the virile poet Hippolytus). Such was my attachment to the reading I have just sketched, and such my fascination with the link between that reading and the presence, actual and virtual, of my old teacher Charles Mauron in the Stevens text, that I found myself pondering what it was that might lead him to overlook (or dismiss) the *Phèdre* intertext.

And then I discovered that my difference with Stanley Cavell was, unexpectedly, in the way of an indirect quotation of his own work. "What Did Derrida Want of Austin?," as it happens, is a text as committed to the memory of an inspiring teacher as anything I have written here. The semester spent with Austin in 1955, Cavell writes, was on the order of a "conversion experience." [2] And his essay, daunting in its eloquence, takes the form of defending the specific originality of Austin from Derrida's assault (in a text that, coincidentally, I co-translated more than a quarter of a century ago) by insisting at some length on all that Derrida missed by failing to respond to an example, cited by Austin, from Euripides' *Hippolytus*. In the seminar following the paper at Bucknell, Cavell specifies the accusation: "[Derrida] neglects the inscription of tragedy in that text, Austin's citation from Euripides' *Hippolytus*." [3]

THIS IS surely not the occasion to rehearse aspects of the Austin-Derrida encounter. It has occurred to me that the two philosophical endeavors might be heuristically encapsulated in two extremely close and entirely incompatible propositions. Austin: My word is my bond. Derrida: *Ma parole bande*. Moreover, if one were to engage a defense of Derrida in this context, it might begin by noting that Cavell himself is prepared to admit that Austin (himself) appears to have misinterpreted, though to excellent purpose, the crucial passage from the *Hippolytus*.

What leaves me perplexed and not a little exhilarated is my sense that my reading of the Stevens excursus at Pontigny, and by implication my supplement to Stanley Cavell's reading, appears to be nothing so much as a masked citation of Cavell's own critique of Derrida: in the orbit of a revered teacher (Cavell's Austin, my Mauron), a claim is made that everything turns on perceiving (or not) the presence of a version of the Hippolytus myth in an enigmatic text. With Stevens's phrase about "unexpected genealogy" hovering close by, it may be wondered if ever a "critique"—but surely at this level of inter-implication the word is inadequate—has been more curiously indebted to what I hesitate to call its object.

NOTES

1. Jeffrey Mehlman, "Chiasmus: A Memoir," in *Parallax* 8, no. 1 (2002): 123–36.

2. Stanley Cavell, *Philosophical Passages: Wittgenstein, Emerson, Austin, Derrida* (Oxford: Blackwell, 1995), 43.

3. Ibid., 70.

Postscript

Response to Mehlman

Stanley Cavell

I DO NOT doubt that Jeffrey Mehlman, in his elegant and exuberant response to my remarks, has successfully demonstrated "the *Phèdre* intertext" in Stevens's "Figure of the Youth as Virile Poet" text. When I said that I assumed the obvious candidates—Ariadne and Phaedra—for Stevens's provision to the young poet of a successor to a "mystic muse," one characterized by the poet as "a kind of sister of the Minotaur," were ruled out, I did not regard myself as taking the play *Phèdre* as a whole to be ruled out as bearing upon Stevens's text. I gladly accept Mehlman's sense and evidence that Racine's play is strewn through Stevens's essay. My reason for the exclusion of the half-sisters of the Minotaur as candidates for the poet's muse was Stevens's noting that the youth's muse is "still half beast and somehow more than human." Phèdre is called a monster by Hippolyte and by herself, and she calls her nurse a monster, and both she and Thésée call Hippolyte a monster, but none, I believe, take the epithet to mean that any of these candidates for monstrousness are half-beasts. It seems rather that their crimes (real or imagined) show them the more human. I might also have adduced for my claim Stevens's characterizing the monster/muse as a *kind* of sister—which *might* be taken to mean that she is a half-sister, but equally might be taken to mean that she is *like* a half-sister, hence different; so either alone is arbitrary.

When Mehlman initially in the discussion period after my talk expressed to me his sense of Racine's presence in Stevens's essay, finding it at least as pertinent as Racine's source in Euripides' version of the Hippolytus story, I accepted the theory he broached then with pleasure and predicted that the relative importance for me of the versions must be a function of their contributions to the question of the condition of a youth's discovery or claim that he is a poet. In Euripides' telling, the contribution can be said to be that accepting a promise, allegorically to give your words to poetry, can be fatal—you may be unequal to the prophecy and the poverty this vow implies. In Racine's telling, the fatal promise is one Hippolyte's father, Thésée, exacts from Neptune, not one the nurse exacts from Hippolyte. It is still the nurse who reveals the connection between Hippolytus and Phaedra's passion that Euripides has her confide to Hippolytus and draw the promise of his silence—but Racine's nurse reveals it by reversing the direction, the subject and the object, of the passion (somewhat as if the positions of the pair were seen in a mirror).

I hadn't read Racine's *Phèdre* recently enough to consider the matter on the spot during the discussion at Mount Holyoke, a failure of preparation that I attribute not quite to overlooking or dismissing the play (as Mehlman tentatively suggests) but rather to simple fear of it: there is too much that I do not know, and should know, that stands between me and Racine's text. Yet painful ignorance has not prevented me in the past from approaching, let's say, other monsters of fame. In any case, I have now reread Racine's *Phèdre* and find enough at hand to broach an initial response concerning its competing contribution to the figure or condition of the young poet. No longer a promise to a lethal burden of silence is at issue, but something like its reverse, namely, the burden or risk of speech, more precisely in the Racinian text, the issue of the right to speak, to speak from the heart, not in order to tell the secrets of others—unless this means to tell the secrets they do not know they harbor.

What is at stake for me here is whether Racine's Hippolyte in relation to the monster Phèdre is to be taken as the model for Stevens's youth in relation to his monster/muse, the specific supposition Mehlman rightly charges me with having failed to engage. Let's unfold the issue a little further. The young poet appeals to his new muse for recognition and for her words. These seem the last things Hippolyte would wish to have from Phèdre. Even if we suppose in him an unconscious desire for her, how are we to imagine that a poet, for the sake of his poetry, could desire the recognition of one who is compelled to keep herself hidden from the sun, her origin, desire the words of one who cannot speak of her desire?

We have known from the beginning of the story that Hippolyte lives with the idea that the right to his existence, and to speak of it (perhaps to dedicate it to poetry), must be assigned by fulfilling the task of killing a monster—doing what his father is famous for doing, preserving cities. (This idea of violence and competition at the root of the justification for selfhood does strike me as peculiarly that of a young male. As the justification for speech, it makes even more general sense.) To kill the monster Phèdre would, in Hippolyte's case, again seem to require a reversal, not putting her to the sword, as she begs or dares him to do, but leaving her to her own transfixed imagination.

Mehlman and his account of his teacher Charles Mauron's work on Racine promise to take me further in a direction I wish to follow, for example, to teach me what I was seeing when I said of the virile poet as figured by the youth that "he needs to attract and withstand the indispensable recognition and guidance of a female monster" (perhaps this is itself the inscription of a memory of Racine's play). This seems quite precisely what Hippolyte cannot manage in relation to Phèdre. It is, I suppose, this impotence that prompted my fancy in taking Stevens's idea of a kind of sister of the Minotaur to be a female Minotaur, a monster to counteract as it were the sea's womb's power to destroy the chariot on the descending mountain's edge in which Euripides' Hippolytus is asserting his autonomy against Phaedra. Stevens describes this autonomy as the new, non-mystical muse's power to recognize him as part of the unreal as well as of the real, to give him a voice carrying beyond "his own speech," to which he resigns himself in his first direct invocation of his construction of his muse: "No longer do I believe that there is a mystic muse, sister of the Minotaur" (ambiguous as between addressing the new muse and identifying her as the old, mystic muse). At the end, where he addresses her unambiguously, and asks for her recognition as part of the unreal, this involves an appeal for exchanges of speech "in which your words are mine, mine yours." I glossed this idea of the unreal as the fictional, that which does not (yet?) exist. Stevens, I believe, also describes this as moments of "victory over the incredible," something he is careful to say does not mean that everything becomes purely clear. Perhaps I can, inspired by Mehlman's intervention, say another word about this.

The line Mehlman cites from Racine's *Phèdre*—Hippolyte's assertion, "Le ciel n'est plus pur que le fond de mon coeur"—he discovers to enter into Stevens's argument, which moves from "when we look at the blue sky for the first time…that is to say…experience it and for the first time have a sense that we live in the center of a physical poetry, a geography that would be intolerable except for the non-geography that exists there"—moves from this experience to the conclusion that "few people realize that they are looking at the world of their own thoughts and the world of their own feelings." It affords me something I daresay is similar to the exhilaration Mehlman expresses to find in this same line of Racine's, as I imagine Austin would suspiciously hear it, a point of coincidence with the assertion Austin quotes (near the beginning of *How to Do Things with Words*, his text on the performative utterance), which Euripides gives to his *Hippolytus*: "My tongue swore, my heart did not"—a line whose neglect by Austin's interpreters, the friendly and the not so friendly, Mehlman pivotally notes that I deplore. (And notes as well that I sense Austin falsely to remember the line as permitting Hippolytus' attempt to get out of his horrifyingly destructive promise. I cite it as revealing Austin's impression of it, not as affirming the truth of the impression.)

Austin's suspicion is that Hippolytus claims the metaphysical, or mystical, separation of the private inner from the public outer in order to attest to his innocence, or purity, in denying the validity of his supposed promise. (The philosophical and moral motive Austin declares for his work on the performative utterance is its working to block inexcusable weaseling out of commitments. He cites as his watchword, as noted by Mehlman, "My word is my bond." I have argued elsewhere that the Euripides *Hippolytus* shows that motto to have in it the power of a curse.) In the same way I imagine Austin would decry the line invoking the purity of the sky that Racine gives his Hippolyte: it permits Hippolyte a claim to the metaphysical or poetic relation of the sky to the bottom of his heart in order to attest to an unverifiable, hence unchallengeable, purity of heart in relation to Phèdre's horrifying claim upon him.

But Stevens is also contesting Racine's Hippolyte. I take Stevens's assignment of purity to be interpreted by his speaking of the non-geography that exists in the center of the physical geography of poetry in which we live. The non-geography is what Emerson (in "Self-Reliance") calls "the voice of the mind," the return of our words to us—lost in the region of the merely credible (the world of conformity, the credulous)—by works of genius, which in effect allow us to become credible to ourselves.

Stevens comparably describes "the moment of exaltation that the poet experiences when he writes a poem that completely accomplishes his purpose, [as] a moment of victory over the incredible, a moment of purity that does not become any the less pure because, as what was incredible is eliminated, something newly credible takes its place." This also is ambiguous. Does "because" mean "since," namely, that purity is not diminished since the incredible is replaced by the credible? Or, as I find, does "because" mean "even though," namely, even though something newly credible takes place, happens? The implication in the latter case is that the incredible, or the newly incredible, retains its place. That is, purity, the condition of poetry, the non-geography that allows us to "tolerate" the physical poetry the world makes, preserves the credible taking place within, or out of, the incredible, speech out of the silence of the poetry of the world, which otherwise would leave us intolerably inexpressive, unresponsive, suffocated by significance or by insignificance, having no intelligence of the blank difference (call it the difference between pure imagination and pure reality).

So purity is no longer a question of a violent autonomy, as youth imagines. This is monstrous innocence, not yet human. The youth's invocation of the muse is an invitation as well as a plea, to allow my words to participate in the monstrousness of language as such, over which there is no absolute mastery, but (only) moments of victory. Stevens's prose wish, within the poetry of his prose, for philosophy and its metaphysics is (merely) a human wish for the inhuman. It calls for poetry.

As if to warn against too much enthusiasm with the myth of Hippolytus (how much is just enough?), Stevens writes of the youth, "For this Aeneas, it is the past that is Anchises." Aeneas succeeded in abandoning, if ingloriously, an impassioned woman, leaving the past. But then he had the favor of Neptune, and he got his father off his back.

Henry Church and the Literary Magazine *Mesures*

"The American Resource"

Claire Paulhan

HENRY CHURCH WAS born January 3, 1880, in Brooklyn. He was a descendant of one of the *Mayflower* pilgrims and also of a pharmacist who owned a monopoly on the marketing of bicarbonate of soda in the United States (the source of Church's immense fortune). At the age of twenty-one, Church went to Europe. He studied music in Munich and chemistry in Geneva before beginning a sojourn in Paris in 1905. After his return to the United States, he married for the first time and had a daughter. For Church, however, America was "neither the wind nor the sea gull's cry; it's a façade with nothing behind it. But it's a fine façade, and people are constantly striving to discover what it means." [1]

After a second Parisian sojourn (1910–1912), Church returned to Paris in 1921, accompanied by his second wife, Barbara, whose background was Bavarian and whose father was a rich coal merchant. They settled in Ville d'Avray, on the southwestern outskirts of the city, where they hired Le Corbusier to convert and reconstruct first two and later three contiguous houses, which were then furnished by Charlotte Perriand. Henry Church, a handsome, reserved man with a weak heart, and his chic wife could afford to live the high life: palatial mansions, extensive travel, and spa treatments in the fashionable towns of Old Europe; jewels and evening gowns; memorable fireworks displays in Ville d'Avray, where their garages housed three Bugattis and a Hispano-Suiza. Soon there were rumors about masses of available money; some indelicate artists and gallery owners clamped on to the prosperous couple, perhaps with a view to cheating them, and as a result the Churches felt a certain *"disappointment in their social relationships,"* in the words of Jean Paulhan. A further result was that Henry Church made the acquaintance of a legal and financial adviser, Monsieur Moreau-Lalande, who became his faithful friend.

Moreau-Lalande made it possible for Church to begin a career as a generous but sensible and judicious arts patron: we know that he materially helped artists and writers, that he financed some shows and concerts in the brand-new Théâtre des Champs-Élysées, that he created an association, the "Jeunes Amitiés Internationales," which organized meetings among students from different countries in the 1930s, and that he contributed handsomely to a fund that made it possible for Thomas Mann to leave Germany in 1933.

But Henry Church, who considered himself "a scientist and an autodidact," loved literature most of all.[2] He began writing during his first Parisian sojourn, during which he met Jean Royère and collaborated on his literary magazine, *La Phalange*. Shortly after his third return to Paris in 1921, Church made a modest entry into publishing, founding Les Éditions des Deux Amis, which was soon taken over by La Librairie de France.

Church was the author of a poetry collection, four plays, and several works of fiction. The most important of these include: *Les Clowns* (drawings by Georges Rouault, Éditions des Deux Amis, 1922), *Indésirables* (Librairie de France, Collection des Deux Amis, 1922), and "Bacillus subtilis Artis" (*Mesures*, 1936). Henry Church also translated several plays into French, among them Shakespeare's *Richard III*, G. K. Chesterton's *Magic*, and Georg Kaiser's *Von Morgen bis Mitternacht*.

The American poet Wallace Stevens, who closely followed developments in French literature and culture from his home in Hartford, Connecticut, told his friend Henry Church, "I love to hear from you. You have so thoroughly lived the life that I should have been glad to live."[3]

SINCE THE death of Jacques Rivière in 1925, Jean Paulhan had been the editor in chief of the *Nouvelle Revue Française (NRF)*. He and Church were probably introduced by one of Church's close friends, Paul Boyer, director of the École des langues orientales and also the uncle of Jean Paulhan's first wife. Church and Paulhan began an epistolary relationship in 1934. The two correspondents had the same ambition, a project that must already have brought them together on more than one occasion: to create a new literary review. Church financed and managed the magazine, and Paulhan proposed the material for each issue and directed the editorial work "in secret"—officially, so as not to interfere with his activities as editor of the *NRF*. Their collaborators included the members of the first selection committee, better known as "secretaries of good will"[4]: Bernard Groethuysen, a very close friend of Paulhan; Giuseppe Ungaretti, also closely connected to Paulhan but to the Churches as well; and Henri Michaux. (Later, we find such names as Armand Petitjean, Roger Caillois, Vladimir Nabokov, and Michel Leiris, who exhibited sufficient interest in Church's publishing venture to be considered part of the review's selection committee.) The first order of business was to agree on the title of the new literary magazine, a quarterly, whose first issue was scheduled to appear in January 1935. During the various preparatory meetings held in Ville d'Avray, several titles were put forward. At one time, *Lectures* seems to have been everyone's favorite; Henry Church, for his part, preferred *Lettres* and found the title *Mesures* too prescriptive:

As for *Mesures,* my impression is the same. The reader will think about measurements, about the measures we'll take to impose our aesthetic opinions, about a tendency. That's what I want to avoid; I want the quality of the works we print to be paramount. Besides, as a foreigner, I must avoid giving the impression that I'm interested in exerting any pressure whatsoever on French taste. That's why I prefer *Lettres,* even though I don't find it a completely satisfactory title. It's a bit drab, but at least it has no meaning other than the alphabet and what one does with it.[5]

Nevertheless, the title *Mesures* was the eventual choice.[6] After that, the magazine's general orientation was decided—French and foreign-language poetry and literature, along with spirituality, particularly that of the Far East—and the founders discussed the contents of the first issue. The names exchanged were Marcel Jouhandeau, Jean Grenier, Jacques Audiberti, André Suarès, André Gide, Paul Claudel, Henri Pourrat, Pierre Leyris, Marcel Arland, Jean Prévost, Armand Petitjean, Georges Schéhadé, Pierre Jean Jouve, and Michel Leiris, all of whom already belonged to the *NRF*'s sphere of influence.

Looking through the first issues of *Mesures* that appeared in 1935, one searches in vain for a declaration of purpose, a programmatic text, an address to the reading public, or an appeal, the sort of thing that could be found at that time in the pages of the *Nouvelle Revue Française.* So what was the line that *Mesures* intended to follow? Perhaps the best place to discern the nature of the "magazine's aesthetic"—which, in any case, remained rather informal—is in the unpublished letters of Henry Church to Jean Paulhan, which are preserved in France's Institute of Contemporary Publishing Archives, the IMEC (Institut mémoires de l'édition contemporaine). Thus we find Henry Church, writing in 1937: "Wasn't the doctrine behind *Mesures* our determination not to have one? to create a doctrine through the diversity of the texts themselves?"[7]

It was imperative for them to define, as quickly as possible, a common position vis-à-vis the outside world—that is, vis-à-vis writers. This seemed to pose a problem for Church, who was normally somewhat formal: "I'm not sure how inflexible we'll have to be," he writes to Paulhan. "I think this will probably be more difficult for you, since you know the authors. I wonder whether we shouldn't create a fictitious person and give him the last word; then we could say, 'The boss thinks your submission isn't exactly what we needed or what he was looking for.' It seems to me that we must try to get Valéry, Gide, or Claudel, one of the three, especially for the first issue, but how do we turn one of them down if we don't like what he submits?"[8] Whatever the solution to this problem, the two agreed that *Mesures* wouldn't give regular column space to any writer, whoever he might be, nor would the magazine publish lectures or papers already delivered in another venue.

Jean Paulhan alone received manuscripts submitted to the review; his address in Chatenay-Malabry appeared on the *Mesures* masthead until the end of its days. And it seems that those manuscripts were forwarded only to Henry Church. Moreover, Church felt a constant urge to do away with the selection committee, "whose role is so subordinate,"[9] or, by contrast, to call for committee meetings more regularly and more often "and talk about nothing but the magazine."[10] Church feared that the meetings would degenerate into the proceedings of a literary circle with an unchanging roster of members.

Since Church wanted to be more than just the magazine's sponsor, he was a very sedulous member of the selection committee; he had, moreover, his own method of judging submissions: he would read manuscripts aloud to his wife, discuss them with her, digest her opinions, and sometimes reprise them, rather pithily, in his letters to Jean Paulhan. Whenever Church traveled to Spain and elsewhere, he tried to persuade writers to send their work to *Mesures.*

Church also edited translations, but he wouldn't review page proofs. He found this activity too tiring, even though in his letters he often claims that he hasn't done anything in the course of the day except read about a dozen newspapers. Nevertheless, he examined very attentively the texts that Jean Paulhan proposed for inclusion in *Mesures.* These were mainly essays in criticism, reflections on language; Church appreciated their "sinuous, obscure style,"[11] though he confessed that he didn't understand a great deal of what he read. Paulhan's essay "The Secret of Criticism," which appeared in the July 1938 issue of *Mesures,* struck Church as the clearest of his colleague's writings.

Church always had great faith in Paulhan and modestly agreed to work on his own pieces under the other's guidance. Thus, Church had first consigned the text of his piece "Bacillus subtilis Artis," which appeared in *Mesures* on January 15, 1936, to René Daumal for rewriting, and it was later reworked by Paulhan. The latter had refined it too much, Church thought, and he longed to put certain awkward expressions and rough patches back into his text. Church and Paulhan also worked together for a long time on another of Church's pieces, referred to under the vague title of "Letters from M. de Hohenhau," whose subject seems to have fascinated Jean Paulhan.[12] When Henry Church's writings were published posthumously in the *hommage* that Paulhan devoted to him, their baroque spirit surprised the friends and relatives of the taciturn arts patron.

WITH THE exception of Katherine Anne Porter, who was invited to Ville d'Avray in 1936, Church doesn't seem to have associated with the English-language writers who were living in Paris at the time. But he read the authors who were currently being read in the United States, not without consulting Sylvia Beach, who played the role of lookout or scout for the smugglers, the translators. One such author, for example, was William Faulkner. Church found one of his short stories "disappointing; less good, it seems to me, than his better-known stories, but interesting all the same. We can certainly publish it."[13] Another author was Theodore Dreiser: "Dreiser has a volume of short stories, *Twelve Men,* which I'm rereading at the moment. It's written in a pretty flat, drab style, and there's not much going on in the plot. Nevertheless, it's not without power. I don't think Dreiser's short stories are very well known in Europe."[14] Some essays by Henry Miller, which were "teeming with obscenities,"[15] failed to find grace in Church's eyes, but he read Miller's novels with interest and wanted to have them translated by Raymond Queneau.

But the role of *Mesures* in presenting American writers to its audience became more incisive with the publication of the July 1939 edition of the magazine, an issue devoted entirely to North American literature (well before the better-known "American" numbers of *Fontaine* or *L'Arche*). This "extraordinary issue," as Henri Pourrat called it, was introduced by Jean Paulhan, who wrote: "The reader should not expect a detailed and complete portrait of American letters.... We simply feel that the present collection, despite what it may lack in completeness, is sufficiently alive, worthy of interest, and, in more than one way, surprising. If the expression weren't slightly pretentious, we would gladly call this issue 'The American Resource.'" There follows a selection of texts written by twenty-four authors, among them Washington Irving, Edgar Allan Poe, Walt Whitman, Emily Dickinson, Vachel Lindsay, Hart Crane, John Peale Bishop, Langston Hughes, Archibald MacLeish, John Dos Passos, Wallace Stevens, and William Carlos Williams.

IN 1937 THE photographer Gisèle Freund was commissioned to take a series of official photographs for *Mesures.* The subjects included some of the members of the selection committee already mentioned, as well as Adrienne Monnier (who handled administrative matters for the journal until the end of 1937), Sylvia Beach, and Germaine Paulhan.

Jean Paulhan's second wife, Germaine (1885–1976), handled the magazine's secretarial work, as she had done since the late 1920s for the *NRF,* that is to say, with an iron fist inside a velvet glove. Church reported that he had experienced a serious episode of cardiac arrhythmia after she vehemently upbraided him on the subject of the April 1935 issue, which threatened to be too large. The typography had to be noble, broad, and spacious, the paper had to be thick, and the number of pages could not exceed two hundred. Producing a handsome magazine was Church's project; keeping it luxurious, in spite of everything, was an essential goal for Paulhan.

At the end of March 1935, Jean Paulhan wrote to Henry Church that *Mesures* had finally exceeded two hundred subscriptions. Among the subscribers was an American woman married to a maharajah, which, Paulhan wickedly added, "diminishes the achievement."[16] For the most part, authors were paid one hundred francs per page, which was unusually high for the time. Evening gatherings called *"Mesures* soirées"—also known as "sessions dedicated to *Mesures"*—were held at Adrienne Monnier's home, where they brought together authors who would read a few pages of their work, already published or to be published in the future, before a cultivated audience.

BUT WHEN Church went over the 1938 accounts, he arrived at this unhappy conclusion: "For expenses falling between 28,000 and 30,000 francs per issue, the receipts were on the order of 1,070 francs.... This result, after four years of efforts, is pretty poor. It seems to me that we should ask ourselves whether we ought to continue." Since he wished to persevere, Church proposed to reduce the number of pages and the type size, to abandon the idea of hiring another person to manage the magazine (Roger Caillois had been under consideration), to stop including expensive authors (Fargue and Claudel), to cut back on advertising, to eliminate the press section, to dissolve the selection committee, and, finally, to reduce the price of the review, "because, if I've understood this correctly," Church wrote to Jean Paulhan, "our readers belong to the left-wing popular front and feel embarrassed to hold such a luxurious item in their hands."[17] But the real problem lay elsewhere.

"In spite of the variety of the fourth issue," Church wrote to Paulhan at the end of the first year, "I'm not at all satisfied. I wonder if we're not just running in place. What we have to do is find some young people. The stuff in *Mesures* is too arid, too sterile. We have to put some pep in it. Besides, it seems to me that *Mesures* is still too much in thrall to the *NRF.* Of course, I recognize the difficulties. How should we go about it? Write a manifesto for young authors?[18] But the work of several young authors was already appearing in the pages of *Mesures:* among others, there were Jean Tardieu, Dominique Rolin, and Henry Thomas, who at twenty-five published his first poems there. René Char, introduced by Paul Eluard in 1937, could have been one of them, had Henry Church not rejected his work, as he also tried to do in the case of Denis de Rougemont.

Although today one might discern in its table of contents a few attempts to build a bridge to the modernity of the time, attempts that made *Mesures,* at its best, a magazine operating within a specific intellectual area—the Collège de Sociologie, post-surrealism, mystical thought, early existential philosophy, Oriental spiritualism, the rereading of ancient texts—one could say that *Mesures* was mainly a laboratory for the *NRF,* and that Paulhan was able to publish pieces in *Mesures* that the gray eminences of rue Sébastien-Bottin (Gide, Schlumberger, Gallimard) would have either refused to print or contested for a long time after their appearance. It is probable that Jean Wahl, Emile Picq, Roland Purnal, and Jean Vaudal weren't exactly welcome at the *NRF,* despite their talent; that Marcel Jouhandeau wrote more than the *NRF* would publish; that André Suarès was not in the odor of sanctity there; and that Marcel Arland, André Breton, Henri Michaux, and Louis Aragon were hardly averse to being published by Jean Paulhan in something other than the *NRF.*

These literary maneuvers, this review-related duplicity/duality, were not very well received at Gallimard, where people must have wondered what game Paulhan was playing, pulling the strings of double magazine direction and reiterating with *Mesures* what he had already done with *Commerce;* Gaston Gallimard might well have frowned upon this, but he had no fault to find with Paulhan, who continued to run the *NRF* impeccably. In June 1937, after Paulhan declined to publish Raymond Queneau's *Chêne et Chien* in the *NRF* on the grounds that there wasn't enough space, Queneau wrote back to him: "No more space? No doubt, that's because the *NRF* is made to *Mesures.* But not to mine." [19]

This weak distinction between the table of contents in *Mesures* and its counterpart in the *NRF* had more than one perverse effect: not only the impression that the reader sometimes had of reading the same review, but also a certain ennui. For a trustworthy verification of this assessment, let's turn to Henri Michaux, member of a selection committee that was unable to play its role of making proposals and issuing validations, who in 1939 gave vent to some pent-up feelings in a letter to Jean Paulhan: "Why don't you finally lay out the truth for Mr. Church, who claims to be seeking it? Tell him the reason his magazine doesn't sell is that it's boring. There are never any surprises. And if for once someone submits something amusing [some poems by Prévert], even something uniquely amusing, you see the result [rejection by Church, relayed by Paulhan]!" [20]

WHAT BECAME of *Mesures* during the war?

The Churches left Europe on July 11, 1939, but they didn't lose contact with their French friends; *Mesures* continued to appear at the beginning of the war, with the heartfelt support of its founder, who sent a telegram from the Plaza

Hotel in New York on October 27, 1939: "We think as you do—friends and Giraudoux—*Mesures* must indeed continue. Send manuscripts quickly."

Henry Church was generously concerned about writers who might be in need, and he asked Jean Paulhan to point any such out to him. Thus René Daumal, Jean Vaudal, Pierre Emmanuel, Alexeï Remizov, and Bernard Groethuysen all started receiving subsidies very early in the war; these lasted as long as money could circulate between the United States and France. Church wrote in a fury, "The freedom to send you cannons and airplanes has been granted me, but the freedom to sail on the sea and return to my home seems more remote than ever." [21] The idea of going home—that is, to France, to Ville d'Avray—so tormented him that he took some difficult steps toward becoming a naturalized French citizen in order to obtain a return visa, but then thought better of it: "What good would it do to get naturalized? I'd never be anything but a pseudo-something-or-other." [22]

Up to and including the delivery of the magazine's second 1940 number (April 15), Jean Paulhan and Henry Church were able to keep up the publication of *Mesures*. Paulhan's eldest son brought posters featuring the review to the Office of Censorship to get permission to put them up. But when Abbeville, the site of the Paillart printing house, capitulated, the jig was up: "Events have made the decision for us." [23]

In this last issue there was no mention of the possibility of an interruption in publication, nor any suggestion that *Mesures* might come to an end. Although Paulhan was forced to step down as editor in chief of the *NRF* in June 1940—surrendering his post to Pierre Drieu de la Rochelle, who had the support of the Nazi *Propagandastaffel*—he tried throughout the course of that year to restart *Mesures* and to secure the production of the third 1940 issue. Its contents were to include pieces by Franz Hellens, François Mauriac, Raymond Queneau, Jean Guérin (i.e., Jean Paulhan himself), and Jean Guéhenno, authors whose presence in the proposed table of contents demonstrates that this issue of *Mesures* was meant to be aggressively Resistance-oriented. During summer 1940, Paulhan hoped to reestablish the magazine in Nîmes, where the mayor had offered appropriate premises for the refugees of the *NRF* in exile, and then in Carcassonne, where Joe Bousquet confidently promised to provide the means for printing *Mesures*. There was even talk about extending the name of *Mesures* to cover the activities of a small publishing house. But the German grip on occupied France was tightening inexorably, and since (according to Henri Michaux) Church himself seemed hesitant, in the fall of 1940 any notion of continuing to publish the review in France was abandoned.

For his part, Church proposed to take the review in hand in New York, working out of the Plaza Hotel, where he and his wife had taken up residence. Later, after coming into contact with several French writers and philosophers—among them Jean Wahl—at Mount Holyoke College, where the Entretiens de Pontigny were held from 1942 to 1944, Church and his friend Wallace Stevens had the idea of persuading Jean Paulhan to come to the United States. Church was certain that he could endow a poetry chair for Paulhan at Harvard, and Stevens's talk at Mount Holyoke College, "The Figure of the Youth as Virile Poet," began as a description of the kind of poet who might be right for the job. We should note here that Jean Guéhenno was also

Signatures of Wallace Stevens (upper right), Marianne Moore, Henry and Barbara Church, J. P. Bishop, and others. "Register," MS 0768, Entretiens de Pontigny records, 1942–45, Mount Holyoke College Archives and Special Collections.

considered for this chair, but in the end neither he nor Paulhan was to cross the Atlantic.

During the Occupation, another American in Paris, another "American resource," Florence Gould, took over from the Churches, generously organizing get-togethers for writers as her predecessors had done in the 1930s. Guided by her devoted supporter Jean Denoël, Florence Gould continued the ritual of opulent, elegant dinners and cocktail parties in the 1960s, but that's another story.

Also during the Occupation, a copy of *Mesures* helped to save François Mauriac and Jean Blanzat, two ardent members of the Resistance. At the time, the members of the insurgent network formed around the Musée de l'Homme and *Résistance,* to which Mauriac and Blanzat both belonged, were falling one after the other. It was agreed that in case of danger, Jean Paulhan would prop up a red copy of *Mesures* in the window of his apartment in the rue des Arènes. Mauriac was being hidden by Blanzat, one of Paulhan's neighbors, and he could see Paulhan's window from his place of refuge. Early in May 1941, when the Gestapo came to arrest Paulhan for the first time, he managed to give the prearranged signal. Mauriac was thus able to put himself out of harm's way, while my grandfather was led off into custody.

To celebrate the liberation, Church wanted to print a special issue of *Mesures;* compelled to abandon this project, he nevertheless talked about returning to France, despite all the difficulties: "All that, of course, depends on whether you want to start over again with *Mesures,* which I think is the case." [24] The Churches eventually returned to France in 1946. Their houses in Ville d'Avray were in bad shape; the Germans had occupied them, stored weapons and gasoline in them, which they used to set them afire before escaping in Church's Bugattis.

Shortly afterward, on April 4, 1947, Church died suddenly of a heart attack in New York. When *Mesures* reappeared, finally and for the last time, it was at the instigation of Jean Paulhan, who gathered together all the former contributors to the magazine in the 1930s for a tribute to Church in April 1948. Paulhan's contribution was titled "Henry Church, or the School of Modesty."

After Church's death, Paulhan remained in touch with his widow, Barbara. Paulhan was quite fond of her unpredictability and her engaging volubility; he was frankly under no obligation to her and felt genuine friendship for her. For her part, she continued to entertain herself and her friends, arranging luncheons, dinners, and cocktail parties, always glad to invite people whom Paulhan wanted to see. When Wallace Stevens was in search of philosophical writings that had their own inherent poetry—eventually published in his essay "A Collect of Philosophy"—Barbara Church helped solicit contributions, approaching Paulhan and others.

ON DECEMBER 29, 1937, at the midpoint of the *Mesures* adventure, Jean Paulhan wrote to his friend Louis Planté: "It seems to me that I can be proud of *Mesures;* it is the handsomest magazine in Europe. Maybe its positions are a little inflexible, but they are never low. Maybe it is a bit esoteric, but no review of pure literature can avoid being so from time to time. The truth is that the journals and little magazines of Geneva, Brussels, London, and New York often say that *Mesures* does honor to France; the French press, however, says this sort of thing more seldom."[25] Here one finds summarized the whole philosophy of the literary review that was the means by which Henry Church sought his way, with application, modesty, and generosity. He should get the final word, for Church, a lucid representative of the "American resource" that has often sustained French letters, had perceived from the beginning the strange way in which literary reviews resemble the people who produce them: "No doubt," he wrote to Jean Paulhan on June 21, 1945, "*Mesures* will be an anachronism. So am I, I'm sure, and maybe you are, too."

Translated by John Cullen

NOTES

1. Henry Church to Jean Paulhan, October 11, 1939, Archives Jean Paulhan, IMEC, Paris.

2. Undated letter from Henry Church to Jean Paulhan [1935], ibid.

3. Wallace Stevens to Henry Church, January 28, 1942, in *Letters of Wallace Stevens,* ed. Holly Stevens (New York: Knopf, 1966), 401.

4. Jean Paulhan to Valéry Larbaud, October 7, 1934, in Jean Paulhan, *Choix de lettres,* 2 vols., ed. Jean-Claude Zylberstein, Dominique Aury, and Bernard Leuilliot (Paris: Gallimard, 1986), 1:329.

5. Henry Church to Jean Paulhan, September 30, 1934, Archives Jean Paulhan, IMEC.

6. *Métamorphoses* would become the title of a little collection edited by Jean Paulhan and published by Gallimard between 1936 and 1963; many authors whose work was printed in *Mesures* also appeared in *Métamorphoses.*

7. Henry Church to Jean Paulhan, August 17, 1937, Archives Jean Paulhan, IMEC.

8. Ibid.

9. Henry Church to Jean Paulhan, October 4, 1935, Archives Jean Paulhan, IMEC.

10. Ibid.

11. Henry Church to Jean Paulhan, July 14, 1938, ibid.

12. Paulhan's letters to M. de Hohenhau (the name of a character who appears in Henry Church's "Bacillus subtilis Artis"), dated 1935, are perhaps a response to Church's text. They can be read in Paulhan's *Traité du ravissement,* ed. Yvon Belaval and Jean-Claude Zylberstein (Paris: Périple, 1983).

13. Henry Church to Jean Paulhan, July 25, 1935, Archives Jean Paulhan, IMEC.

14. Henry Church to Jean Paulhan, October 4, 1935, ibid.

15. Henry Church to Jean Paulhan, February 8, 1937, ibid.

16. Jean Paulhan to Henri Pourrat, March 29, 1935, Archives Henri Pourrat, Ambert.

17. Henry Church to Jean Paulhan, July 21, 1937, Archives Jean Paulhan, IMEC.

18. Henry Church to Jean Paulhan, October 4, 1935, ibid.

19. Raymond Queneau to Jean Paulhan, June 2, 1937, cited in a footnote in *Correspondance, 1926–1962: Michel Leiris et Jean Paulhan,* ed. Louis Yvert (Paris: Claire Paulhan, 2000), 87.

20. Undated letter [1939] from Henri Michaux to Jean Paulhan, Archives Jean Paulhan, IMEC.

21. Henry Church to Jean Paulhan, November 10, 1939, ibid.

22. Henry Church to Jean Paulhan, February 12, 1940, ibid.

23. Henry Church to Jean Paulhan, June 5, 1940, ibid.

24. Henry Church to Jean Paulhan, June 21, 1945, ibid.

25. Jean Paulhan to Louis Planté, December 29, 1937, in Paulhan, *Choix de lettres,* 2:40.

III

Art and Artists

The remoteness of modern art is not merely a question of language, of the increasing "abstract-ness" of modern art. Abstractness, it is true, exists, as the result of a long, specialized internal development in modern artistic structure. But the crisis is the modern artist's rejection, almost *in toto,* of the values of the bourgeois world. In this world modern artists form a kind of *spiritual underground.*

—Robert Motherwell, "The Modern Painter's World" (August 10, 1944)

The artists—Chagall, Masson, Motherwell, Louise Bourgeois, Stanley Hayter—came to Pontigny-en-Amérique and so did the art critics, including the Italian art historian Lionello Venturi, who issued the invitations, and the scholar (and husband of Bourgeois) Robert Goldwater, whose work on primitive art had great influence among the artists assembled. In retrospect, the date of assembly, in late August 1944, is as interesting as the particular mix of participants. The war seemed all but over, and artists exiled from their Paris studios, such as Masson and Chagall, looked forward to resuming interrupted careers. What they could not know at the time was that a seismic shift was about to occur in Western art. Certain young Americans based in New York, such as Motherwell and Pollock and Rothko, were on the verge of taking European influences such as Surrealism in radically new and unexpected directions. During the Mount Holyoke gathering, Venturi took issue with Masson's defense of Surrealism; Venturi, according to the journalist Elizabeth Wallace, who witnessed the exchange, "drew out of his vast storehouse of learning devastating refutations of André Masson's surrealist statements." These were prewar battles, however. It was the young philosopher-turned-painter Motherwell who, in his first major theoretical statement, laid out some of the still inchoate claims for abstraction and spiritual exploration that would drive New York School painting for the next decade and a half. In this section, three art historians delve into this rich matrix of cultural transition—from Surrealism to Abstraction, from Paris to New York, from prewar to postwar. Jed Perl discerns as much continuity as rupture in the transition, finding shared tenets of Romanticism among the significant artists and theorists of the era (including Wallace Stevens). Mary Ann Caws explores her friend Motherwell's coming of age as an artist circa 1944. And Romy Golan takes a fresh look at the career of the anti-Fascist Venturi, who—in a spirit of political engagement—combined the long views of art history with up-to-the-minute art criticism.

Romantic Reverberations

Jed Perl

In 1941, Eugene Jolas, the friend of Joyce and editor of *Transition*, was living in the United States, where he assembled *Vertical: A Yearbook for Romantic-Mystic Ascensions*. The book, published by the Gotham Book Mart in New York, included poems, essays, classic texts by Kleist and Victor Hugo, a cover design of an ascending snake by Calder, and drawings of Romantic idols, including Kleist and Dionysus, by André Masson, one of the artists who participated in Pontigny-en-Amérique. Jolas, who there is reason to believe was himself a visitor to Mount Holyoke, announced in *Vertical* that "Romanticism is not dead." He argued that the Romantic revolutions of the eighteenth century, which had been "paralyzed by the advent of the positivist-mechanistic age," were now at last resurgent. "We are again in the midst of a Romantic revolution in the arts—and in life—which is sweeping across continents with the force of a tidal wave. It is part of the apocalyptic sensation which we all experience in the present social convulsions accompanying the war, and it is also the expression of vast creative forces that are preparing the way for a spiritual resurrection."[1]

Although Jolas was right to emphasize the importance of Romanticism in the mid-century years, the future of Romanticism was not as promising as he believed. While Romanticism was on the move, this development was closer to paroxysm than to revolution. What we see in the 1940s and 1950s is the extraordinary final fireworks of the Romantic sense of art and life, of the belief that men and women exist in a thrillingly and even terrifyingly organic relationship with nature, with culture, with history. Certainly these Romantic reverberations could be felt at Pontigny-en-Amérique. Masson, who chaired one of the sessions about art, had been present at the beginnings of the Surrealist movement, which the critic Cyril Connolly referred to in his 1944 book *The Unquiet Grave* as "Romanticism's last stand."[2] He had broken with Breton, the ringleader of the Surrealists, but he was surely aware that in the 1930s, at the time of official French celebrations of the hundredth anniversary of the premiere of Victor Hugo's *Hernani*, a defining event in the battles between Romanticists and classicists, Breton had argued that the Surrealists were the inheritors of the Romantic tradition. Working in America in the early 1940s, Masson was painting a series of poetic portraits of historical figures—from Heraclitus to Leonardo and Kleist—whose interest in mystery and metamor-

Signatures of Masson, Motherwell, Bespaloff, Bourgeois, Hayter, and others. "Register," MS 0768, Entretiens de Pontigny records, 1942–45, Mount Holyoke College Archives and Special Collections.

phosis made them icons of Romantic thinking and feeling, and who shared some of Masson's fascination with tumbling, reeling, careening sensation. Another visitor to Pontigny was Marc Chagall, whose levitating lovers and topsy-turvy interminglings of far-flung times and places reflected a modern man's besotted responses to the wayward Romantic spirit of eastern Europe's Yiddish culture.

Romanticism was also very much on the minds of some of the Americans who spoke at Pontigny-en-Amérique. A few years before Robert Motherwell came to Mount Holyoke, he was taking a seminar at Harvard with Arthur O. Lovejoy on "The Idea of Romanticism," where he focused his studies on the *Journals* of Delacroix, that greatest of all Romantic painters. Although Motherwell did not pursue his scholarly studies, he later wrote—in an introduction to Delacroix's *Journals*—that "the image of Delacroix's alert and cultivated mind constantly rolling, like an ever-changing tide, over the rocky questions of *l'art moderne*, an art made by self-chosen individuals rather than the tribal artists of the past, remained a sustaining moral force in my inner life, as I think it may have in the lives of many artists."[3] And there's more. Robert Goldwater, the art historian who was at Pontigny-en-Amérique, had published in 1938 his pioneering book *Primitivism in Modern Painting*, in which he observed that primitivism and Romanticism, in spite of all their differences, were both "attempts to infuse new life into art by breaking away from the current and accepted formulas"—and were thus attempts "to renew the *essentials* of art."[4] The thread that links Motherwell's and Goldwater's comments is the idea of "self-chosen"-ness, of the "breaking away" from what is "current and accepted," the renewal of essentials. That such a process might involve a return to beginnings, a starting over, occurred to several participants at Pontigny. The printmaker Stanley William Hayter invoked primal experience in the opening words of his book *New Ways of Gravure*, published in 1949. "Engraving," he wrote, "the act of incising a groove into some resistant material, is found as early as the first traces of human activity."[5]

There were many artists in the mid-century years who wanted the act of creation to be a natural, organic act—one that arose from the surprising, evolutionary movements of history, from the unruly spirit of the individual, from the unpredictable nature of materials. This search was a Romantic search, and it was one that was reflected in Wallace Stevens's beautiful account of the growth of inspiration in the essay that he presented at Pontigny-en-Amérique, "The Figure of the Youth as Virile Poet." This young, virile poet, who brings to mind a Greek kouros figure or a young man from Picasso's Rose Period, is, Stevens tells us, "the intelligence that endures. It is the imagination of the son still bearing the antique imagination of the father. It is the clear intelligence of the young man still bearing the burden of the obscurities of the intelligence of the old." This sense that youth will carry, as a matter of heredity, the mark of the past recalls Hayter's image of the modern engraver, still connected to the earliest act of incising. The imaginative intelligence of Stevens's poet is autonomous yet saturated in what has come before, so that what Stevens is offering us is a version of the old Romantic view of the artist in history, organically related to what surrounds him, and, because of that relationship, capable of growing through it and beyond it. Stevens's poet is tender yet strong, a sapling emerging from the rigorous soil of what Stevens calls the "Miltonic image of the poet, severe and determined."[6] There's a delicacy to Stevens's virile poet that suggests not the dark-toned, lowering, labyrinthine work that was being done by the Abstract Expressionists in the early 1940s so much as it foreshadows some of the painting that emerged in New York in the 1950s—compositions by Philip Guston and Joan Mitchell and Fairfield Porter, with their lighter colors, their increasingly fluid compositions, their easygoing optimism.

During the Pontigny sessions, a number of participants insisted that the power of art was grounded in the concrete, the real, the actual. Stevens argued that "the incredible is not a part of poetic truth. On the contrary, what concerns us in poetry, as in everything else, is the belief of credible people in credible things. It follows that poetic truth is the truth of credible things, not so much that it is actually so, as that it must be so."[7] Now, if there was a paradox here, it is one that Hegel, one of the greatest commentators on the Romantic nature of art, had pointed to when he observed that "romantic art must be regarded as art transcending itself, albeit within the boundary of its own province, in the form of art itself."[8] The young poet Robert Duncan, an admirer of Stevens, was saying something similar, in *The Black Mountain Review* in 1955, when he argued that "we owe to the Romantics" the idea "that form is Form, a spirit in itself."[9] The point is that the spirit inheres in the actuality—that, as Stevens put it, poetic truth is credible. This line of thinking is, essentially, anti-idealist. It is also, in a certain sense, anti-abstract. The lecture titled "A Crisis of the Imagination" that Masson gave at Pontigny contains, in a digression in the published version, a critique of the use of the term "abstraction" in relation to the visual arts.[10] Masson observed that the concept of abstraction is more appropriate to philosophy than to painting, for painting is always, in some way, concrete, actual, real. And in saying this Masson prefigured de Kooning's famous attack on the idea of abstraction in his lecture at the Museum of Modern Art in 1951, where he argued that "the word 'abstract' comes from the light-tower of the philosophers," and hoped that they would not shine that light on the visual arts.[11] Masson and de Kooning were not opposed to nonrepresentational painting any more than Wallace Stevens was opposed to obscure allusions in poetry. The point, altogether different, was that the work of art, whether more or less representational, gains its power from its presentness, its hereness, its credibleness, its materiality. Perhaps the idea was stated most clearly by the painter Hans Hofmann, whose ideas would have been well known to Goldwater and Motherwell, and who would have been teaching at his school in Provincetown during the summers when Pontigny-en-Amérique was taking place at Mount Holyoke. Hofmann would hold up before his students a sheet of plain-as-plain-can-be paper and announce in that crazily accented English of his that "within its confines is the complete creative message." [12] What Hofmann was saying was that when you draw a line on a piece of paper, you are creating a world. "Pictorial life," Hofmann asserted, "is not imitated life; it is, on the contrary, a created reality based on the inherent life within every medium of expression. We have only to awaken it." [13]

When Motherwell spoke, in his Pontigny lecture, of formalism, I think we can understand him to have meant, as Hofmann would have it, that meaning and metaphor are born out of the manipulation of the artist's most immediate resources—the artist's materials. It was Clement Greenberg's formulation of this idea that has become most famous, and Greenberg was quite explicit about how much he owed to Hofmann. Greenberg was in fact offering a Romantic view of creation when he argued that artistic value emerges from the very stuff of paint and canvas. But if what Greenberg called "modernism" was a form of Romanticism, the Romantic view of the centrality of materials, as we encounter it at Pontigny-en-Amérique and elsewhere in the 1940s, was far more open-ended than Greenberg allowed. If the point was to let your imagination grow through the engagement with the materiality of things, who was to say that a face, a tree, a landscape could not emerge as easily and naturally as a blot, a circle, a jagged line? In the 1940s de Kooning was working both representationally and abstractly. Masson was always interested in moving between images that were more or less representational, more or less nonrepresentational. Hofmann, who talked about returning to landscape painting toward the end of his life, never pushed students in one direction or another; indeed, a number of his finest students began painting still lifes and landscapes and figures in the 1940s, sometimes under the influence of the French painter Jean Hélion, another wartime visitor to these shores who was slated to visit Pontigny.

There was a process of trial and error involved in this willingness to embrace the materiality of painting and leave open-ended the ultimate question of the extent to which the work of art would or would not relate to the world outside the artist's studio. And here we confront another key element in mid-century Romanticism. For this questing spirit involved an exploration of antitheses, oppositions, contraries, dialogues, dialectics—an embrace of dynamic possibilities that could lead to the discovery of an underlying unity. The very arrangement of Pontigny-en-Amerique, with its panels and discussions, was a celebration of the dialectical give-and-take that was involved in learning, in growing. In an essay that she presented at Pontigny, "Feeling and Precision," Marianne Moore observed that "instinctively we employ antithesis as an aid to precision"—and although I would not want to make too much of that remark, I do believe that we often underestimate the extent to which dialectical thinking of various kinds shaped the mid-century experience.[14] Among Stevens's notebook entries, some of which were published in the avant-garde magazine *View* in the early 1940s, we find a taste for oppositions. In the poem "Connoisseur of Chaos," when Stevens begins by announcing, "A violent order is disorder," we are in the realm of the dialectic.[15] And in his Pontigny lecture Stevens observed that "the simple figure of the youth as virile poet is always surrounded by a cloud of double characters."[16] Students of intellectual history speak of the gradual rejection in the 1940s of dialectical thinking, at least of a Marxist variety of dialectical thinking, but dialectics, contraries, antitheses come in many varieties. In an essay in *The Magazine of Art*—which was edited by Goldwater, a Pontigny participant—Jacques Barzun argued that Romanticism's "aim is to bring into a tense equilibrium many radical diversities, and it consequently produces work that shows rough texture, discontinuities, distortions—antitheses in structure as well as meaning. From the classical point of view these are flaws; but they are consented to by the Romanticist—indeed sought after—for the sake of drama. They are not oversights on the artist's part, but planned concessions to the medium and the aim it subserves."[17]

Masson, speaking at Pontigny on the "Unity and Variety of French Painting," insisted that in spite of the variety of French painters—who included classicists and Romantics, Fauvists and Cubists—they were also united by "their passionate engagement with their craft, their consciousness of the possibilities of art."[18] In Masson's account of French painting, muscular contrasts between artists' differing sensibilities add to the richness of art. In spite of their differences, artists whose work appears as opposite as night and day—Poussin and Delacroix, for example—sometimes turn out to be pursuing similar goals. Masson praised Poussin for his fusion of extremes: order and passion, intellectuality and plasticity. The process by which a thesis and an antithesis create a synthesis, conventionally attributed to Hegel, was only the beginning of the dialectics that were in the air in the 1940s, which included Hofmann's push and pull, Mondrian's verticals and horizontals, the black and white of some of de Kooning's perfervid abstractions, the division of art-historical styles into classic and Romantic, Nietzsche's Apollonian and Dionysian, Freud's ego and id. Kenneth Burke, early in the 1930s, had published a book called *Counter-Statement*. Nietzsche, revered by many artists, although a critic of the dialectic, had offered in "The Will to Power as Art," as a response to the decadence of religion, morality, and philosophy, "the *counter-movement: art*." [19] Perhaps the most succinct description of how these dialectical processes affected the visual arts appeared in 1950, in the introduction that Motherwell wrote for an exhibition at the Kootz Gallery titled "Black or White." Motherwell observed that "if the *amounts* of black or white are right, they will have condensed into quality, into feeling." [20] The conciliation of contraries—as Blake, another figure much discussed in the 1940s, might have put it—became the vehicle for the expression of emotion.

A gathering such as Pontigny-en-Amérique must have been fueled, at least in part, by a Romantic desire to conciliate contraries. And there were in the 1940s and 1950s a whole range of more or less established institutions where artists sought to engage with antitheses, oppositions, contraries, dialectics: they included Black Mountain College in North Carolina; Forum 49 in Provincetown; and, in New York, the Hofmann School, Hayter's Atelier 17, Subjects of the Artist (a short-lived school of which Motherwell was one of the founders), and the Artists' Club (which had at least in part been modeled on the social clubs in old Italian neighborhoods). All of these institutions echoed the institutions of the Romantic past. Socially, the coming of Romanticism in the eighteenth century was characterized by a collapse of old family ties and rigid class distinctions. Romanticism was a freewheeling community, often of the young, who made their own kinds of families and communities—their elective affinities. There were gatherings of artists and writers; there were informal schools; and there were freely selected father figures—Goethe, most famously. The mid-twentieth-century years, a time of tremendous social upheaval, turned out to generate a recapitulation of this Romantic search for and discovery of elective affinities. Pontigny-en-Amérique was part of this development—an improvised educational experience, bringing together in unexpected ways Europeans and Americans, the young and the old, philosophers, writers, and artists.

Stanley William Hayter had originally founded his printmaking studio, Atelier 17, in Paris, and then, during the war, he reopened in New York, where he not only encouraged a revival of intaglio printmaking but also gave American artists some opportunities to encounter Europeans who were working there. A. Hyatt Mayor, the curator of prints at the Metropolitan Museum of Art, offered a resonant description of the impact that Hayter had on young artists—a description that catches something of the communal spirit of the war years. Artists, Mayor announced, "have clustered around [Hayter] like athletes who discover a natural leader for their games." The teacher functioned "like a magnetic field that knits haphazard particles into lines of force. This invigorating interplay of endeavor and opinion among young and old, aspirants and masters, is doubly precious here in the United States where artists often lose strength in solitude. Individualism makes itself more rugged, not less, by learning where to merge itself in a common effort."[21] That individualism might be sharpened through the intense experience of a new kind of group was very much a part of the story of how the virile young poet discovered his true self. And this search for self in turn had older Romantic reverberations, for at Pontigny-en-Amérique the communal aspects of the quest for enlightenment were felt to echo the organization of the great monasteries and universities of medieval Europe, which for many of the participants in the original Pontigny conferences, held at a Cistercian abbey in Burgundy, were viewed through a medievalizing nostalgia that had been an aspect of Romantic experience since the eighteenth century.

There was a let's-try-it spirit to Pontigny that was typical of artistic communities in the 1940s—a coming together to see what came of it. And there was perhaps a sense that it was only in the organic community, the truly Romantic community, that a truly organic art, a truly Romantic art, might be born. That a calamity such as World War II should have created the possibility for new alliances was, as Eugene Jolas suggested, an affirmation of the old Romantic mystery of organic processes, by which upheavals could turn into opportunities, by which the horrors of the war years could generate new insights, new discoveries. If American artists found in Hayter or Hofmann new masters—or, as Mayor put it, the leaders of their games—it was Hitler and the war, strange to say, that had made this possible by bringing Old World artists to the shores of the New World. And of course the Europeans who helped to knit "haphazard particles into lines of force" also included many philosophers and authors and composers. You feel all the exhilaration of discovering a new, elective community in the impressions that Mary McCarthy (who translated Pontigny participant Rachel Bespaloff's essay on the *Iliad*) and Randall Jarrell have left of their visits to the Morningside Heights apartment of Hannah Arendt, who not long after arriving in the States had participated in Pontigny-en-Amérique. In Arendt's presence, the toughest, most exacting, least forgiving New York intellectuals were awestruck, giddy kids, drawn into the encompassing aura of a woman who had the talismanic power of a sort of long-lost older cousin with an extraordinary experience of the world. It was in the community freely convened, the Romantic community, that new ideas came into being, which leaves us in no doubt as to why some of Arendt's pages, in *The Human Condition,* should be devoted to an ideal of community in ancient Greece. Like Hayter's primal incised line, Arendt's invocations of ancient Greece suggest an expectation, altogether serious in its abiding Romanticism, that the past will function not as a fixed model but as a shock administered to the present, a shock that will in turn spring the lock that opens the future.

NOTES

1. Eugene Jolas, "Romanticism Is Not Dead," in *Vertical: A Yearbook for Romantic-Mystic Ascensions,* ed. Eugene Jolas (New York: Gotham Book Mart Press, 1941), 157.

2. Cyril Connolly, *The Unquiet Grave* (New York: Harper and Brothers, 1945), 102.

3. Robert Motherwell, introduction to the Viking Compass Edition of *The Journal of Eugène Delacroix,* trans. Walter Pach (New York: Viking, 1972), 7.

4. Robert Goldwater, *Primitivism in Modern Painting* (New York: Harper and Brothers, 1938), 181.

5. Stanley William Hayter, *New Ways of Gravure* (New York: Pantheon Books, 1949), 18.

6. Wallace Stevens, *Collected Poetry and Prose,* ed. Frank Kermode and Joan Richardson (New York: Library of America, 1997), 675.

7. Ibid.

8. G. W. F Hegel, *The Philosophy of Fine Art,* trans. F. P. B. Osmaston, vol. 1 (London: G. Bell and Sons, 1920), 108.

9. Robert Duncan, *Black Mountain Review* 5 (Summer 1955): 210.

10. André Masson, *Le plaisir de peindre* (Nice: La Diane Française, 1950), 57–58.

11. Willem de Kooning, *Collected Writings* (Madras: Hanuman Books, 1988), 40.

12. Hans Hofmann, *Search for the Real and Other Essays* (1948; reprint, Cambridge: MIT Press, 1967), 42.

13. Hans Hofmann, "The Color Problem in Pure Painting—Its Creative Origin," in *Hans Hofmann,* ed. James Yohe (New York: Rizzoli, 2002), 51.

14. Marianne Moore, *Predilections* (New York: Viking, 1955), 5.

15. Stevens, *Collected Poetry and Prose,* 194.

16. Ibid., 676.

17. Jacques Barzun, "Romanticism: Definition of a Period," *The Magazine of Art* (November 1949): 244.

18. Masson, *Le plaisir de peindre,* 39.

19. Friedrich Nietzsche, *The Will to Power,* ed. and trans. Walter Kaufmann with R. J. Hollingdale (New York: Random House, 1967), 419.

20. Robert Motherwell, *The Collected Writings of Robert Motherwell,* ed. Stephanie Terenzio (New York: Oxford University Press, 1992), 72.

21. A. Hyatt Mayor in Stanley William Hayter et al., *Atelier 17* (New York: Wittenborn, Schultz, 1949), 4, 6.

Robert Motherwell and the Modern Painter's World

Mary Ann Caws

The greatest adventures, especially in a brutal and policed period, take place in the mind.

Robert Motherwell, "The Modern Painter's World" (1944)

Robert Motherwell is my topic here: I knew him, loved him, and discussed at length with him his relation to the painting and poetry of France and of America, to other arts such as music, and, most particularly, his relation to literary Symbolism—especially to the ur-Symbolist Stéphane Mallarmé, whom I have spent so much time translating—and to Surrealism, a far more difficult issue. I had first been in contact with him through running the journal *Dada/Surrealism,* for which he was the art adviser, and then, through his asking me to translate a book about him, and subsequent to that, conversing with him about his friend Joseph Cornell, whose diaries and source files I was editing.[1] Motherwell pointed out to me that while Cornell was closest to the Symbolists, he himself was and had always been closest to the Surrealists, a topic to which I will return.

Fortunately, Motherwell's own background was fascinating to me, as it was to him. Growing up in California, he had spent many of his school hours poring over the *Encylopedia Britannica,* with its brightly colored illustrations. Then, on a tennis court, as I remember it, he had met Michael Stein, Gertrude's brother, whose collection of modern art bowled him over. He had originally thought of translating the journal of Eugène Delacroix into English, and then of becoming a philosopher. Yet, through the encouragement of the great art historian Meyer Schapiro, Motherwell began to take drawing lessons with Kurt Seligman, who was part of the Surrealist group in exile in New York.

He never ceased, from then on, working as an artist, and as a writer. By far the most intellectual of the New York painters, Motherwell wrote many seminal essays on aesthetics and ethics, and the place of the artist in the world around him. He preferred creative friends, and had many of them: Joseph Cornell, Octavio Paz, Lukas Foss, Rafael Alberti, and other poets, musicians, and painters.

His relationship to the world of the arts was the motivation for one of his most crucial and interesting essays, a revised version of his talk at Pontigny-en-Amérique, to which he was invited through the Surrealist André Masson. This was the period in which the ten-day-long discussions that had originated at Pontigny, in French Burgundy, had moved over to Mount Holyoke, where one of their leading lights, the philosopher Jean Wahl, was teaching. Originally having planned to deliver a rather philosophical treatise on the nature of abstraction itself, Motherwell realized that was scarcely appropriate to the audience on this occasion, and then changed his title, at Lionel Abel's suggestion, from "The Place of the Spiritual in a World of Property" to "A Modern Painter's World"—a bit more palatable, a bit less self-congratulatory about his would-be bohemian self. The son of a banker, he very much wanted to be on the romantic and artistic side of things, and not on that of the bourgeois and the privileged: repeatedly he would say to me how he didn't want to be confused with T. S. Eliot, for example, who had the same sort of general background. This issue remained one of great delicacy, for Motherwell the aesthetic was in no way Motherwell an ascetic: he loved fine cars, food, and drink. Nevertheless, what he cared about was his voracious reading, his impassioned painting, and his truly sensitive writing in reaction to what he read and thought and saw, in himself and in others. He had a generosity of spirit which was unfailing, and it was this that many of us who knew him loved in him as well as his great talent for living and for art.

The general topic for his talk was the distinction between individualism and objectivism, as he saw them at that period, in 1944. Even as Motherwell insisted that "great art is never extreme," he set up the two poles of Surrealism and abstraction, and opted for the latter. For him, Surrealism held a contradictory position: "They have been the most radical, romantic defenders of the individual ego. Yet part of their program involves its destruction.... That part is the unconscious, the romanticism of the individual, the pure ego, not touched by the world." As he described it, the Surrealist move was toward the "dark forest" of automatism, a passive acceptance of whatever the unconscious offered, thus, for him, the feminine attitude. His own preferred attitude, as we see clearly in his painting, is often of the opposite type: the large, gestural kind we tend to associate with a masculine stance. One of the main issues is, of course, how to ally an extraordinary sensitivity to color and form with that largeness of gesture.

Motherwell, speaking for the other "Abstract Expressionists"—a term I am thinking of here in quotation marks, given the original hesitation over the term by Motherwell and others—preferred the domain of chosen form, an active will, therefore presumably masculine, toward what he called the "felt expression of modern reality."[2] This "feeling" had to include both mind and body, which rather left Symbolism behind, and since for him mind meant conscious choice, it also, in the long run, left behind Surrealism—at least in principle, as the painter was moving toward formalism, abstraction, and willed expression. In this move toward *ab-straction,* or the drawing forth of elements from something, to *ab-stract* them, there still remained a double possibility: either the drawing of subject matter from the self, so that the painter's individual personality is the main element expressed, or then the socialization, the objectification of it into something more "mature," as he expresses it. Those are the bare bones of his argument in this essay about the spiritual mission of art in a material world.

Now, Motherwell had been very close indeed to the Surrealists during their exile in New York, and acted as their interpreter to New York and to American ways of living, as they cared about it: for things as small as where you get the best olive oil, and as large as society's various and ongoing connections with the endlessly spreading world of art. It was in particular Roberto Matta to whom he was drawn: they went together to Mexico, on which trip Motherwell would meet his first wife, Maria; and it was Matta who gave him the idea of the "doodle," the mark or line you lay down spontaneously, which breaks the ice or the terribleness of the white page, and permits a further creative spurt. It was this emphasis on the power of the spontaneous, on the initial impulse supposed to free the unconscious into a fruitful productive mode, that concerned him. And it was this idea that he then transmitted to the other painters of what we call the New York School.[3]

One anecdote about Motherwell's relation to Surrealism has always seemed to me of particular interest, transcending the merely anecdotal. Motherwell was Breton's translator for a while, for Charles Henri Ford's publication *View,* in New York. This relationship ended, it seems, over Motherwell's deep concern at Breton's casual dismissal of the distinction between the words "conscience" and "consciousness" in English, given the convergence of these terms in the French *conscience.* This distinction may seem trivial, but I think it was not. Breton didn't see the difference, whereas, for Motherwell, it made a morally crucial difference, to which the Surrealist leader was deaf. Breton was famously tone-deaf, but this was being perception-deaf. This difference, over the word and over his relation to Breton, was to bother Motherwell all his life, and has a bearing on his subsequent relation to the Surrealists.

The difference relates even to the public-private split about which Motherwell was and remained so sensitive, in that one's private conscience about one's own actions is to be distinguished from one's public consciousness about a situation beyond the personal. His discussion of the split in this essay raises some ticklish points that I will only brush over very lightly. For the public stance, in a time of bourgeois values, of the artist who represents a refusal of those values, the artist chooses, according to Motherwell, large canvasses:

thus, his *Elegies* manifest the felt expression of a chosen "moral indignation at the character of modern life"—a longing for a sort of bohemianism of the mind. Until societal values change, he says, artists will "not find positive liberties in the concrete character of the modern state.... [M]odern artists form a kind of *spiritual underground*." [4] And then there is the private move: that is, the move to formalism until some radical revolution in the values of modern society comes about, which seems at this moment, as it seemed then, especially unlikely. Thus his interest in the private expression, his delight in the collage of the individual story, and his use of the small size occasioned by individualism.

Now the prickly thing here, at least to my way of thinking (or rather seeing), is his criticism of Picasso's *Guernica* as somewhat ill-fitted to large public expression: "It expresses Picasso's indignation, as an individual at public events. In this it is akin to Goya's *Los Desastres de la Guerra.* The smaller format of etchings, or even of easel paintings is more appropriate." [5] He feels this as more efficacious and more befitting an individual horror. The comparison here would be with his *Elegies,* of course, related to a parallel event from a different period: the tragedy of Franco's Spain. His *Elegies* are small and large, black and white and sometimes tinged with blood, or covered in blue. They come, as all tragedy comes, writ large and small.

It is entirely true that Motherwell's collages and smaller works closely related to his private life. I am thinking of the magnificently crimson *Je t'aime,* or another of his small works with lettering on it, a studio painting: *Jour la Maison Nuit la Rue.* His collages were often formed of objects sent to him, like a packet of Gauloises in his favorite color—so distinctive that it is called Motherwell blue—or a wrapping from the publishing house of *NRF* (particularly appropriate since it was the group of the *Nouvelle Revue Française,* including Jean Wahl, that was at the origin of Pontigny-en-Amérique). These *papiers collés,* or the collage of disparate forms, have within them the idea of "sendings," like Jacques Derrida's conception of the *envoi* or of the postcard: here we see a personal relic in a formal setting.

There is setting and there is setting out. From the bars of *The Little Spanish Prison* of 1941–1944, reminiscent in its yellow and the small red stripe of the colors of the Mexico he had just visited, to the collage now called *Mallarmé's Swan* of 1944, with its suggestion of a sail setting out across the water, the psychological distance is severe. This was the year of Motherwell's participation in Pontigny-en-Amérique, and I take it as some sort of sign of his generosity that he should have changed the title from *Mallarmé's Dream,* as he once meant to call it, to *Swan,* in a double homage to his friend Joseph Cornell,

Jour La Maison Nuit La Rue (1943), Robert Motherwell. Art © Dedalus Foundation, Inc./Licensed by VAGA, New York, N.Y.

who remembered it that way, and who had made his own collage in honor of Mallarmé's famous swan poem, starting, "The virgin, lively, and lovely today" ("Le vierge, le vivace et le bel aujourd'hui"), and to Mallarmé the Symbolist, as Motherwell was beginning to set out on his own path.

Of all the stories he used to tell, the one that remains with me the most clearly is that of the *Opens*. One day he saw in his studio a canvas leaning on another canvas, as both leaned against the wall. There he saw a door opening out, like those French windows of his childhood. Finally, he upended that opening, making of it a true window, so that the spirit could find its own space upward. This had to do also with the vastness of American expression, to which Motherwell was endlessly committed. Think of his large canvases, of his *Reconciliation Elegy* in the National Gallery in Washington, D.C.'s East Gallery as it takes up all the space of a wall. Public and great indeed.

But to my way of thinking, his *Opens* show Motherwell in his own greatness best of all. They recall the spontaneity of Surrealism, openness being the very definition of that state of readiness—the *état d'attente*—that was Surrealism's lyric comportment, as Breton phrased it. We know how ripeness was

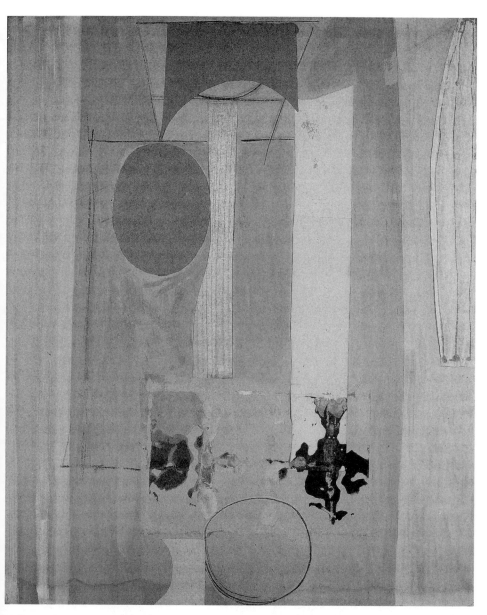

Mallarmé's Swan no. 2, Robert Motherwell (1944). Art © Dedalus Foundation, Inc./Licensed by VAGA, New York, N.Y.

all for Lear, and how readiness was all for Hamlet: Surrealism as a movement called upon both, in what Breton termed the kind of acceptance the Surrealists made of the condition of living, which he found totally unacceptable.

One of his *Opens,* the *Mediterranean Blue,* reminds us of Motherwell's heartfelt connection to Provincetown and its galleries, in particular the Long Point Gallery, of which he was the key founder. He felt that its atmosphere was full of the Mediterranean blue he could see from his cottage on Commercial Street. He would say to me, about his porch overlooking the sea: "Look! This is my Paris café." His series of spontaneous works called the *Lyric Suite,* with the spurt of paint hurled up against the top, above the sea wall signed "Motherwell," were part of his Provincetown experience also; they were interrupted at the death of David Smith, Motherwell's friend, and never picked up again.

And his *Night Music* collages, their title paying homage to Alban Berg, have, no less than his *Elegies,* a tragic air to them. At this point, ethics and aesthetics merge, and the public and the private. This is perhaps the place to call upon Matthew Arnold's *Culture and Anarchy,* with its memorably firm distinction between the Hellenic or the aesthetic point of view as opposed to the Hebraic or Judeo-Christian, ethical point of view, with a strictness of conscience. Such a spontaneity of consciousness (conscience and consciousness work together here) as that practiced by the Surrealists would be closer to the aesthetic or Hellenic than to the ethical. And yet, and yet…What the *Opens* signify is, I think, a whole panoply of possibilities that have no need to be spelled out: about the private and the public, about what we believe and what we create.

Permit me to leave open a great deal about Motherwell, about his writing, his thinking, and his painting. Mostly, I would like to leave open—as, after all, he always did—the interpretation of his move, both verbal and visual, both conceptual and material, in his always double creative manifestation, from Surrealism to abstraction. I truly believe that he was able to retain his fidelity to both. This was part and parcel of his vision, its collage form and its epic content. And part of what he wanted so much to share with all of us.

NOTES

1. Stéphane Mallarmé, *Selected Poems and Prose,* ed. Mary Ann Caws (New York: New Directions, 1983); Marcelin Pleynet, *Robert Motherwell,* trans. Mary Ann Caws (Paris: Daniel Papierski, 1990); *Joseph Cornell's Theater of the Mind: Selected Diaries, Letters, and Source Files,* ed. Mary Ann Caws (New York: Thames and Hudson, 1993).

2. Robert Motherwell, "The Modern Painter's World," talk given at Pontigny-en-Amérique, August 10, 1944, reprinted in *The Collected Writings of Robert Motherwell,* ed. Stephanie Terenzio (New York: Oxford University Press, 1992), 28–35; the expression is found on 28–29.

3. Actually, the Surrealist writer Robert Desnos had, long before Matta, found that tracing a line on the page led him into his most valuable drawings: the scribble or doodle was to set loose the creative imagination.

4. Robert Motherwell, "The Modern Painter's World," in Terenzio, *Collected Writings of Robert Motherwell*, 29.

5. Ibid., 30.

The Critical Moment

Lionello Venturi in America

Romy Golan

Lionello Venturi was the only art historian invited to come to the Pontigny encounters at Mount Holyoke, and he came twice.[1] The decision to invite Venturi was significant. No European art historian in exile had his credentials as an anti-fascist. If his physical stature was unusual—a gentle giant in the photographs shot at Mount Holyoke, he is always towering somewhat clumsily above his colleagues—his moral stature was equally unusual, especially in the dismal moral landscape of the twenty years of Italian Fascism.

Venturi was born into an old bourgeois family from Modena in central Italy. His father, Adolfo Venturi, was the patriarch of academic art history in Italy. Lionello was named professor of art history at the University of Turin in 1919. In August 1931 he was one of the very few professors—and the total number is truly striking, twelve in all—who refused to swear allegiance to Mussolini's regime, as was required from all professors. As a result, these twelve had to step down from their academic positions and endure professional limbo. Whereas most of them were in their sixties and seventies and about to reach the age of retirement anyway, Venturi was entering the prime of his career. He had just been offered, and had accepted, his father's position at the University of Rome, Italy's most prestigious chair in the history of art. Neither a communist nor a Jew (the oath took place seven years before the racial laws were instituted, and only four of the twelve professors who refused to take it were Jewish), nor a particularly militant anti-Fascist, Venturi refused the oath simply as a liberal. And while the majority of those twelve professors chose to remain in Italy, hoping to keep a low profile, Venturi chose instead to leave.[2] Venturi was the only art historian among the twelve professors (the others were in the sciences, law, or history), and the only Italian art historian of renown living in exile in the United States during the Second World War. He went first to Paris, but after the French defeat by the Germans in 1940 and the advent of the collaborationist Vichy regime, he decided to move on to America. He lived in New York City until 1945. Venturi had some independent means but still needed money. While living in Paris, he wrote books, advised art dealers and museum curators on acquisitions, and produced the first *catalogue raisonné* of Cézanne. Only in America, during the war years, did Venturi take on a more public stance. Joining what seems to have become a lecture circuit for many academic émigrés during those years, he spoke at Johns Hopkins in 1940, Berkeley in 1941, and Chicago, Detroit, Philadelphia, and Mexico City in 1942. In New York he taught at the New School for Social Research, the hub for European scholar émigrés, in 1943–44. It was toward the end of the war, when he was already contemplating a return to Italy, that he became, in the true sense of the word, an *intellectuel engagé.* In a series of articles written for the left-wing publication *The New Leader,* he lashed out at the Americans and the British for siding, after the liberation of Italy by the Allies and the fall of Mussolini, with the Italian monarchy and the corrupt government of General Pietro Badoglio.[3] Calling for a clean break with the Fascists' *ventennio* (their twenty years in power), Venturi co-signed, with six fellow Italian intellectuals in exile, "An Italian Manifesto." The text, published in *Life* magazine in June 1944, condemned the Allies' expedient support of what had been a Fascist monarchy and what they now called a "demo-fascist" government.[4]

It was his work, however, and not just his liberal political views that made Venturi's position untenable after Mussolini's takeover. The essence of his argument—from the time of the publication of his first book, *Il gusto dei primitivi* (The Taste of the Primitives), in 1926, to his *History of Art Criticism* of 1936 and its follow-up, *Art Criticism Now,* in 1941—was twofold. The first principle of his thought was that art criticism and art history were inextricably interwoven, indeed, that they were one and the same thing. As he posited at the outset of *Art Criticism Now,* the publication of the series of lectures he delivered at Johns Hopkins University a year after his arrival in the United Sates in 1941: "A critic's taste is always based on the art of his day. What he has learned from past ages is useful in checking his ideas. He judges past art with the experience of the present, which makes present, and contains, the whole of the past. Therefore his aim, even if he studies the art of the past, is always to make suggestions for, to take a stand in relation to, contemporary artists."[5] The manuscript version of his introduction to those lectures was even more explicit: "Perhaps there are some who hold that an apology should be offered for discussing criticism in a university. And I am fully aware that today criticism is scorned by 'scientific-minded' scholars on the grounds of its subjectivity. But I believe that history is subjective too, or else it is not history at all, and the science of art is a false science. Art criticism is our only means of understanding a work of art as art.... The final step in the history of art must be and is art criticism."[6] This statement, which might have been taken for granted in the 1930s in literary criticism, was radical within the field of art history. The second principle of his art history, and perhaps the most daring one, was his conviction that the art object was first and foremost a discursive object. It is in the writings about art that one grasped what reception theorists have called "the horizon of expectation" of the works themselves.

Although he seems to have participated in a number of panels at Mount Holyoke College, only two talks are listed in the conference proceedings. "La valeur absolue de l'art et la valeur relative du goût," delivered on August 6, 1942, was the last lecture on a panel devoted to art to which Venturi had invited the intellectual historian George Boas and three fellow exiles: the painters Marc Chagall and André Masson, and the Italian musicologist Vittorio Rieti. The other lecture, "Le problème italien d'aujourd'hui," was delivered on a panel devoted to politics. Venturi must have spoken extemporaneously and in French, as almost everybody else did in the informal atmosphere of these gatherings. No texts for his talks can be traced either in his archive kept in the Art History Department of the University of Rome or those kept at Mount

André Masson, Lionello Venturi, George Boas, and Marc Chagall at Mount Holyoke College, 1943. MS 0768, Entretiens de Pontigny records, 1942–45, Mount Holyoke College Archives and Special Collections, 0768-5-30.

Holyoke. All we have are the titles. Since they correspond, however, to articles he published at the time, we can infer with some certainty what he said.

Venturi's first contribution must have irritated at least two of his guests on the panel that morning. In their respective lectures, "Unité et variété de la peinture française" and "Quelques impressions sur la peinture française," Masson and Chagall had tried to outline what might be considered the absolute constants of French art. Asserting the innate preference of the French for concision over abundance, in line with the famous French "sense of measure" represented by Poussin and Seurat, Masson's argument was, like Chagall's, a cautionary one. He stressed the importance of "le fait pictural" over anecdote in paint and the picture as a self-contained organism, but argued that the free brushstroke had to be kept in check. He invoked the example given by the French artists of the past from Poussin to Corot to Cézanne, even up to Cubism, as a bulwark against the anti-humanist tendencies lurking in Dada and Surrealism.[7]

For Venturi it was, on the contrary, the relative, historical, and context-specific value of taste that prevailed over the absolute value of art. This question had been fervently debated in the eighteenth century, at the outset of modern aesthetics, but had been more or less abandoned since the early nineteenth century. Hegel had found the contingency of taste intolerable and had thus eliminated it from his aesthetics. The question of taste was reintroduced by Benedetto Croce, a figure of cardinal importance for Venturi as for many Italians of his generation. Croce was an idealist who believed in the immanence of the work of art, but he recognized in *Problemi della critica* of 1911 the tension that existed between, on the one hand, the synthesis necessary to the production of a work of art, and, on the other, taste, which was irrevocably heterogeneous. Croce got around the problem by asserting that viewing (and by extension the writing of art criticism) was aimed at the reconstruction of the synthesis of the work of art. He stipulated a mirroring relation between the making of art and writing about art. Venturi departed from Croce in an attempt to break the paralysis inherent in Croce's exegetic circularity between production and viewing. Taste allowed one to grasp how the artist was able to synthesize the elements that make up the work of art. But he also insisted that taste, being selective rather than synthetic, was precisely the faculty that allowed one to distinguish what was synthetic and transcendent in a work of art from what was not.[8] By confusing aesthetics with criticism, Venturi warned, people had come to believe, for instance, that Johann Winckelmann's infatuation with classicism in the mid-eighteenth century, which he tried to pass off as absolute and timeless aesthetic laws, was in fact tied to the taste, that is, the worldview of his day. Closer to the present, the defense of classicism waged by the painter and critic André Lhote was, far from being trans-historical, part and parcel of the conservative political climate known as the "Call to Order" in post–World War I France.[9] Attention to the history of taste thus allowed one, he claimed, not only to document but also to discern and untangle the inevitable ideological component of the history of art.

Such views proved incompatible with Fascism. Thus, while Croce managed to remain above the fray and reemerge as an Italian grandee who, although he had remained at home, had been untainted by Fascism, Venturi's writings proved to be an immediate irritant. *Il gusto dei primitivi* provoked a debate as soon as it came out in 1926.[10] The book traced the taste for, or what one may call the drive toward, what Venturi terms "the primitive" in art. Venturi proceeded from the seminal Crocean premise that the "classical," as opposed to the style-specific concept of "classicism," was a moment of inspiration reborn every time art was created. Venturi deployed the primitive as a critical meta-historical (as opposed to trans-historical) concept. The primitive was reborn each time an artist broke away from the demand for naturalism or from academic routine (for Venturi, often synonymous with classicism) in favor of intuition, or what Venturi calls "revelation." Venturi's belief in the discursivity of the art object was made evident by the book's format. Part one, the bulk of the book, was titled "La critica della critica" and dealt, from a modernist viewpoint, with the critical undoing of classicism in favor of direct expression. Beginning with Plato, Venturi moved on to Giorgio Vasari, Winkelmann, and Hegel, and ended, after a long chapter on John Ruskin, with the "pure-visibility" theories of the late-nineteenth-century German Konrad Fiedler. Much shorter, and reading almost like a coda, was part two, "Il gusto dei primitivi e l'arte," which looked at the artworks themselves. Focusing almost exclusively on painting, Venturi began with Giotto and Botticelli, and skipped over the High Renaissance except for a short passage on the colorist Venetians, on to the eighteenth century. Detecting a kernel of archaism in the late work of the arch-neoclassicist sculptor Antonio Canova, Venturi stressed Canova's influence on the primitivizing tendencies of the German Nazarenes. He then segued into the French Impressionists and their Italian counterparts, the Macchiaioli, and clinched his argument on the last pages with a comparison between Giotto and Cézanne.

The anti-classicist stance in favor of primitivism was not the most striking position adopted in *Il gusto dei primitivi*. Anti-classicism had become almost a prerequisite for early-twentieth-century modernists, and indeed was shared by one of the most prominent Fascist artists at the time, Mario Sironi. The anti-Fascist message of the book lay rather in Venturi's assertion that the drive to the primitive was not a question of style but an attitude: a profoundly moral attitude irrepressibly related to the concept of artistic freedom. The book was published at a critical moment. It came out just as the regime was attempting, through the writings of the likes of Ugo Ojetti, the supreme regulator of art under Fascism, to consolidate a rhetoric of Italian cultural superiority over things foreign. Ojetti held up High Renaissance art (i.e., Raphael) as the gold standard. In 1930 Venturi got embroiled in a heated polemic in the magazine *Arte* against Ojetti's views on recent art expressed in the reactionary review *Pegaso*. Venturi lamented Italy's nationalist obsession with classicism, its provincialism, and its virulent antipathy toward French modernism, especially Impressionism. Cézanne's famous dictum about wanting to "redo Poussin after nature," which Ojetti took as a confirmation that he was a classicist at heart, did not change for Venturi the fact that Cézanne was, like the other Impressionists, mostly indebted to the colorism of the Venetians. In order to be Italian, Venturi maintained, contemporary art had to be European first, and only then Italian. Thus, for Venturi, a Paris-based artist like Amedeo Modigliani was more Italian in his cosmopolitanism than Canova had been, with his inability to shake off neoclassicism—in Venturi's view, a German import to Italy in the early nineteenth century.[11] Venturi was also one of the very few in Italy publicly to condemn the Futurists for their loud embrace of Fascism. The one Italian art movement that, thanks to Filippo Tommaso Marinetti's belief in a pan-European modernism, had both been affected by and itself affected the avant-garde beyond its national borders now adhered to the Fascist mandate of autarchy.[12]

It would have been fitting for Venturi to publish *The History of Art Criticism*—which we recognize today as essentially the first history of art history—in Paris. It was there that he wrote it, and it was Charles Baudelaire who stood as his exemplary art critic. One of Venturi's favorite Baudelairean maxims was: "Pour être juste, c'est à dire pour avoir sa raison d'être, la critique doit être partiale, passionnée, politique, c'est à dire faite à un point de vue exclusif, mais au point de vue qui ouvre le plus d'horizons [To be true, in other words to find its raison d'être, criticism must be partial, impassioned, political; that is to say, it must proceed from an exclusive point of view to also form that point of view which opens onto the greatest number of horizons]." And yet Venturi didn't find a publisher for the book. It was thus not in France but in New York, in English, that *History of Art Criticism* first appeared in 1936. France, as a country where a prominent critic such as Waldemar George (whom Venturi openly denounced at Johns Hopkins) could take what French historians now call a *derive fasciste*, drifting from a defense of Cubism in the teens to an infatuation with neoclassicism in the 1920s, all the way to open praise of Italian Fascism in *L'humanisme ou l'idée de patrie* in 1936, was—in spite of its short-lived socialist interlude from 1936 to 1938—no longer the most congenial setting for Venturi's book. He did eventually find a French publisher two years later, in 1938. But it took ten years for the book to be published in the language in which it was originally thought and written, in Florence, in 1945. When asked by his New York publisher to write a few lines for the book's jacket, Venturi said, "I wrote this treatise for the American public, because I am aware that the American scholars, students, and amateurs are interested today in the theoretical problems more than the European public." It is in America, then—three years before he even knew that he was going to have to leave occupied Paris and come to live in New York—that Venturi thought he had found his ideal reader.

Still, Venturi's crossover between the art of the past and the art of the present would elude the Americans as well. Leo Steinberg reminisced years later about his moonlighting as an art critic while writing his dissertation on the Baroque architect Borromini at the Institute of Fine Arts. As he put it in the preface of *Other Criteria: Confrontations with Twentieth-Century Art,* the volume of his collected essays on Picasso, Jasper Johns, and Robert Rauschenberg: "The brief reviews in this book were done for monthly magazine columns by a truant art history student. In those days, the mid-1950's, practicing art critics were mostly artists or men of letters. Few art historians took the contemporary art scene seriously enough to give it the time of day. To divert one's attention from Papal Rome to Tenth Street, New York, would have struck them as frivolous—and I respected their probity. Therefore, whenever a fellow student referred to my column, I begged him to lower his voice. He was speaking of my secret life."[13] Indeed, when it came to criticism, Clement Greenberg and Harold Rosenberg, who were emerging during the 1940s as the first major American art critics, steered clear—except, in the case of Greenberg, for the occasional exhibition review on Old Master painting—from anything before Courbet. More important, they steered clear of academic art history. Focusing on contemporary art, a subject that was left virtually untouched by the discipline, was key to their self-definition as critics. The one exception in the United States was Meyer Schapiro, who split his interests between medieval art, Courbet, Seurat, Cézanne, and twentieth-century abstraction.

Meanwhile, under the impact of the dozens of German and Austrian émigrés then settling in American academia, art history was about to take not a progressive, as one might have expected, but a conservative turn. It is of some significance in this context that the most important influence on Venturi's work should have been the so-called Vienna School of art history. Venturi's championing of these Viennese as the fathers of contemporary art history and criticism took place in the United States just as these European émigrés, many of whom had been deeply affected by the Viennese, set out to recoil from this body of work. At the turn of the century, Alois Riegl and Franz Wickhoff, the founding figures of the Viennese school, wrote about the art of ancient Rome from a point of view profoundly inflected by the most recent avant-garde of their day: Impressionism. The *Kunstwollen*—the term coined by Riegl meaning "the will to form," and which, many have argued, is what Venturi meant by "taste"—of the Romans in their sculpture reliefs was characterized by an optical effect of dematerialization as opposed to tactile solidity, and by the ever-shifting chromatic effect produced by chiaroscuro. Inspiration continued to come for the next generation of Viennese from contemporary art. It was via German Expressionism and the artists of Die Brücke that Riegl's follower Max Dvorak had rediscovered El Greco in 1906, and it was via the phantasmagoria of Surrealist painting that Hans Sedlmayr revisited Brueghel in 1931.[14] And yet even the Viennese, as Schapiro noted in 1938, had ultimately focused in their writings on the art of the past, alluding only indirectly to the parallel between their ways of seeing and contemporary art.[15] They never saw what was for Venturi the ideological imperative to investigate the parallel between their readings of the art of the past and contemporary art and criticism.

The most significant case of this recoil in the United States from the Viennese was Erwin Panofsky. Deeply affected, back in the 1920s, by the anti-classical, modernist ethos of the Vienna School, Panofsky later came to perceive the radical formalism of the Viennese as a dangerously over-interpretive approach to the art of the past. He found refuge in the textual documents, and in iconography, a method that even in its more intuitive mode, iconology, restricts the range of interpretation of the work. This was a method Venturi found flawed, as he stated in his 1941 Johns Hopkins lectures, because of its stress on content over form, and even content as opposed to form.[16] For Panofsky and his followers, moreover, the classicism of the Italian High Renaissance emerged as the repository of humanist and universal values. Panofsky's retrenchment has been interpreted as a repression of the unbearable uncertainties visited by Nazism upon his life and that of his fellow exiles. Venturi, persona non grata as he might have been to his Fascist co-nationals, was of course neither Jewish nor German, and so had no need to repress the images of fragmentation and disintegration that he had found in the writings of the Vienna School.[17]

"The greatest danger in art and criticism today," he wrote in 1942, "is the lack of sincere, natural feeling and emotion, and the emphasis on intellectual abstraction."[18] Such statements, and Venturi's lifelong equation of the painterly stroke with political freedom, proved to be profoundly attuned to the American *Kunstwollen* of the war years. "Thirty-six years after his death, Cézanne is more alive than ever, standing behind the best efforts of painters, sculptors, and architects today," he claimed in "Cézanne, Fighter for Freedom," in *Artnews* in 1942. "The primacy of sensation, surface effects, lack of artistic finish, all these contrasting principles impel us towards Cézanne and his contemporaries today, when he stands as a symbol of the freedom his countrymen are fighting for, just as much as thirty years ago." [19] Meanwhile, in reaction to rhetoric of "degenerate art" voiced by the Nazis, Venturi's antipathy toward classicism had hardened even further. In a talk titled "The So-Called Malady of Modern Art," delivered in 1942, he stated: "Modern art reveals the ills of mankind. Because of that it is wholesome, if courage and freedom represent health. After the First World War, believing that art was sick, painters, sculptors, critics and politicians tried to cure it with drugs such as the revival of neo-classicism....The revival of classicism in art was a fascist remedy. And history will confirm that it was necessarily fascist: it suppresses the imagination." [20]

"Art is creation while war means destruction, and yet history teaches us that some of the most brilliant periods in art occurred during wars: i.e., Phidias, Giotto, Giorgione," Venturi would go on to write in "The Arts in Wartime" in the *Museum News* the following year. "This is because the great characteristic of art is freedom of the imagination. This war, more than any other war, is about freedom from oppression. It is a world civil war." [21]

Venturi's taste led him to embrace, after his return to Italy, the young generation of *pittura informale,* the Italian version of Abstract Expressionism. The leitmotifs of his 1950s essays on Birolli, Afro, Corpora, Scialoja, Vedova, and others were liberation, spontaneity, and the importance of the imagination. Buzzwords of art criticism both in the United States and in Europe throughout the 1950s, these were concepts that already sounded a little passé by the time his book *Italian Painters of Today* appeared simultaneously in Rome and New York in 1959. What was unusual about the book was Venturi's willingness, in contrast to the defensive tone of his French and Italian colleagues, to embrace what he recognized to be at this historical juncture the primacy of the painters of the New York School. The true radicals, he argued, the ones whose practical attitude had found its expression not in a flight into idealist geometric abstraction but in the concrete, everydayness of *matière,* were the Americans. The Italians, though less radical than the Americans, were also less refined than the French. Refinement, Venturi was now ready to recognize—and here he begins to sound like Clement Greenberg—by the 1950s had become a curse.

Venturi's preference for the free painterly gesture and his mistrust of any kind of theory also proved to be his blind spot. Thus Venturi championed the maudlin archaizing of Modigliani rather than the "alienation effect" of the transgressive classicism of Giorgio De Chirico, the other Italian in self-imposed exile in Paris before World War I.[22] And it was in Chagall that he saw the confirmation of "a victory of the poetic spirit and of *fantasia*" (both very Crocean concepts) over the "intellectual dryness of Cubism." In Chagall, the doubly exiled Jew who fled first the Russian pogroms to France and then occupied France to America, rather than in the globetrotter Marcel Duchamp, Venturi found his paradigm for the cosmopolitan artist. Chagall alone, he wrote in 1944 in the New York exiles' review *France-Amérique,* had managed to bridge East and West, Judaism and secularism, folk tradition and modern urbanity, in a single, universal humanity.[23] His dislike of theory in art led Venturi to ignore the exiled Surrealists, the most important avant-garde European presence during his years in New York. Like Greenberg, he considered them besotted by psychoanalysis and too literary to be "true" painters.[24] While he might have warmed to André Masson the man during their years in America,[25] it took Venturi years to warm to Masson the artist. It wasn't until the late fifties, once he was able to associate him no longer with Surrealism but with the pictorial sensibility of *peinture informelle,* that Venturi wrote a short essay on Masson for a gallery exhibition in Rome.[26]

Venturi's second talk at Mount Holyoke, "Le problème italien d'aujourd'hui," must have been derived from an essay titled "Considerazioni inattuali sulla critica d'arte in Italia," which he published that summer in a journal called *Quaderni Italiani.* Its title was taken from Nietzsche, and the piece was an adamant indictment of the untimeliness of his co-nationals. Anti-Fascists now believed, Venturi argued, that Italian art criticism had achieved a certain primacy in the world. They were unfortunately mistaken. This illusion, in Venturi's view, was symptomatic of Italy's cultural isolation and the all-pervading influence of Fascism. The fact that Italians did not partake in the reaction after World War I against the avant-gardes of the late nineteenth and early twentieth centuries could not be attributed to any particular progressive flair on their part, he argued. It was because Italy saw itself as always already classical because of the undisputed hegemony of the heredity of the Renaissance on its culture. The Italians simply did not distinguish between classicism and neoclassicism. France, England, and the United States had made the mistake of retrenching into classicism after the war, but in those countries there were also other currents. Everywhere nationalism in aesthetics had been tempered, willingly or not, by the recognition of the primacy of France in the modern age. Not so in Italy, where Impressionism was skipped over in favor of Klimt. Since the Renaissance, Venturi contended, Italian art had not managed, except for Tiepolo and Guardi, to surpass what was produced across the Alps. The best modern art had originated in Holland, Spain, and France, and diffused itself around the world. This art would have to be studied if the next generation of Italians wanted to get anywhere after the war. Italian art criticism bore a heavy responsibility in all this: "It had failed to fulfill its duty."

The urgency of Venturi's tone was that of the *Quaderni* as a whole. The journal, which was printed in Cambridge, Massachusetts, and published four issues from 1942 to 1944, was launched as a sequel to the review by the same title edited in Paris in the early 1930s by the anti-Fascist activist Carlo Rosselli. Its publication had been dramatically curtailed by Rosselli's assassination by Mussolini's envoys in 1937. Stirred by the spirit of resistance elicited by the entry of the United States into the conflict on the side of the Allies in 1942, the journal, published in Italian, was intended for a double readership. It was addressed, as stated in its editorial, to fellow Italian anti-Fascists in America, an atomized group that tended to be uninformed about the deeds of anti-Fascists back home (namely, their enrollment alongside the loyalists in the Spanish civil war, to which the journal dedicated a whole issue in 1943). Most important, however, the journal stretched a hand back to comrades in Italy. One particular group was singled out: the new generation of university students.

It is telling of Venturi's impact on the younger generation that the chief editor of the *Quarderni,* in whose living room the magazine was printed, was Bruno Zevi. A young architect and architectural historian, Zevi had left Rome in 1939, after the declaration of the racial laws, to study architecture with Walter Gropius at Harvard. Zevi would become the most resonant voice for an anti-Fascist modernist architecture upon his return to Italy after the war.[27] In *Towards an Organic Architecture,* a book written during his exile in America and published upon his return to Italy in 1945, Zevi almost single-handedly made the tremendous postwar European reputation of the American Frank Lloyd Wright.[28] Wright epitomized for Zevi—as he had for Venturi in *Art Criticism Now*—an emotional, humanist alternative to what both men had come to perceive as the cold, inhuman functionalism of the machine aesthetic. This aesthetic, which triumphed in the United States under the impact of the two German architects in exile, Gropius and Mies van der Rohe, had been particularly problematic in Italy. There the machine aesthetic had served, via the group known as the "Rationalists," as one of the most powerful instruments in the construction of the myth of a progressive Fascist modernism.[29]

In 1945 Venturi was offered, once again, the chair of art history at the University of Rome. There he alternated courses on the Baroque with classes on contemporary art, a mix unheard of in the university curriculum of the Eternal City. His lectures became the rallying point for an entire generation of Italian scholars. In listening to Venturi, Giulio Carlo Argan, Cesare Brandi, Francesco Archangeli, and Maurizio Calvesi—many of them no longer students—were gripped by the moral and political imperative, as Venturi defined it, to become two-pronged.[30] Often taking more daring positions on contemporary art and architecture than Venturi's own, they wrote both on the art of the past and on contemporary art. This situation had no parallel in America, France, Germany, or England after World War II. It took twenty more years and another critical moment in the humanities, that of the "theoretical turn" of 1968, for Venturi's most radical lesson—that of the signal discursivity of art—to be absorbed. "It is about time that we examine systematically the way in which the reception of art and the production of art are indissociable," wrote the French sociologist and theorist Pierre Bourdieu, singling out Venturi, in his book *L'amour de l'art* in 1969. "For indeed it may be said that every work is made twice. Once by the artist and once by the viewer, or better, by the society to whom the viewer belongs."[31]

NOTES

1. Much of this account is drawn from documents in the Venturi archive at the University of Rome. I thank Professor Stefano Valeri, the director of the archive, for making my research in the small room of the Venturi archive at La Sapienza such a pleasurable experience.

2. Helmut Goetz, *Il giuramento rifiutato: i docenti universitari e il regime fascista* (Milan: La Nuova Italia, 2000).

3. Lionello Venturi, "The First Year from the Fall," *The New Leader* 27, no. 30 (July 22, 1944): 5; Venturi, "The Democratic Offensive in Italy: The Inside Story of the Fall of the Badoglio Cabinet," ibid. 27, no. 44 (October 28, 1944): 7; Venturi, "Rome under the German Heel: Why Italians Who Fought Fascism had Badoglio and the King," ibid. 27, no. 50 (December 9, 1944): 7; see also Venturi, "Italy after Fascism," *Current History* (September 1943): 56–60; Stefano Valeri, "Lionello Venturi antifascista 'pericoloso' durante l'esilio (1931–1945)," *Storia dell'arte* 101, n.s. 1 (2002): 11–14 (special issue on Venturi).

4. His co-signers were the conductor Arturo Toscanini, in exile in the United States since 1938; Giuseppe Antonio Borgese, professor of Italian literature at the University of Chicago (the son-in-law of Thomas Mann, he is mentioned in *Life* as one of the twelve professors to have refused to take the oath, although he is not listed among the twelve by Helmut Goetz); Gaetano Salvemini, a leading anti-Fascist who was imprisoned in Italy in 1925 and who, after his release, came to America in 1930, where he taught history at Harvard until his return to Italy in 1948; and Giorgio La Piana, who came to the United States in 1913 and taught church history at Harvard.

5. Lionello Venturi, *Art Criticism Now* (Baltimore: Johns Hopkins University Press, 1941), 7. See John Alford's review in *Art Bulletin* 24 (1942): 403–5, and Venturi's final answer, "Art and Taste," ibid., 26, no. 4 (December 1944): 271–73. The book was also reviewed by Dino Ferrari in

the *New York Times Book Review,* March 29, 1942, positively, for being as sharp as a surgeon's knife.

6. As cited by Claudia Cieri Via, "Lionello Venturi e le lezioni americane," *Storia dell'arte* 101, n.s. 1 (2002): 41–45.

7. Both Chagall's and Masson's essays appeared in *Renaissance,* the journal published by the New School for Social Research, the following year. See *Renaissance* 2–3 (1944–45): 45–57 and 217–23.

8. See Lionello Venturi, "Teoria e storia della critica," *Art et Esthetique* 1, no. 1 (1936), reprinted in *Lioello Venturi: saggi di critica* (Rome: Edizioni Bocca, 1956), 100–220; Venturi, "Croce e la storia dell'arte," *Commentari* 1 (January–March 1953), reprinted ibid., 341–48; and Ricardo de Mambro Santos, "La critica epicentrica. Lionello Venturi tra sintesi del genio e selettivita del gusto," *Storia dell'arte* 101, n.s. 1 (2002): 31–40.

9. Critics' views often ran the risk of being prescriptive rather than descriptive, getting in the way of the artist, he added. See Lionello Venturi, "Sur les limites de la critique d'art," *L'amour de l'art* (October 1938): 306–8; reprinted in *Lionello Venturi: saggi di critica,* 191–98.

10. See Aldo Bertini's obituary, "Lionello Venturi," *Settanta* 2, no. 19 (December 1971), 39–47; and, most important, probably the best essay written on Venturi, Giulio Carlo Argan, "Le polemiche di Lionello Venturi," *Studi Piemontesi* 1, no. 1 (March 1972): 117–24.

11. See three articles from *L'Arte* (January, March, and July 1930), reproduced as "Polemica con Ugo Ojetti," in *Lionello Venturi: arte moderna* (Roma: Edizioni Bocca, 1956), 85–102.

12. See Argan, "Le polemiche di Lionello Venturi.

13. Leo Steinberg, *Other Criteria: Confrontations with Twentieth-Century Art* (New York: Oxford University Press, 1972), vii.

14. See Gert Schiff, ed., *German Essays on Art History* (New York: Continuum, 1988); and Margaret Olin, *Form and Representation in Alois Riegl's Theory of Art* (University Park: Pennsylvania State University Press, 1992).

15. See Meyer Schapiro, "The New Vienna School," *Art Bulletin* (1938), reprinted in *The Vienna School Reader: Politics and Art Historical Method in the 1930s,* ed. Christopher S. Wood (New York: Zone Books, 2000), 439–52. This was the first piece, an otherwise positive review on these Viennese, in an American art journal.

16. See Venturi, *Art Criticism Now,* chap. 5, "Iconology, Laboratory Criticism, and the History of Vision."

17. For this line of argument, see Christopher S. Wood, "Art History's Normative Renaissance," in *The Italian Renaissance in the Twentieth Century,* Acts of an International Conference, Villa I Tatti (Florence: Leo Olschki, 2002), 65–92.

18. Lionello Venturi, "On Aesthetic Intuition," *Journal of Philosophy* 39, no. 10 (May 7, 1942): 273.

19. Lionello Venturi, "Cézanne, Fighter for Freedom," *Artnews* 41, no. 13 (November 15–30, 1942): 16–17.

20. Lionello Venturi, "The So-Called Malady of Modern Art," paper delivered at a 1942 conference on science, philosophy, and religion, 3080 Broadway, New York (institution unclear), Venturi Archive, Rome.

21. Lionello Venturi, "The Arts in Wartime," *Museum News* 21, no. 4 (June 15, 1943): 7–8. For a more flatfooted instance of argument in the pages of *Artnews* see the review by Duncan Phillips (August–September 1942): 20, 45. These articles were written in reaction to exhibitions in New York galleries in 1942–43 such as "War and the Artist" at the Pierre Matisse Gallery (which included works by Picasso, Miro, and Rouault, as well as exiled artists such as Ernst,

Chagall, Masson, and Matta) and exhibitions of Corot and van Gogh at the Wildenstein Gallery in aid of American war relief.

22. See Lionello Venturi, *Modigliani* (New York: American British Art Center, 1930).

23. Lionello Venturi, "Sous le signe de l'École de Paris: Chagall," *France-Amérique,* no. 19 (1944).

24. While Venturi pretended to ignore them, judging from his compulsive gathering of clippings filling a very fat file in his archive, Dali's flirtation with mass culture in the United States, prominently featured in two spreads in *Life* magazine in 1941 and 1945, must have been a source of irritation for him. See my essay "On the Passage of a Few Persons through a Rather Brief Period of Time," in *Exiles and Émigrés: The Flight of European Artists from Hitler* (Los Angeles: Los Angeles County Museum, 1997), 128–46.

25. See Masson interview with Deborah Rosenthal, *Arts Magazine* (November 1980): 94.

26. Lionello Venturi, *André Masson* (Rome: Galleria dell'Attico, 1959).

27. The other editors were fellow émigrés, the scholars Renato Poggioli, Enzo Tagliacozzo, and Aldo Garosci.

28. Bruno Zevi, *Verso un'architettura organica: saggio sul pensiero architettonico negli ulitimi cinquant'anni* (Turin: Einaudi, 1945); English edition published 1950.

29. On this question, see Cesare de Seta, "Cultura e architettura in Italia tra le due guerre: continuità e discontinuità," in *1919–1943: Razionalismo e architettura in Italia* (Venice: Biennale, 1976), 13–17.

30. See Enrico Crispolti, "Brevi riflessioni su Venturi e l'arte del proprio tempo," *Storia dell'arte* 101, n.s. 1 (2002): 145–48.

31. Pierre Bourdieu, *L'amour de l'art* (Paris: Éditions de Minuit, 1969), 76.

IV

Creativity and Crisis

Professor Maritain, when lecturing on scholasticism and immortality, spoke of those suffering in concentration camps, "unseen by any star, unheard by any ear," and the almost terrifying solicitude with which he spoke, made one know that belief is stronger even than the struggle to survive. And what he said so consciously, was poetry. So art is but an expression of our needs, is feeling, modified by the writer's moral and technical insights.

Marianne Moore, "Feeling and Precision" (1944)

Pontigny-en-Amérique was a meeting place not only of nationalities but also of academic disciplines, in a more intimate setting than a traditional institution of higher learning. A term such as "interdisciplinary" does not do justice to the fusion of diverse ways of thinking that one finds, for example, in Gustave Cohen's evocation of the Middle Ages, Claude Lévi-Strauss's analysis of culture, or Jacques Hadamard's analysis of creativity in mathematics. Such bold syntheses arose—as the writers in this section make clear—in conversational refuges like Mount Holyoke amid the crises and chaos of the war years. This section opens with an overview, by the scholar Nadia Margolis, of the consuming interest in the Middle Ages among Pontigny participants. We get two contrasting perspectives on the extraordinary career of Pontigny organizer Gustave Cohen: Sorbonne professor, man of the theater, "Mr. Middle Ages," war hero, ambivalent Jew. Helen Solterer lays out Cohen's paradoxical achievement as an ardent nationalist and promoter of "la France éternelle." Jeffrey Mehlman examines the cultural ramifications of Cohen's anti-Semitism. Solterer and Mehlman reveal contrasting strands of discipleship deriving from Cohen's teachings. Solterer traces the heroic efforts of one of Cohen's young actors in the rescue of Jewish children in occupied Vichy. Mehlman explores the ways in which the poet Louis Aragon adapted some of Cohen's ideas for his own politically uneasy uses. The section concludes with two explorations of interdisciplinarity. Andrew Lass evokes the seminal exchanges between Lévi-Strauss and Roman Jakobson that changed the face of at least three disciplines (anthropology, linguistics, and literary theory) and gave birth to the complex of approaches we now call Structuralism. Lass notes along the way how both thinkers drew inspiration from the intellectual and aesthetic currents of Surrealism. Donal O'Shea connects the dots between Hadamard's great achievements in number theory and his arresting insights—inspired by earlier exchanges with the poet Paul Valéry and others—about the workings of "invention" in mathematics. O'Shea argues that the multidisciplinary encounters at Mount Holyoke contributed to this "turn," from pure mathematics to the theory of creativity, in Hadamard's thought.

Medievalism and Pontigny

Nadia Margolis

"Nos yeux reçoivent la lumière des étoiles mortes [our eyes register the light of dead stars]." So began André Schwartz-Bart's 1959 novel of the Holocaust, *Le dernier des justes (The Last of the Just)*, which came to mind as I first read through the Pontigny dossier in the Mount Holyoke College Archives in the summer of 1995.[1] The voices in the participants' *Régistère*, having lain silent within yellowing pages for decades, echoed their protestations from 1942 to 1944. My stumbling upon this archive attests to Mount Holyoke's on-line catalogue back then—meticulous in ways ahead of its time—and to my own lucky penchant for discovering research gems in unlikely places (as when I located, back in the summer of 1990, the obscure Bibliothèque Jeanne d'Arc, full of rare classics in the history of the right-wing royalist group known as the Action française, in the Paris phone book). Upon seeing the archive's detailed citation on my screen (arrived at simply by typing "Gustave Cohen" into the search field), replete with names and places I recognized but had never associated with the Five College area, I was stunned. I phoned the Mount Holyoke Archives librarian, Patricia Albright, and asked permission to see the file right away, to which she readily assented, so eagerly in fact that, by the time I had made the twenty-minute drive, she had the file there waiting for me, neatly arranged on a separate table along with pencils and a pad of paper. "Just like the Bibliothèque nationale," I thought to myself wryly. Perusing the mosaic Pontigny file spontaneously synthesized for me not only my research and that by others (notably Angus Kennedy, a fellow medievalist at Glasgow, for whom I had been sifting through material on Gustave Cohen during the war), but also personal recollections of family and of friends from that time: my father (who landed at Omaha Beach wielding antiaircraft guns, then returned after the war as a Harvard student on the GI Bill to study with Nadia Boulanger) and various former refugees and Résistants (fighters in the French Resistance).

To backtrack a bit, in order to situate my comments within my own scholarship: as a French medievalist working in the later period (fourteenth and fifteenth centuries)—unlike my more "classical medieval" (i. e., twelfth century: Chrétien de Troyes, Marie de France) colleagues, who tend to study romances and poems *about* heroes and damsels in the courtly love arena or epic battlefield—I deal with authors who are often *themselves* the hero-narrators of their own works, such as Christine de Pizan (1364/5–1430?), usually political or moral-historical poems and prose with little patience for Arthurian reveries and for whom old-style chivalry had become a warmongering nuisance. The liminally boring (even when expressing passionate conviction), earnestly ponderous nature of these late medieval texts (late thirteenth to early fifteenth centuries), compared to the seductions of twelfth-century romance, tend not to tell stories as did their earlier counterparts; rather it was their authors' writing of the work (when, for whom, and why) that constitutes the story, the exploit. Their theater was likewise heavily moral and learned, their comedy mordantly irreverent. These were poets and commentators composing amid extreme political upheaval, sometimes in mortal danger for their beliefs: *engagé* writers centuries before Sartre and Camus, though existentialism would never have caught on in the anti–self-deterministic Middle Ages. But late medieval authors did seek to improve the world around them by reminding their influential patrons of the lessons of Greece and Rome as a means of remedy and, failing this, consolation after disasters such as the French loss at the battle of Agincourt (1415). After Agincourt, Paris and other areas of France were occupied by the English and their French sympathizers (the Burgundians)—occupied not just militarily but also intellectually, as the invaders slaughtered both soldiers and scholars as of 1418 and then seized control of the Sorbonne, the University of Paris. It was the pro-English Sorbonnards who, despite their French birth, would help the English cause by, for example, condemning and burning Joan of Arc.

Five hundred and thirty years later—if it is not too simplistic an analogy to make—when the Nazis invaded and occupied Paris, similar events occurred: French-born Nazi collaborator scholars took over the university. Their incursions were facilitated by the Statut des Juifs (Anti-Jewish Statute) and anti-Freemason ordinances, aimed at the two groups predominant in academe. More generally, as in the Hundred Years' War, French national pride—indeed identity—was on the line; the intellectuals knew it, and the more courageous spoke out. Not surprisingly, some self-identified with Joan of Arc, bypassing her Catholic and Vichy affiliations. Among the Jewish academics persecuted by Vichy, two of the most remarkable were the renowned medieval historian Marc Bloch (1886–1944) and the medieval literary historian Gustave Cohen (1879–1958): the former stayed and fought in the Resistance (codename "Narbonne"); the latter fled Paris and eventually moved to the United States. Cohen would join the Catholic philosopher Jacques Maritain (1882–1973) and the art historian Henri Focillon (1881–1943), among others, in founding the École Libre des Hautes Études in New York, from which the Mount Holyoke Pontigny colloquia, founded mainly by Cohen and Jean Wahl, would emerge as a summer spin-off, whose unique initiating aura would be recaptured in Cohen's *Lettres aux Américains*.[2] This would prove to be a glorious experiment—a *moment privilégié* for Mount Holyoke, for the Franco-American intelligentsia, and for the history of the survival of civilization.

My interest in this specific enterprise arose not merely from admiration for Cohen's pioneering, creative work in medieval literature, but even more so from my attendance at one of the colloquia of Pontigny's ancestor, then postwar continuator: those held at Cerisy-la-Salle in Normandy, in a series organized by R. Howard Bloch and Alain Boureau on medievalism and modern literary studies in July 1994. Intriguingly enough, too, the Cerisy colloquia are held at the stately pastoral summer residence of France's greatest nineteenth-century medievalist, Gaston Paris (1839–1903), who himself had played his part as an *engagé* medievalist by testifying as an expert witness in the Dreyfus trial in the late 1890s.[3] These discussions sparked my fascination with how medievalists made the modern world go 'round via the reception history of various legendary and historical characters, for example, Joan of Arc (1412?–1431), whose afterlife far exceeds her mortal one in many areas. In the wake of my Mount Holyoke Pontigny and Cerisy research and his own, Angus Kennedy then published his findings on Gustave Cohen, revealing how, during his period of flight from Paris to southern France, Cohen sustained himself both spiritually and financially through teaching courses on Christine de Pizan and Joan of Arc, while instilling the proto-feminist poet's and her warrior-maiden doppelgänger's fortitude within his students.[4] Other colleagues too would soon publish relevant works on medievalism, and most pertinently on medieval literature and the twentieth-century exilic imagination.[5]

Marc Bloch died before a firing squad in 1944 shouting the same words as some of those Pontigny members signing the register at Mount Holyoke: "Vive la France!"[6] In that same year, Gustave Cohen, having fought his war abroad, would return as soon as the Nazis and their collaborators left, taking his customary place before the students in the amphitheater (or so legend has it) and exclaiming, after three years' enforced absence, "As I was saying..."

NOTES

1. André Schwartz-Bart, *Le dernier des justes* (Paris: Seuil, 1959), 11.

2. Gustave Cohen, *Lettres aux Américains,* 2nd ed. (Montreal: Éditions de l'Arbre, 1943).

3. Another of that Cerisy session's participants, Ursula Bähler, would publish her work as *Gaston Paris dreyfusard: le savant dans la cité,* preface by Michel Zink (Paris: CNRS, 1999).

4. Angus J. Kennedy, "Gustave Cohen and Christine de Pizan: A Re-reading of the *Ditié de Jehanne d'Arc* for Occupied France," in *Sur le chemin de longue eétude...actes du colloque d'Orléans. Juillet 1995,* ed. Bernard Ribémont (Paris: Honoré Champion, 1998), 101–10.

5. See, for example, the *Journal of Medieval and Early Modern Studies* 27 (Fall 1997), "Medi-

eval Studies under Fire," edited by Helen Solterer, which covers what we might call heroic medi-evalism through different manifestations of twentieth-century oppression, especially World War II.

6. See Carole Fink, *Marc Bloch: A Life in History* (Cambridge: Cambridge University Press, 1989), 321.

Gustave Cohen at Pont-Holyoke

The Drama of Belonging to France

Helen Solterer

Gustave Cohen, the medievalist and man of the theater, limped onto the Mount Holyoke campus in the summer of 1942, an ardent advocate of France.[1] Just two years earlier, he had been stripped of his post at the Sorbonne by the Vichy government and its anti-Jewish statutes. He fled to America. Exile made him all the more determined to militate for his chosen country back in Europe.

Other European intellectuals followed his lead. Dozens of them converged on western Massachusetts to attend the meetings that Cohen had organized with American and other refugee colleagues. When one of them arrived at the crossroads that is the village of South Hadley, she asked in her heavily accented English, "Where is Pontigny?" The refugee was thinking of the genteel colloquia that had been held in France during the thirties, under the shadow of a Romanesque abbey. A local woman understood her question differently; she pointed to the campus of Mount Holyoke College and answered, "There."[2]

It did not take long for this motley crew of foreign aliens to settle in. Within a few weeks, their sessions were in full swing on the lawn. When a representative of Roosevelt's government was sent to observe them, he reported back to Washington: "The impression was that the French university was the host, and the Americans, as well as the foreigners were merely the guests, as had been the case back in the student days in France."[3]

How did Gustave Cohen manage to transform this sleepy college campus into an outpost of French culture? Why would Roosevelt's government have cared? What was the effect on those who remained in France? Against the odds, Cohen carried on fighting for France. In the wake of the Great War, he had begun campaigning energetically within the university world. Tapping into his theatrical know-how, he had worked as a cultural propagandist for the Third Republic throughout the twenties and thirties. Cohen longed to represent the cult of the nation, and with the prospect of another world war, to promote "eternal France." The political polarization and its intensifying anti-Semitism did not deter him. On the contrary, they spurred him on. His was a zealous lifelong effort of belonging to France, animated theatrically and driven by bittersweet conflict.

Mutilé de guerre

Gustave Cohen, born and raised in Brussels, was one of thousands of foreign Jews who had signed up for duty in the French army during World War I.[4] "God," the Yiddish proverb said, "lived in France"; many of these men chose to fight for the country whose Republic promised freedom and fraternity, and welcomed them officially with an egalitarian hand. Cohen was wounded severely in the first year on the western front.[5] Like some 4 million other French soldiers, he was a *mutilé de guerre*—a war invalid. Unlike most of them, he seemed almost proud of his condition. He had gone into battle, charged up with the language of sacrifice and holy war; and he came out of no-man's-land, blasted by shrapnel, and still speaking of "glorious wounding."[6] Despite the injury that pained him for the rest of his life, the experience of trench warfare did not turn him into a pacifist. It seemed instead to quicken his zeal for the kind of mystical nationalism that was engulfing Europe.[7]

As a soldier, Cohen envisaged his actions through the filter of French literature. He had seen Charles Péguy, the socialist activist, march off to the front, his head full of Joan of Arc mysteries, offering himself up to the nation like the girlish warlord. This generation had grown up learning how to configure events through literary personae and scenes, especially those from medieval theater. The Dreyfus affair had already, surprisingly, initiated them into this practice. Many intellectuals resorted to casting this political controversy according to one drama that we associate with the Christian Bible and its story of Jesus' Passion.[8] They had all participated in describing the court-martialed Captain Dreyfus as a Jewish sacrificial victim for the French Republic—on the left as on the right, among Jews as well as Catholics.

As a scholar, Cohen knew this French tradition of the Passion play inside out. Writing the first extended study of medieval religious and secular theater had established him as a leading intellectual authority.[9] Cohen had taken up where his predecessors, the philologist Gaston Paris and the man of letters Baron James de Rothschild, had left off. In 1878 they had brought out a vast cycle of these plays, called *The Mystery of the Passion* and *The Mystery of the Old Testament,* in order to publicize the vitality of early French communities. Cohen had been hooked by this theater. He saw how it bound different social groups during the Hundred Years' War. The medieval mystery play looked to be a potentially rich model for patterning the political world, in his own times, as much as during the fifteenth century. Cohen was also proud to put himself in the line of Rothschild; the baron had been distinguished as a "true heartfelt Frenchman by publishing the Mystery Plays that reflected the way the French of the past understood the history of Israel."[10] Inspired by such a lineage,

Cohen downplayed the gamble of a Jewish intellectual turning to Passion scenes to dramatize commitment to the nation. He was single-minded in his ambition to become an impresario for France.

World War I gave Cohen the scholar-soldier an occasion to theatricalize his nationalism. After he had recuperated from his injury, he composed a presentation that traced out the major episodes in the veteran's story. The draft, life in the barracks, trench warfare—all leading up to that moment of "glorious wounding." [11] He proceeded in the manner of a *meneur de jeu,* or stage manager of a mystery play, orchestrating a string of scenes so as to encourage the public to assume them personally, including the scene of suffering. Through his actions, he was also inserting himself heroically into this scenario. He was out to present himself as an exemplary French citizen—not only in France, where he had returned, but also abroad, outside the war zone, in neutral Holland, where he gave his presentation, and where he still held a post teaching French literature.

COHEN'S WAR record was one factor that helped him to gain his first university post in France. He went on from Amsterdam to Strasbourg. Many fellow scholar-soldiers saw appointment in this Alsatian frontier town recaptured for France as vindication of French *civilisation* over German *Kultur.* University work amounted to a battlefield of sorts; heroism in one could be extended in the other. Cohen imagined the defeated Germans saying, "We'll pardon Cohen for fighting against us, but we'll never forgive him for taking Gröber's chair of medieval literature." [12] In his mind, the originary sign of a superior French civilization was the Middle Ages, and professing it an act of patriotism. Gaining such a chair was part of proving his Frenchness. This was a campaign that vaulted him, along with his medievalist colleagues, historian Marc Bloch and art historian Henri Focillon, to the capital, where he won the most prestigious chair in medieval literature at the Sorbonne. [13]

In Paris, throughout the 1930s, Cohen made a name as a charismatic teacher. Far from the remote *maître* intoning lectures in a dark amphitheater as if no one else were there, Cohen mobilized the students. Provincials and Parisians such as Roland Barthes, Marcel Schneider, and Jacques Chailley, émigrés from Russia, colonials from Syria and Madagascar, all were inspired by his enthusiastic challenge to dramatize their required reading. [14] This international youth group came together to put on medieval farces, satirical sketches known as *dits,* as well as religious theater. Their first play, Rutebeuf's *Miracle of Théophile,* told the story of a seductive Faustian bargain. It presented Théophile, an ambitious Parisian clerk fallen on hard times; Salatin, a foreign, fast-talking huckster, who cajoles him into signing up with the devil;

and Mary, an idealized woman who plucks him, in the end, from disaster. Taking on these roles triggered an intense experiment in identification for this group. "By putting themselves into the skin of their characters," Cohen claimed, "by regaining both their spirit and passions, my young people have been able to give another existence to literature that seemed dead." [15] These actors were asked to do more than assume their dramatis personae in ways that confirmed Stanislavsky's notion of acting as assimilation. Their commitment was supposed to run deeper: a commingling of actor and persona, a becoming-medieval. Animating personae of a literature that many cherished as distinctively French created a virtual laboratory of nationalism. For Cohen, the student revivals verged on acts of national identification, and they performed them across the country in a Tour of France.

What happened in Cohen's acting lab makes us, in retrospect, uncomfortable. The scenes of a down-and-out Parisian Théophile facing off with a Semitic Salatin hustling to cut a deal seem to play into the fears provoked by economic crisis and the numbers of Jewish refugees arriving in town. Today we are alert to the consequences of such extreme identification. When Cohen's students took on the appearance of such French medieval personae, their actions look all of a piece with those of right-wing, anti-Semitic nationalists.

In 1933, however, prominent, anti-racist socialists applauded Cohen and his unknown young actors. The critic Benjamin Crémieux praised the group for provoking "some of the strongest emotions in the theater in over ten years." [16] The lesson was not lost on the left. In 1938 Léon Blum's Popular Front made sure to enlist Cohen and his students in their own efforts to show their patriotism. The minister of culture, Jean Zay, called on them to perform at the ceremony inaugurating the restored Cathedral of Reims. [17] This time they put on the twelfth-century biblical drama of Adam and Eve, assuming the roles of First Man and Woman and Enemy before the main façade that had been smashed by German bombs twenty years earlier. Framed by a setting that had aroused such indignation and fierce loyalty, their personae gained a patriotic charge. The young actors participated theatrically in re-sanctifying Reims as war monument and national shrine. Their medieval dramatis personae were also taken to represent the first French citizens; in Zay's terms, they were democratic workers, struggling to make do in an imperfect world.

As the group of actors won this kind of attention across the country, Gustave Cohen emerged as a public authority. More and more, he was recognized as a first-string cultural propagandist for France. He became, according to the press, "Mr. Middle Ages." This nickname, however fanciful, conveyed the lure of his theatrical revivals. His romantic impulse propelled him to believe that, entering into this age, he could activate this imaginary patrimony.

While he attempted to initiate another generation into this theatrical way of becoming and acting French, he insisted on exemplifying national figures for his fellow countrymen.

There is something troubling about Cohen's headlong desire to represent a nationalistic cult as Mr. Middle Ages. The first audiences of the students' revivals included far-right extremists who were tracking him. One *Action Française* journalist reported: "When you talk about medieval theater, you say Cohen, just as you say Littré for dictionaries.... [O]riginally I wanted to entitle my article: Mr. Cohen or the Good Jew." [18] This anti-Semitic sniping targeted him because he represented a subject that the far right was determined to monopolize nationalistically. He was by no means the only medievalist of Jewish background who was attacked. Yet, unlike Marc Bloch, for example, he was a foreign-born intellectual breaking into the French scene, and his successes drew particular scorn. His prominence served as a lightning rod for nationalistic animosities toward the Jewish Outsider. His success with the student revivals also bred contempt because his power of identification with France was increasingly persuasive to the general public. At the time of such attacks, Cohen continued to give himself over to representing the French Middle Ages. He did so completely, to the point of considering converting to Catholicism. The single-mindedness of this born-again Frenchman had put blinkers on him. He could not see that belonging to the nation through this radical, theatrical identification would never change the attacks of the extreme right against him.

A New Stage

When the "phony war" hit in the early autumn of 1939 and Cohen saw the next generation drafted like his own, his diagnosis was melodramatic. "This is the most tragic October that we've gone through together," he wrote his student-actors, "since most of you have responded to the call of our fatherland in danger. When I say fatherland, it is not only our beloved France. It's also our Middle Ages that must be defended, our cathedrals. If you protect them with your bodies, they can be spared new, irreparable wounds." [19] Against what we see today as better judgment, Cohen carried on obsessively representing the Middle Ages—the French, Catholic Middle Ages. This cult of the nation was so visceral, so imaginatively deep for him that he could not help but see it as a living body incorporating people with monuments. At the center of his cult remained the sacrificial wound infused with its aura of French mystery which he continued to project everywhere he turned.

When, little over a year later, the Vichy regime used a newly imposed statute to remove him from his Sorbonne post, there was no more talk of bodies on the line. Like many other Jewish World War I veterans, he pleaded with the same Marshal Pétain who had decorated his military service. "Is it really in the interest of young people to deprive them of a teacher who worked with them to revive ancient mysteries," he wrote in December 1940, "the young people whom you support with such fervor?"[20] Cohen did not wait for an answer. As Vichy bureaucrats were arguing over a response, he was on his way to New York via the not yet occupied south of France, and Lisbon.

Throughout the war, Vichy bureaucrats continued arguing over his case. The Parisian Bureau of Jewish Affairs drafted a decree sometime in 1942: "Considering that Professor Cohen increased the intellectual prestige of France through the theatrical tourneys of his students; considering that Lieutenant Cohen proved his military qualities through World War I; considering all the services that he rendered to the French State we decree that the interdictions to teach be lifted." It was never signed. Cohen never learned that Vichy was considering giving him a dispensation, something that would probably have relieved him and justified his admiration for Pétain.

Instead, the shock and danger of Vichy's anti-Semitic rejection exacerbated Cohen's fundamental histrionic reflex. So did American exile. Over nearly three years from the late summer of 1941, Cohen was indefatigable in dramatizing the cult of France. He sized up the new world, as Archibald MacLeish saw European refugees doing, as "merely a new stage for an old play."[21] Still, the dramatic form of his activities did change. The scenario of self-sacrifice that he had derived from the French medieval Passion and tried out with his student actors was too painful to repeat. It had licensed once again the deaths of many young men, including one of his students. It also sharpened the destructive contradiction that he was harboring: all his theatrical propaganda for France did not outweigh, in Vichy's view, his ethnic and national origins. Cohen let this scene of sacrifice drop and devised in its place a sentimental mix of images from troubadour poetry and romance that still bore his characteristic medieval signature.

Fresh off the boat in New York, Cohen got involved in developing an émigré university à la française, along with the intrepid Alvin Johnson at the Free School, and fellow refugees Henri Focillon and Jacques Maritain.[22] Founding this École Libre des Hautes Études in February 1942 extended his nationalistic cult abroad. It rendered France dynamically, through its rival actors of every political persuasion, from communist to Vichy loyalist. A French University of America acted to transfer the scene of combative continuity. It substantiated the dream of a nation unshaken by attack. With de Gaulle's imprimatur sought by Cohen, it began to put into play another cult of "Free France"—all for American consumption. The impresario was making the pitch to Roosevelt's government to garner his support for the operation.

Cohen spoke out at the inauguration of the École Libre as if he were the only founder. "In my life," he said, "I've attended three great spectacles: the Victory parade of American troops after the Great War, recapturing the University of Strasbourg for the French in 1919, and today." In the public sphere—theater of symbolic actions—all three events celebrated his visions of the French nation. The New York event was a tragic-heroic rendition. "There is only one France, Eternal France," Cohen proclaimed, "she who never tires of creating new forms of art and thought."[23] Cohen was himself flamboyantly assuming the same role of the nation, as if the only enemy were the foreign aggressor.

The only thing eternal about this France was its divisiveness. The École

Portrait sketch of Gustave Cohen. Fonds Jean Wahl/Archives IMEC.

Libre was a notorious political free-for-all. No matter how often Cohen insisted on declaring theatrically the unity of France, the group that he had helped assemble in Greenwich Village kept on disrupting it. They argued interminably over whether to ally the school with de Gaulle or not. The greater their antagonism, the stronger Cohen's idealism grew. No matter how hard he tried to realize the medieval image of the beloved lady-country, his fellow refugees refused to take it on, exploring instead indigenous Haida masks, or Surrealist *objets trouvés* scavenged on city streets. The ceaseless creativity that Cohen wanted to enact and promote abroad turned out to be a turbulent scene of conflict over academic freedom—the flipside of his experience with the student actors.

Franco-American Play on the College Lawn

As the Free School was taking shape contentiously in 1941–42, Cohen turned to other projects. He was boiling over with ideas for dramatizing the French cause; he was, he admitted, "a maniac for creating happenings."[24] What happened through that unusual summer get-together for European refugees that became known as Pontigny-en-Amérique was a further rehearsal for Cohen's drama of Eternal France. This time, his chief accomplice was a former student, Helen Patch, head of the French Department at Mount Holyoke. He first imagined the college catering to francophone refugees who could carry on as if they had not found themselves in the American countryside. His model was Pontigny, the dignified causeries among European scholars following World War I.[25] It was simply a matter of relocating this model from the French province elsewhere. The enterprising New Englander Patch saw it differently. She conceived of the summer colloquium instead as a kind of academic CARE package for displaced scholars. "We Americans who are longing to keep *real* France alive here in America lean upon the courage and integrity of such as yourself," she wrote in response to Cohen's first inquiry in the New Year 1942. "Do let us help wherever we can until such time as France may be restored to her own beloved land."[26] Patch knew how to invoke the larger-than-life feminized nation, mimicking Cohen's style in order to get the project under way.

Together, the pair proposed a plan to the president of the college, Roswell Ham. Cohen had high-flying notions about the scholars reflecting on French literature, aesthetics, and politics in the besieged West; Patch followed up with budgets, calendars, and housing arrangements.[27] The Sorbonnard played the great thinker to the activist with common sense. Patch knew that the U.S. military had requisitioned Mount Holyoke for defense courses during July and August. The students were to march around campus on their way to becoming WAVES—the Women's Auxiliary Volunteer Service.[28] It was easy to envisage another sort of war effort: the French refugees coming to the college, living in the dormitories, and conducting an extraordinary summer school. She was also imagining Americanizing them slowly—whether they were aware of it or not.

"It's a far cry from Pontigny in Burgundy to South Hadley, Mass.," one local professor remarked.[29] Yet many exiled intellectuals did make the trip to participate in the sessions. "Pont-Holyoke," as it became known affectionately, began by creating the impression of a national transplant grafted onto this bucolic campus. The foreigners arrived in the Connecticut River valley by train, and made their way to campus. They crossed the green, passing the tomb of Mary Lyon, "the founder of Mount Holyoke Female Seminary, 1797–1849," in the direction of Porter Hall. Every day, the expatriates went to work on the lawn outside their dormitory. They frequented the cafeteria, and the local hangout, in search of wine and coffee. They signed up for extracurricular activities, swimming in the nearby lake and, during the evenings, playing charades and swing dancing in the Wilder recreation room. For fifteen dollars a week, these bearded men and middle-aged women adjusted to the rhythms of life at a women's college.

The locals were taken with them. These exotic people had shown up without much advance warning, followed by a trail of wives, poodles, and children. The *Holyoke Transcript-Telegram* reported that these transplants made Porter Hall look like the Grand Hotel. Others told Helen Patch that "the entire village suddenly became French."[30]

The odd group assembled was, in fact, a polyglot mix of French, Belgians, Russians, Swiss, Italians, and Spaniards. Most of them were leaders in the Free School: political scientist Boris Mirkine-Guetzevitch, mathematician Jacques Hadamard, philosopher Alexandre Koyré, film director Jean Benoît-Lévy, or people such as poet André Spire and philosopher Denis de Rougemont.[31] But there were other exiles who came: psychoanalyst Raymond de Saussure, art critic Lionello Venturi. Cohen and Patch were also sure to invite various political dignitaries: the former prime minister of Belgium Paul van Zeeland, and Amé-Leroy, a French diplomat and the counselor to Aristide Briand, a leading spokesman for the notion of a European republic between the wars. In their ranks were militants actively involved in the anti-Nazi propaganda war: André Morize with the Free French Information Service, and Geneviève Tabouis, journalist and founder of the first newspaper in exile, *Pour la Victoire.* Then, at the last minute, Jean Wahl arrived, all skin and bones. The Sorbonne philosopher and protégé of Bergson had escaped from Drancy, the Nazi concentration camp outside Paris, and landed in Baltimore just weeks earlier.[32] All in

Boris Mirkine-Guetzevitch, Gustave Cohen, and Jacques Hadamard at the Entretiens de Pontigny Conference, Mount Holyoke College, 1942. MS 0768, Entretiens de Pontigny records, 1942–45, Mount Holyoke College Archives and Special Collections.

all, the intellectuals whom Cohen and Patch had persuaded to come were a cross-section of Europeans, some of whom spoke school French and others only broken English.

Cohen quickly gave this diverse crowd symbolic shape. "It's necessary to continue discussion between men of all nations," Cohen told the Springfield newspaper on the opening day, "no matter what political party they may join." He was counting on setting up a form of group activity reminiscent of the post–World War I era, a "League of Nations in miniature," he would say later, a "Geneva size small." [33] Cohen was happy to promote this model of an international assembly that surpassed any single nation so long as France remained its raison d'être. The gathering represented an older vintage of his international student actors back in Paris, whose theatrical coming-together was to reinforce a belief in French cultural superiority. Patch knew Cohen's strategy inside out, and translated it explicitly. "If many among you are exiles and émigrés," she told the first Pont-Holyoke participants, "we too, the Americans, are exiled from France. We who love France will join efforts here in discussions of our new Pontigny, to secure France, and to protect her, inviolable France…our spiritual mother." For Patch, bolstering the privilege of French culture came before promoting any internationalist value. And it had all the qualities that Cohen espoused: the heroic, the mystical, and the feminine. Cohen synthesized them in another image that he cherished from medieval literature—the troubadours' lady love, at once hetero-erotic dream and beloved homeland. "At Pontigny," he declared in South Hadley, "Fighting France became Beloved France, as vital in the spirit as on the battlefield."[34] His words suggest one final dramatic act of becoming. Since the figure of sacrifice was untenable in American exile, he revived the romantic figure of *amor de long*—love from afar—that sublimated the internecine violence engulfing France. At the time, too, when the Gaullist camp was shifting the name from "Free France" to "Fighting France," Cohen was working to idealize the nation in another medieval vein, and in doing so, to keep at a distance the conflicts that threatened him.

At Pont-Holyoke, in the very first groups assembled to listen to the refugees, the representative of Roosevelt's government took notes on Cohen and his operation. Richard Lachmann was an undercover officer of the newly formed Office of Strategic Services, which evolved later into the CIA. In his eyes, the former Sorbonne intellectual looked very much a "type of conservative Frenchman, far too patriotic, and with little knowledge of everyday politics." Yet the officer credited him with inspiring and directing the events at Pont-Holyoke in its first year. While Cohen the actor was maudlin, at odds with what was happening in the world around him, his actions were assessed as surprisingly productive. They moved others to pursue their own brand of cultural activism for France. The Strategic Services officer communicated back to Washington how impressed he was by the "forceful demonstration" mounted at Pont-Holyoke "against the widely publicized theory of French decadence."[35] This was also true for other European and American participants in the events, starting with the poet-philosopher Jean Wahl, who would take the organizing and intellectual lead from Cohen in the two years that followed.

In the second group that gathered in the summer of 1943, there were also Americans who were touched by Cohen the showman—in spite of themselves. Wallace Stevens confessed to his friend and fellow participant John Peale Bishop that "somehow or other, I can't help licking the feet of people like Professor Cohen."[36] The excessive, overeager side of Cohen made him wary; yet the activist side—if not Mr. Middle Ages, then the middle-aged impresario of French culture—stirred the American poet. It was another poet who was in attendance who speculated about Cohen's effect on Stevens. Marianne Moore wondered whether her confrère was sufficiently intrigued by Cohen that he went on to his own experimentation with French medieval literature in poems such as "Certain Phenomena of Sound."[37]

What, then, did Cohen expect to enact through events at Pontigny-en-Amérique? A romanticized national unity? European thought? An updated "Nouvelle France" in foreign New England? From the outset, Pont-Holyoke encompassed all these competing parts. Cohen was exercising his penchant yet again for mounting events that put French culture into living action. He remained a romantic national scene-setter. But as the École Libre had made amply clear, once the scenes were organized, the players developed them independently of his peculiar nationalistic imagination. Unlike his student actors, they took no direction. When Pont-Holyoke was inaugurated in the summer of 1942, it had Cohen's trademark of a collective functioning theatrically as a laboratory for French cultural superiority; its symbolic significance, and indeed its intellectual substance, was up for grabs.

The Gift for Theater

Cohen's will to dramatize his belonging to France through such sentimentalized medieval personae and plots looks pathetic to us now. Over a lifetime punctuated by war, he clung to one scenario for the nation that seemed to demand self-sacrifice. The attractive, explosive act of the born-again Frenchman had possessed him. When that failed, he dug in, drawing on an idealistic scene with its simple profession of love that he wished desperately would vindicate him and many others. In American exile, from New York to South Hadley, Cohen took on a role resembling that of the medieval troubadour for France: a militant, sweet-talking servant on bended knee before the beloved lady— distant, unattainable, and decidedly unreal. It is sad to think of him unable to recognize the contradiction at the heart of his nationalistic dramas.

Still, the actions of Cohen the impresario were pathetic in a second sense. His commitment to France was moving to people both at home and in America.

There is one little-known, surprising example of the influence of Cohen's theatrical activism that takes us back to France. It introduces the principal actor of Cohen's group, Moussa Abadi, a Middle Eastern Jew from Damascus who began training with them within months of arriving in Paris as a scholarship student. From 1933 on, critics praised this anonymous amateur for his performances in medieval mystery plays, farces, and satirical *dits.* When he played the role of Salatin in the *Miracle of Théophile,* his strong, accented voice drew audiences in, his vivacious manner often captivating them. When he played the role of Judas Iscariot in the principal French medieval Passion play of Arnoul Gréban, he was applauded as someone whose acting had "an awful grandeur about it." He was known to perform with "hot blood and a cool head."[38]

When war struck, Abadi refused to leave France. He chose instead to go underground. In an act of Jewish Resistance, he organized with his partner, the physician Dr. Odette Rosenstock, a network for hiding children in Nice.[39] They began to work in tandem with the Catholic archbishop of Nice, Monsignor Paul Rémond, who was persuaded by Abadi to let them use the archbishop's residence as command central for their clandestine rescue operation.[40] Together they reconnoitered Catholic and Protestant establishments that would take children in; they fabricated identity cards, baptismal certificates, all the documentation necessary to turn Jewish children strategically—on paper—into young Christians. When Alois Brünner, the commander of the Drancy concentration camp, roared into Nice with the Gestapo in September 1943, Abadi, Rosenstock, and Rémond went into action. We know today of some two hundred children they saved from a particularly brutal campaign of deportation. The actual number of children rescued is probably much larger.

Many decades later, toward the end of his life, Abadi spoke publicly about his wartime actions. He gave a Holocaust testimony in 1995 to the French scholar of modern Jewish history Annette Wieviorka.[41] As he remembered his earliest days in France, he began by evoking Gustave Cohen. He spoke with affection of his mentor—his engaging presence, his commitment to young people. The rough-and-ready student, newly arrived from the Middle East, relied on his teacher's example.

Abadi shaped his testimony through many medieval theatrical roles, animating it with their verve and dark humor. It was his insider knowledge of the *Miracle de Théophile* that had first brought him to the attention of Archbishop Rémond. During the first eerie days after Abadi and Cohen had fled Paris, they met up again in Nice, where they began presenting dramatic renditions of medieval literature to while away the time. The archbishop came to their performance, and Cohen proudly introduced his protégé to him. Months later, Abadi would capitalize on this chance encounter with Rémond, using their common pleasure in medieval literature as a password of sorts to enter an elite Catholic world. Once he was through this door, it enabled him to convince the cleric that they could operate together as a team. Out on the streets, Abadi continued to draw on his medieval role-playing to develop a modus operandi for his undercover work. The part of a feisty rascal from Rutebeuf's satirical *dits* or of a biblical figure from a mystery play was useful to him as a cover for dealing with the risks of being caught, or even as an entrée into other religious establishments. Through these roles, he knew viscerally how to put on an act. This helped him to "pass" on the street, undetected, and to go about his Resistance work, largely undisturbed, as Monsieur Marcel, the codename he adopted. Abadi/Marcel was so good at this tactic of clandestine role-playing that it led him to attempt some unlikely, dangerous stunts. He performed scenes from Gréban's *Mystery of the Passion* for audiences in Nice.[42] It even took him as far as the Catholic seminary, where the archbishop had asked him to give his young priests training in public speaking, instructing them how to preach sermons.

Yet it was in Abadi's training of Jewish children where we find the most remarkable signs of his theatrical talent and discipline. In a cloistered Poor Clare convent in the foothills of Nice, Abadi helped to initiate some of the children in role-playing. Together with Odette Rosenstock, he simulated scenes of daily life with them, showing them how to develop a role out of a few scraps: a new birthplace out of a Moroccan town found on a school globe; a new name out of fiddling with their own, Sarah becoming Suzanne, or out of a heroine from a girls' magazine, like Lisette; and, most important of all, a character out of gestures and voice. For hours at a time, Abadi and Rosenstock drilled the children in ways to assume false identities, equipping them for living under duress and protecting them from close scrutiny, arrest, and deportation. Their practice grew out of Abadi's earliest experience with acting and performing. So does his 1995 testimony, which bears trace elements of his theatrical experiences, including the part of Jesus, the Jewish rabbi, from the French Passion.

In his own description, Moussa Abadi had taken Cohen's theatrical direction to heart, with some profound differences. His drama of belonging to France meant neither sacrificing his Jewish sense of self nor giving himself over to a romantic idealism. On the contrary, his acting French by assuming medieval roles was self-affirming, combative, and extraordinarily generous. The traditions of the mystery play and farce provided a creative resource for Abadi in his Resistance work, against almost every expectation, both then, in the 1930s and the war years, and again in 1995, when he looked back.

Side by side, Cohen the impresario and Abadi the activist give us a bittersweet sense of the commitment to France during those war years. For all his zeal, Cohen could not reckon with what was actually happening. Taken with the medieval personae—sentimental and sacrificial—he was blind to the real suffering. During those summers of 1942–43, in South Hadley, his cult of "Beloved France" could not help those most in distress. Back in Nice, Abadi was keenly attentive to the pain of many fleeing Jewish refugees. He fought back, refusing to die sacrificially for France. He dedicated himself instead to the most vulnerable group there. Cohen's gift of theatrical culture was indispensable to him. Abadi transformed it into one dramatic form of action that proved lifesaving for many children.

NOTES

1. This essay comes from my forthcoming book *Playing for Life: Medieval Roles for Modern Times*. I am thankful to Chris Benfey and Karen Remmler for creating an inventive colloquium to reflect and build on all the Pontignys. I thank Chris Benfey especially for introducing me to Cohen's American connections and discussing with me this unlikely assembly of poets.

2. "Allons à Pontigny!" unsigned article, *Pour la Victoire*, no. 29 (July 17 1943): 12. Gustave Cohen reports the incident as well in "Un Pontigny franco-américain," *L'Age d'or* 1 (1945): 51.

3. "Symposium of the French University in New York at Mount Holyoke College, August 17 to September 11, 1942," submitted by Richard Lachmann to Heckscher. National Archives, Washington, D.C., Office of Strategic Services files, French 529, 6. Jeffrey Mehlman introduced material from the Office of Strategic Services into the debate about refugee life in his book *Emigré New York: French Intellectuals in Wartime Manhattan, 1940–1944* (Baltimore: Johns Hopkins University Press, 2000), 25–26, 101, 133, 181–83. For the wider circuit involving American intelligence experts and foreign refugees, including especially French and Germans, see Robin W. Winks, *Cloak and Gown Scholars in the Secret War, 1939–61* (New York: William Morrow, 1987); and Barry M. Katz, *Foreign Intelligence: Research and Analysis in the OSS, 1942–45* (Cambridge: Harvard University Press, 1989).

4. Philippe-E. Landau, "Les Juifs de France et la Grande Guerre, 1914–1941: un patriotisme républicain" (thesis, University of Paris, 1991), 1:121–31, published as *Les Juifs de France et la Grande Guerre: un patriotisme républicain, 1914–41* (Paris: CNRS Editions, 1999), 50–57. See also his article "Juifs français et allemands dans la Grande Guerre," *Vingtième siècle* (July–September 1995): 70–76.

5. Archives nationales, Paris, Papiers Gustave Cohen (hereafter Papiers GC), 59 AP, 1, 1914–21.

6. On this ideology and language of sacrifice as they defined the French war effort, see Stéphane Auzoin-Rouzeau and Annette Becker, *14–18: Understanding the Great War* (New York: Hill and Wang, 2002), the section titled "Crusade" (French original, *14–18, Retrouver la guerre* [2000]); Annette Becker, *War and Faith: The Religious Imagination in France, 1914–1930* (New York: Oxford University Press, 1998), 94–95 (French original, *La Guerre et la foi: de la mort à la mémoire 1914–1930* [1994]). Ivan Strenski trenchantly analyzes the implications of this model; see his *Contesting Sacrifice: Religion, Nationalism, and Social Thought in France* (Chicago: University of Chicago Press, 2002).

7. See two analyses: Conor Cruise O'Brien, *God Land: Reflections on Religion and Nationalism* (Cambridge: Harvard University Press, 1988); and, more recently, the brilliant reflection of Amin Maalouf on the consequences for today's world, *In the Name of Identity: Violence and the Need to Belong* (New York: Arcade, 2001) (French original, *Identités meurtrières* [1996]).

8. Christopher Forth, "Bodies of Christ: Gender, Jewishness, and Religious Imagery in the Dreyfus Affair," *History Workshop Journal* 48 (Autumn 1999): 17–39.

9. Gustave Cohen, *Histoire de la mise en scène dans le théâtre religieux français au Moyen Âge* (Paris, 1905–6); see the complete *Bibliographie des oeuvres de Gustave Cohen* (Paris: Honoré Champion, 1955); and Christophe Charle, *Les professeurs de la faculté des lettres de Paris: Dictionnaire biographique, 1909–1939* (Paris: CNRS, 1986), 60–62.

10. Gaston Paris and Baron James de Rothschild, *Le mistére du Vieil Testament*, vol. 3 (Paris: Société des Anciens Textes Français [SATF], 1878–91), iii. Publication of this multivolume work continued, even after the baron's untimely death in 1881.

11. "Souvenirs et impressions de campagne d'un officier français," presented to the Société Nederland-Frankrijk, Amsterdam, reported in the newspaper *L'Echo Belge*, January 19, 1918. Newspaper clipping in Papiers GC, 59 AP, 1, 1914–21.

12. Gustave Cohen, *Ceux que j'ai connus* (Montreal: Éditions de l'Arbre, 1946), 144.

13. Olivier Dumoulin, "La tribu des médiévistes," *Genèses* 21 (December 1995): 120–33.

14. See my essays "The Waking of Medieval Theatricality: Paris, 1935–1995," *New Literary History* 27, no. 3 (Summer 1996): 357–90; "Jouer les morts: Gustave Cohen et l'effet théophilien," *Équinoxe* 16 (Fall 1996), 81–96; "Performing Pasts: A Dialogue with Paul Zumthor," in a special issue of the *Journal for Medieval and Early Modern Studies* that I edited, "European Medieval Studies under Fire, 1919–1945" 27, no. 3 (Fall 1997): 595–640.

15. Gustave Cohen, "Expériences théophiliennes," *Mercure de France* 273 (February 1, 1937) : 456.

16. Benjamin Crémieux, "Le miracle du théâtre médiéval," *Nouvelle revue française* (April 1935): 649–50.

17. Archives nationales, Paris, F17, 15726, folder 15, 1.

18. "La chronique des théâtres," *Action française*, March 12, 1937.

19. Letter in undated bulletin, Bibliothèque de France, Département des arts du spectacle, Fonds Théophiliens.

20. Archives nationales, Paris, F 17 25416.

21. Archibald MacLeish, "French Culture in America," *Pour la Victoire*, no. 43 (October 31, 1942), 1.

22. On the history of the development of the idea of a French university in America, much good work has been done recently; see Laurent Jeanpierre, "La politique culturelle française aux États-Unis de 1940 à 1947," in *Entre rayonnement et réciprocité: contributions à l'histoire de la diplomatie culturelle*, ed. Alain Dubosclard, Laurent Grison, Laurent Jeanpierre, Pierre Journoud, Christine Okret, and Dominique Trimbur (Paris: Publications de la Sorbonne, 2002), 85–116, esp. 95–97; the most complete version of Jeanpierre's argument is found in his thesis (University of Paris, 2004); Emmanuelle Loyer, *Paris à New York: Intellectuels et artistes français en exile, 1940–1947* (Paris: Grasset, 2005); François Chaubet and Emmanuelle Loyer, "L'école libre des hautes études de New York: exil et résistance intellectuelle (1942–1946)," *Revue historique* 302, no. 4 (2000): 939–72; Aristide Zolberg with the assistance of Agnès Callamard, "The École Libre at the New School, 1941–46," *Social Research* 65, no. 4 (Winter 1998): 921–51; Peter Rutkoff and William B. Scott, "The French in New York: Resistance and Structure," *Social Research* 50, no. 1 (1983): 185–214.

23. Gustave Cohen, *Lettres aux américains* (Montreal: Éditions de l'arbre, 1943), 62.

24. "Vous savez que j'ai la manie de ces créations-là." From a speech, "Impressions d'exil aux États-Unis," delivered in Nice, at the Centre méditerranéen, April 10, 1946. See the typescript, Municipal Archives, Nice, France.

25. See Claire Paulhan, ed., *De Pontigny à Cerisy. Un siècle de rencontres internationales* (Paris: Éditions de l'IMEC, 2002); François Chaubet, *Paul Desjardins et les Décades de Pontigny* (Villeneuve d'Ascq: Presses universitaires du Septentrion, 1999) ; and Jean-Paul Aron, *Les modernes* (Paris: Gallimard, 1984), 55–63.

26. Helen E. Patch to Gustave Cohen, January 7, 1942, Mount Holyoke College Archives (hereafter MHC Archives), "Entretiens de Pontigny, box 1, folder 1.

27. See Laurent Jeanpierre, *"Pontigny-en-Amérique,"* in this volume; and Nadia Margolis, "Exiles in Arcadia: Gustave Cohen and the Colloques de 'Pontigny-en-Amérique' (1942–44)," *French Studies Bulletin* 57 (Winter 1995): 12–14.

28. Patch to Cohen, January 7, 1942; brochure for Industrial War Training Program, MHC Archives, box 1, folder 6; "Martial-Minded Maidens," *Mount Holyoke News,* May 14, 1943.

29. Ruth J. Dean was another medievalist at Mount Holyoke who served as a correspondent for the *Times Literary Supplement* during the war years. See her letter of January 10, 1943, and the article "Pontigny Revives," *TLS,* March 6, 1943, 115.

30. "An Experiment in International Understanding," March 5, 1943, MHC Archives, box 1, folder 6.

31. See Gustave Cohen's handwritten list of intellectuals invited and general subjects to be discussed, MHC Archives, box 1.

32. "I arrived in the American waters and then saw the American police on July 31, 1942." Jean Wahl, "Autobiographie," Fonds Jean Wahl, IMEC, Paris.

33. Gustave Cohen, "Un Pontigny franco-américain," *L'âge d'or* 1 (1945) : 49

34. Gustave Cohen, "La leçon de Pontigny," *Pour la victoire,* September 19, 1942, 6. Cohen was building on the remarks made on the opening day by Patch ("Typescript of Announcement," MHC Archives, box 1, folder 3).

35. OSS—Fr 529, 7–9, National Archives, Washington, D.C.

36. Wallace Stevens to John Peale Bishop, August 25, 1943, Wallace Stevens Papers, Huntington Library, San Marino, Calif.; quoted in Alan Filreis, *Wallace Stevens and the Actual World* (Princeton: Princeton University Press, 1991), 112.

37. Quoted in Filreis, *Wallace Stevens and the Actual World,* 112.See Patricia C. Willis, ed., *The Complete Prose of Marianne Moore* (New York: Viking, 1986), 445.

38. For reviews of Abadi's performances, see Bibliothèque de France, Département des arts du spectacle, Collection Rondel 4364, no.57, "Les hesitations du traître, ses élans infirmes vers un repentir impossible ont une grandeur affreuse qui ont été exprimés avec un talent remarquable par celui—là qui—aucun acteur ne veut être nommé—jouant le rôle du juif Salatin dans le Miracle [de Théophile]" ; "Les Théophiliens: Judas et la Farce de Maître Pathelin," *Revue des deux mondes,* April 1, 1937, 669; Yves Bonnet, *Le Soir,* May 14, 1937; *Revue des Jeunes,* November 10, 1937.

39. Les Anciens de la résistance juive en France, and Jean Brauman, Georges Loinger, and Frida Wattenberg, eds., *Organisation juive de combat, résistance/sauvetage, France, 1940–45* (Paris: Autrement, 2002), 409–11.

40. Ralph Schor, *Un évêque dans le siècle: M. Paul Rémond (1873–1963)* (Nice: Éditions Serre, 1984), 23, 54, 116–25.

41. Videotaped interview of Moussa Abadi and Odette Rosenstock Abadi with Annette Wieviorka, April 18–19, 1995, deposited at the Archives nationales in Paris, through the Association Témoignages pour Mémoire.

42. Théophiliens file, Fonds Abadi, IMEC, Paris.

The Tiger Leaps

Louis Aragon, Gustave Cohen, and the Poetry of Resistance

Jeffrey Mehlman

Surely Walter Benjamin, who had been at Pontigny in 1938, would have been at the Mount Holyoke Pontigny colloquia of the war years, and the pathos of those gatherings owes not a little to his absence. Benjamin called one of his protracted meditations preliminary to the Arcades Project "Zentralpark"—largely because he no doubt imagined himself working out the Baudelairean issues those pages deal with while strolling through Central Park in Manhattan. What would the final format of the Arcades Project have been? And might there not have been a Mount Holyoke *Konvolut*—a folder of citations and observations assembled in anticipation of a lecture in South Hadley? Such are the questions that bring a particular pathos to the events we are commemorating here.

If we don't know where the Arcades Project would have ended up, we have precise knowledge of where it began. A letter of May 1935 from Benjamin to Theodor Adorno details a febrile night spent reading Louis Aragon's *Paysan de Paris,* a book that so affected Benjamin that he was unable to read more than two or three pages at a time. Such would have been the "beginning" of Benjamin's "dialectical fairy tale."[1] Now it happens that the "Paysan de Paris" was making a very Baudelairean reappearance in French letters at the very time of the Pontigny-en-Amérique meetings. For he resurfaces in Aragon's Resistance poem "Le Paysan de Paris chante." Paris is a dreamscape from which the city, across which Baudelaire appears to be stalking, is about to awaken, and the awakening itself is imagined in terms of an "Heure H," an hour of liberation.[2] In its conventional metrics, what Cyril Connolly called "the controlled heaving swell of [its] Baudelairean alexandrine[s]," and in its altogether unconventional rhymes, the poem is a characteristic achievement of France's leading poet of the Resistance. It was, moreover, a poetry that came with its own poetics, and it is to a consideration of that poetics, which will bring us a step closer both to Benjamin and to South Hadley, that I now turn.

The text in which Aragon sets forth what was at stake in his wartime verse is titled most provocatively "La leçon de Ribérac ou l'Europe française" and is centered on a biographical episode.[3] Emerging, in late June 1940, from the inferno of Dunkerque, Aragon finds himself in the southern town of Ribérac. He is suddenly struck by the fact that Ribérac was the native town of the medieval Provençal poet Arnaud Daniel, inventor of the sestina, an artist so esteemed by Dante that he is the only figure in the entirety of the *Commedia* granted the privilege of speaking a language (Provençal) other than Italian. That serendipitous insight descends on Aragon with the force of revelation. It was out of Ribérac, in troubled times, that the genius of French poetry had shone forth, in the Middle Ages, to "invade" and conquer all of Europe. And now, opines Aragon, in the wake of France's military collapse, Ribérac emblematizes the prospect of a new and redemptive spiritual conquest of Europe by French verse.

THE KEY point is the resonance between the two moments at Ribérac and the elation it elicits. As Aragon puts it, what transpired in twelfth-century French letters, a development whose emblematic figure Arnaud Daniel would be, was of such moment that "it could be explained only by [or in terms of] the present epoch" (123). It is as though the dialectic of history had come to a standstill, time had stopped, in the flickering affinity between twelfth-century and twentieth-century Ribérac. In the middle of catastrophe, the poet and would-be revolutionary stages what Benjamin called a "tiger's leap into the past," liberating, in its redemptive pretension, what the German would call a "chip of messianic time."[4]

Before long Aragon is evoking a second medieval poet, Chrétien de Troyes, whose oeuvre enacts a first and crucial consolidation of what had been invented by Arnaud Daniel, for Chrétien represents the marriage of the courtly, idealizing traditions of the Provençal south and the realistic conventions of the Celtic north. He thus becomes emblematic of France—unified and triumphant. And it is here that Aragon's poetics broach the Mount Holyoke Pontigny gatherings, for establishing the centrality of Chrétien de Troyes's achievement was said to be the scholarly accomplishment of none other than the organizer of Pont-Holyoke, the Sorbonne medievalist Gustave Cohen. In Aragon's pregnant words, it was Chrétien's fate to await "que M. Gustave Cohen enfin vint" for his true importance to be acknowledged (128). The diction is crucial. For it recalls "Enfin Malherbe vint" of Boileau's *ars poetica,* the recognition of a crucial turning point in neoclassical France's sense of itself.

There is, in sum, a nice symmetry in our constellation. Benjamin, the Jew who never made it from Paris to South Hadley, claimed to find his principal inspiration in Aragon. And Aragon, elaborating his Resistance poetics, claimed to find his principal inspiration in Gustave Cohen, the Jew who did make it from Paris to organize the colloquia at South Hadley. The importance of the poetry of Provence, in its relation to the north, was a live topic among the émigrés of New York. For Denis de Rougemont, the troubadors of Provence were crypto-Catharist mystics and their mystique of self-destructive passion, displaced from the private to the political sphere, the principal inspiration for the Nazism that had driven so many from Europe to these shores.[5] For Simone Weil, to the contrary, the civilization of the south, during the Albigensian crusades, had been the object of a virtual genocide on the part of the north, a holocaust every bit as violent as whatever one might lay at the door of the Nazis.[6] Thus Rougemont, with his proleptically Nazi south, and Weil, with her prodigiously victimized south, stood on opposite sides of the issue. What both shared, however, was a sense of the crucial discontinuity between south and north. In drawing on Cohen, Aragon evokes a more organic, less modernist vision of the question. France, then divided, must be restored to its unified essence.

We have spoken of Cohen, in flight from France, as a Jew, but he was a curious Jew indeed. Nothing seems to have made him prouder than the respect he enjoyed from "notorious anti-Semites" such as Barrès.[7] Moreover, if he was happy to enjoy the respect of many an eminent anti-Semite, he was equally intent on eschewing what he called "philosemitism," a practice that consisted in favoring marriages between Jews, "thereby perpetuating a problem whose disappearance or solution through mixed marriages would be eminently desirable."[8]

The problem, in sum, was the survival of the Jews themselves. Thus, whereas Hitler was intent on doing away with the Jews, and Vichy, jealous of its bureaucratic autonomy, attempted to convince the Germans that the Jewish problem was one that it was eminently equipped to resolve, a Jew—or Israelite—such as Gustave Cohen, in his *Lettres aux Américains,* seems intent on affirming that the Jewish "problem" is one that Israelites such as himself, to use what Cohen himself called the "polite" form, ought to be left to dismantle through intermarriage.[9]

All this is a reminder of just how marginal the Jewish question may have been in the eyes even of those suffering its consequences during World War II. Yet there was something irreducibly Jewish about Gustave Cohen. Indeed, anyone who could arrive in New York City, the world capital of Jewry, during World War II and pretend to see in the skyscrapers nothing so much as a "forest of Gothic cathedrals," as Cohen did, would have to be a Jew.[10] Cohen, the man who, according to Aragon, invented the centrality of Chrétien de Troyes. It was Cohen's successor at Yale, Howard Garey, who once suggested, following a similar logic, that Chrétien himself may have been Jewish. Why? Because, claimed Garey, we possess a manuscript in which the name is written "Chrestien li Goys," and any man calling himself Christian the Goy would have to be Jewish. According to Aragon? The logic may be contagious. For any man, I would suggest, *that* prepared to worship his wife, Elsa, in *that* hyperbolic a fashion, would have to have been a homosexual, as Aragon, in fact, was.[11]

But I anticipate. Let us isolate four salient points from the "Lesson of Ribérac":

1. A will to step out of history: the moment of defeat improbably coincides with a rush of "immense pride in invading Europe *poetically*" (124).
2. The utter elation with which the poet, in Ribérac, seems infused on what turns out to be, after all, the occasion of a devastating French defeat.
3. A postulate that the mirage of France triumphant was to be infused with a medieval and overtly Catholic sense of things.[12]
4. The new poetry of Resistance, like the old poetry of courtly love, would be dependent on a poetics of "contraband" or *"double jeu."*[13] One would deceive the censors by publishing poems that were overtly—but only overtly—unthreatening to the status quo, as in those hermetic poems of the courtly tradition which allowed poets cryptically to "celebrate their Ladies even in the presence of their Lords" (138).

WHAT IS striking in these elements—so central to the poetics of Resistance—is how they cohere in a constellation which is precisely that of collaboration. Consider: First, contemporary historiography has pinpointed the Vichy error in 1940 in assuming that because France had lost its battle, the world war was indeed over. In this, the decision of Vichy was effectively to step out of history. Second, at the same time, as Maurras put it, the defeat of the Third Republic was a "divine surprise" that had come totally unexpectedly in the form of an apparent catastrophe.[14] Third, the new France of the National Revolution was a harking back to ancien régime (if not overtly medieval)—and fundamentally Catholic—values. Finally, the new regime insisted that to the extent that it collaborated with the Germans, it was only because apparent collaboration was the subtlest ruse of Resistance. Vichy's ongoing alibi was that it was engaged in a *double jeu*.

The alignment of four elements from Aragon's Resistance poetics with analogous elements from the ideology of collaboration, it will be objected, is a mirage, and the objection would be well founded. Proof of the fundamental opposition between the two might take the form of a consideration of Drieu la Rochelle's venomous response to "La leçon de Ribérac" in the pages of the collaborationist journal *Emancipation Nationale* (October 11, 1941). Drieu, mocking the "marvelous patriotic effusion" that has suddenly overcome the ex-Surrealist, suggests that Gustave Cohen may have had greater appeal for Aragon than Chrétien de Troyes; moreover, the Chrétien whom Cohen allows

Aragon to promote is said to be "borderline *communisant*."[15] In sum, France's preeminent literary collaborator, the former friend (and sometime lover, it is now believed) of Aragon, was quick to denounce the poet as a Jew-loving communist, a charge that could easily have led to a death sentence.[16] The opposition between Resistance and collaboration could not have been more marked.

Yet consider Aragon's response to Drieu, the poem "Plus belle que les larmes":

> Ah si l'écho des chars dans mes vers vous dérange
> S'il grince dans mes cieux d'etranges cris d'essieu
> C'est qu'à l'orgue l'orage a détruit la voix d'ange
> Et que je me souviens de Dunkerque Messieurs.[17]

The remarkable fact is that the poem-response to Drieu, replete with a masked reference to the Communist Party Congress of 1937 in Arles, was published in a Tunisian journal at the request of the Vichy governor, Admiral Esteva, who could not quite figure out what Aragon was talking about. This is what the poet calls "making use of *l'hypocrisie vichyste*."[18] It remains, of course, to determine to what extent a deceptive exploitation of the hypocrisy of the adversary remains uncontaminated by the very hypocrisy it pretends to oppose. It is that kind of consideration which, after the war, would allow Jean Paulhan, combating the purge, to view Drieu and Aragon as morally twinned mirror images of each other.[19]

If one wanted to peel Aragon away from the ideology of collaboration—despite the medievalism, despite the more than decorative Catholicism, despite the nationalism, despite the curiously elated sense that the fall of France opened up remarkable poetic possibilities, and despite the poetics of "contraband" or what Vichy would later call *double jeu*—it would be in terms of the very different Middle Ages his poetry claimed to champion. For the Middle Ages of Aragon, steeped in the traditions of courtly love and poetry, pretended to be a kind of feminist revenge and "prodigious reaction," cultivated in medieval courts abandoned by the Crusaders, against "feudal barbarism" (125). (Indeed, Aragon's poetry was as overtly feminist in its implication as Wallace Stevens, in his Mount Holyoke excursus on "male" centuries and "virile youth," was by implication anti-feminist.)[20] In France, the representative of what Aragon calls a misogynistic "nietzschéisme au petit pied" was Montherlant, who comes in for some abuse in "La leçon de Ribérac" (127). But behind Montherlant lay the Nazi vision of a barbaric and virile Middle Ages. Which is why the text ends by evoking the difference between Chrétien de Troyes's valiant Perceval and Wagner's homosexually panicked Parsifal—all to the advantage of Chrétien de Troyes.

The will to take (French) poetry back from Wagner is an implicit—but remarkably illuminating—gesture in the direction of a poet not usually associated with Aragon: Mallarmé. For the great minimalist was obsessed with the threat posed by Wagnerian maximalism. His answer—to the plenitudes of Wagnerian myth and archetype—was the Gallic abstraction of structure.[21] Whereas Aragon—as the discussion of Perceval makes clear—would supplant Germanic myth with Gallic myth: "les mystères français."[22] "Brocéliande," for example, a call to Resistance set in an Arthurian forest haunted by "the sorcerers of Vichy and the dragons of Germania," ends up with a section called "Le ciel embrasé" that sounds not a little like a French version of *Götterdämmerung:* "renversant le ciel que les dieux étoilaient."[23] Moreover, "Brocéliande" is studded with Mallarméan allusions: "Mais le bel autrefois habite le présent" harks back to Mallarmé's "bel aujourd'hui."[24] The flamboyant vestiges of a "solar cult" manage to mobilize what Mallarmé's most erudite reader, Bertrand Marchal, has identified as Mallarmé's primordial obsession.[25] But it is Aragon's difference with Mallarmé that deserves underscoring in this context. Take Aragon's most celebrated poem of the Exodus, "Les lilas et les roses." It is a heartbreaking meditation that juxtaposes the sublime landscape of early summer and the desperate Frenchmen fleeing the German advance: "le démenti des fleurs au vent de la panique."[26] Now, it would be possible to delineate the *structure* of Mallarmé's poetry in terms of an abstract opposition between white and red, emblematically lily and rose.[27] Indeed, all in Mallarmé takes place along the infinitesimal line establishing that difference. Mallarméan structure versus Wagnerian myth, on the one hand; Aragon's Gallic myth versus Wagner's Germanic myth on the other. To have countered myth with myth was admittedly a lesser challenge, though no mean one.[28] And certainly not deserving of the obloquy that Benjamin Péret, in a famous polemic, called *Le déshonneur des poètes.*[29]

SHORTLY AFTER the war, Jean Paulhan and Dominique Aury together published an anthology of French wartime texts, associated with the Resistance, under the title *La Patrie se fait tous les jours.*[30] One of the most revealing is an Aragon poem which is in fact the conclusion of *Le Musée Grévin,* the long polemical work Aragon published under the pseudonym François la Colère in 1943. In the Paulhan-Aury collection it is called "Auschwitz," and its subject is indeed the concentration camp. It is an inferior poem, but no less revealing for that:

Ce sont ici des Olympiques de souffrance
Où l'épouvante bat la mort à tous les coups
Et nous avons notre équipe de France
Et nous avons ici cent femmes de chez nous.[31]

This is an Auschwitz not for Jews but for (French) women, and the poem, which may have been inspired by the "convoi des femmes" of January 24, 1943, is addressed to them in the very Christian mode of a collective "Hail Mary": "Je vous salue Marie" modulates to the plural "Je vous salue Maries de France" and finally to "Je vous salue ma France"—with not a mention of Jews. Moreover, the notion that fear beats out death in the Olympics of suffering, that the principal thing we have to fear is fear itself, makes of this Auschwitz anything but the locus of the insuperable and unfathomable evil with which it has since become associated.

Aragon's "Auschwitz," in sum, with its Hail Marys and its indifference to the unmentioned Jews appears to be an anticipation in verse of the scandal of the Carmelite monastery established at Auschwitz some years back. Yet it was in no way a source of scandal. As such it can serve as a reminder of how different our contemporary perception of the French experience of the war is from that of those who actually lived through it. Recently the historian Pierre Nora has referred to the contemporary French as the "Bousquet generation."[32] The implication is that the figure who has transfixed the generation is René Bousquet, the Vichy head of police, who had arranged with the Germans in the summer of 1942 for the French police to proceed independently in rounding up Jews for deportation. The genocide of the Jews, that is, whose emblematic venue was Auschwitz, was the limit case around which a generation defined itself. The title of the Paulhan-Aury collection, *La Patrie se fait tous les jours,* suggests that their focus too is the self-definition of a generation. But if such be the case, it is a self-definition that has quite simply no room for Jews—not even and above all at Aragon's Auschwitz. As though Aragon, in a single poem, had invented Holocaust denial...before the Holocaust.

This is entirely in keeping with the notion we encountered in Gustave Cohen himself, Aragon's guide to the Middle Ages, according to which the best solution to the Jewish problem would be allowing Jews the freedom to self-destruct through assimilation and intermarriage.

BENJAMIN's "tiger leap" into the past was undertaken with an eye, however blind, to the messianic future. For which reason it may be useful, in conclusion, to examine, however schematically, two cases of futurity relating to Aragon's wartime poetry.

The first is the five hundred–page volume *Le fou d'Elsa* (1963), arguably the poet's major effort of the postwar period, which is built around a metaphysical resonance between the tragic fall of Paris in 1940 and the no less tragic fall of Granada, in the course of (or resulting in) an Islamic holy war, or *jihad*, in 1492. The madman of the title wanders around Granada, mystically enthralled with the poet's beloved Elsa, a woman who does not yet exist, and who will serve as this (Muslim) Dante's Beatrice. Having written the Jews out of his very Catholic Auschwitz, Aragon, as it were, would make amends by expanding the sphere of victims of World War II beyond the case of the French alone, and ends up with a vision of Muslim *jihad*, holy war as the appropriate supplement to the Marxist vision of civil war. Everything is caught up, Aragon interestingly suggests, in a temporal paradox: the madman of 1492 with his mystical access to Aragon's muse of 1942, but also the fact that Arabic, a language without a future tense, would soon be the language of a people without a future. And then, as if to clinch our point, Aragon, in a book-length interview with François Crémieux, reveals that his thoughts on futurity and its absence, the nub of the book, are all inspired by a classic work of historical linguistics: *Le système verbal sémitique et l'expression du temps* by Marcel Cohen.[33] Consider the constellation: on the one hand, Aragon's Resistance poetry, culminating, in the Paulhan-Aury anthology, in an "Auschwitz" without Jews, in whose margins lay the scholarly achievement of Gustave Cohen, who had his own benign solution to the "Jewish problem"; on the other, the mystical future (or past) of that wartime experience, a Granada whose fall is said to anticipate the fall of Paris ("notre Grenade à nous"), the prospect of an ancient *jihad*, in whose margins lay the scholarly achievement of Marcel Cohen.[34] And this as communicated to a journalist whose very name, Crémieux—that of the decree of 1870 conferring citizenship on Jews, but not Muslims, in Algeria—was an incitement to anti-Jewish violence in North Africa and beyond.[35]

A second future of sorts for Aragon's Resistance poetry concerns the poem that resulted in Vichy's first seizure and suspension of a literary review and, as such, a first acknowledgment of Aragon's poetics of "contraband."[36] The poem was called "Nymphée" and the journal, suspended for two months, *Confluences.* The occasion of "Nymphée" was to all appearances literary: a casual reading of the neglected Racine tragedy *Mithridate.* Mithridate, the ancient Middle Eastern potentate and perpetual thorn in the hide of the Roman Empire, lived long enough to see his son Pharnace collaborate with the invading Romans. Pharnace, that is, is a figure of the collaborator, and the poet evokes him, in his treachery, awaiting the incoming ships of the predatory Romans:

Lui qui désespérait déjà de leurs galères
Enfin les voici donc ces vainqueurs qu'il aida
Ils ont mis à venir la lenteur de l'éclair
Leur triomphe est le sien sur ses propres soldats.[37]

Note the Blitzkrieg flashing in the "éclair" of the third line. The poet sympathizes with the aging king, betrayed by his son, offers up a near Baudelairean development on the depression gripping a thousand "absurd objects," trifles whose charms will go unperceived by their new and brutal owners, and eventually closes his Racine to dream a happier ending ("le dénouement qu'exige une France exaltée").[38] A classic poem of Resistance, then, that Vichy's minister of information had every reason to seize. Yet it is enough to reopen Racine to detect a quite different Mithridate and a very different political prospect: a cruel Middle Eastern despot, first seen "on the banks of the Euphrates"; the greatest thorn in the side of the Western superpower, known for his defeats but also for his longevity; an infamous dabbler in poisons, the chemical warfare of his day. And then there is the horrendous strategy that Racine reveals in act 3: skirmishes against the Western superpower are ineffective, Mithridate suggests, for her designs on our treasure are intractable; what is needed, it is proposed, is a daring new plan, allowing Terror (la Terreur) to rise out of the "marshlands" and strike the capital, Rome, itself. Racine, in sum, has provided the smoking gun, the link between Middle Eastern despot and international terrorism, that Colin Powell sought in vain. But wait. No sooner does the despot announce his mad scheme than French critics begin to find him, in his folly, vaguely Shakespearean, grandiose, and, to that extent, sympathetic. And it is that sympathy, afflicting a "vieux roi malheureux contre qui tout conspire," which survives in Aragon's poem.

Two futures for Aragon's poetry of Resistance, in sum: from "Nymphée" and the stunned sympathy of a French readership before the folly of a Middle Eastern despot's aspirations to international terrorism; from the fall of Paris ("notre Grenade," as it is called in Le fou d'Elsa) to the pathos of jihad. For all its retro accoutrements, there are few bodies of poetry, alas, that pack as contemporary a wallop as the Resistance poetry of Louis Aragon.

NOTES

1. Walter Benjamin, Correspondance, vol. 2 (Paris: Aubier, 1979), 163–64.
2. Louis Aragon, La Diane française (Paris: Seghers, 1946), 111.
3. Louis Aragon, Les yeux d'Elsa (Paris: Seghers, 1942). Page references in the text are to this edition.

4. Walter Benjamin, *Illuminations* (New York: Schocken, 1969), 261, 263.

5. Concerning Rougemont in New York, see my *Émigré New York: French Intellectuals in Wartime Manhattan, 1940–1944* (Baltimore: Johns Hopkins University Press, 2000), 61–84.

6. Concerning Weil in New York, see ibid., 85–103.

7. Gustave Cohen, *Ceux que j'ai connus* (Montreal: Éditions de l'arbre, 1946), 95; Cohen, *Lettres aux Américains* (Montreal: Éditions de l'arbre, 1942), 63.

8. Cohen, *Lettres aux Américains*, 77.

9. Or through conversion. Cohen himself converted to Catholicism in New York in 1943. See Claude Singer, *Vichy, l'Université et les Juifs: les silences et la mémoire* (Paris: Les Belles Lettres, 1992), 247. According to Stephen Steele ("L'Après-guerre de Gustave Cohen et les institutions françaises," *Nottingham French Studies* 42, no. 2 [Autumn 2003]: 43), that gesture, deemed to have been undignified, would have cost Cohen the support of Georges Duhamel in his failed quest to occupy the seat in the Académie française relinquished by the disgraced Charles Maurras. On the circumstances of Cohen's conversion, see as well Helen Solterer, "The Waking of Medieval Theatricality, Paris, 1935–1995," *New Literary History* 27, no. 3 (Summer 1996): 357–90.

10. Cohen, *Lettres aux Américains*, 30.

11. On Aragon's homosexuality, both before and after the death of Elsa Triolet, see Jean Ristat, *Avec Aragon* (Paris: Gallimard, 2003); and Pierre Daix, *Aragon* (Paris: Flammarion, 1994), 409, where mention is made of the "scandal of a friendship a bit too tender for a young man" in 1942.

12. On Aragon's newfound "respect for a faith he would never share," see "De l'exactitude historique en poésie," in *La Diane française*, 102.

13. See Olivier Barbarant, *Aragon: la mémoire et l'excès* (Paris: Champ Vallon, 1997), 122.

14. Stephen Steele, in "La place de la nation dans le Moyen Âge de Gustave Cohen et de Louis Aragon," *Rivista di Letterature Moderne e Comparate* 8, no. 1 (2000): 74, speculates wryly on what terms Gustave Cohen might have found to praise his predecessor had he been successful in his campaign to replace Maurras in the Académie française.

15. Louis Aragon, *L'oeuvre poétique*, vol. 9 (Paris: Livre Club Diderot, 1974), 404.

16. On Aragon's unconventional "attempts at gymnastics" with Drieu in the 1920s, see Ristat, *Avec Aragon*, 96.

17. "Ah if the echo of tanks in my verse disturbs you / If strange shrieks of axles screech in my skies / It is because the storm has destroyed the organ's angel voice / And I can still remember Dunkerque, Messieurs." Aragon, *Les yeux d'Elsa*, 82.

18. *Aragon parle avec Dominique Arban* (Paris: Seghers, 1968), 141.

19. See Gisèle Sapiro, *La guerre des écrivains* (Paris: Fayard, 1999), 623. For additional discussion of Paulhan's postwar critique of the Resistance, see my "Writing and Deference: The Politics of Literary Adulation," in *Genealogies of the Text* (Cambridge: Cambridge University Press, 1995), 97–112.

20. See Wallace Stevens, *The Necessary Angel: Essays on Reality and the Imagination* (New York: Vintage, 1951), 52.

21. See Stéphane Mallarmé, "Richard Wagner: rêverie d'un poète français," in *Oeuvres complètes* (Paris: Gallimard, 1945), 541–46, a meditation on the dissolution of myth or "legend" by abstract—or musical—thought.

22. Cohen, *La Diane française*, 162.

23. "Overthrowing the heavens constellated by the gods." Ibid., 96, 184.

24. Ibid., 162.

25. See Bertrand Marchal, *La religion de Mallarmé* (Paris: José Corti, 1988).

26. "The flowers disputing the winds of panic." Louis Aragon, *Le Crève-coeur* (Paris: Gallimard, 1946), 40.

27. As in, say, "Toast funèbre": "Pourpre ivre et grand calice clair," which are wine and cup, but also lily and rose. See my *"Ad centrum,"* in Denis Hollier and Jeffrey Mehlman, *Literary Debate: Texts and Contexts* (New York: New Press, 1999), 168–86.

28. See Marchal, *La religion de Mallarmé*, 182, for a poetic proposal analogous to Aragon's that was issued by Catulle Mendès in the context of efforts to find an adequate French response to Wagner.

29. Benjamin Péret, *Le déshonneur des poètes* (Paris: Pauvert, 1945), 82. Péret attacked the "reactionary" mix of Christianity and nationalism in Aragon's Resistance poetry.

30. Jean Paulhan and Dominique Aury, eds., *La Patrie se fait tous les jours* (Paris: Éditions de Minuit, 1947).

31. "These are the Olympics of suffering / In which fear beats out death at every turn / And we have our French team / And we have here a hundred women from back home." François la Colère [Louis Aragon], "Auschwitz," ibid.

32. "Tout concourt aujourd'hui au souvenir obsédant de Vichy," interview with Pierre Nora by Robert Solé and Nicolas Weill, *Le Monde,* October 21, 1997.

33. Louis Aragon, *Entretien avec François Crémieux* (Paris: Gallimard, 1964), 76.

34. Louis Aragon, *Le fou d'Elsa* (Paris: Gallimard, 1963), 29.

35. Concerning the Crémieux decree, see my "Sad News: *L'antisémitisme nouveau est arrivé,"* *Contemporary French Civilization* 27, no. 2 (2003): 277–96.

36. Pierre Seghers, *La Résistance et ses poètes* (Paris: Seghers, 1974), 201.

37. "He who already despaired of their ships / Finally they're here, then, the conquerors he helped / Theirs was the slowness of lightning in arriving / Their triumph over his soldiers is his own." Aragon, *La Diane française,* 130.

38. The reference to Racine brings us back to the first poem I mentioned, "Le paysan de Paris chante": "Peut-on déraciner la croix du Golgotha / Ariane meurt qui sort du labyrinthe [Can the cross of Golgotha be uprooted / Ariadne dies leaving the labyrinth]." The labyrinth will turn into the Paris Métro; Ariane was Phèdre's ill-starred sister.

Poetry and Reality

Roman O. Jakobson and Claude Lévi-Strauss

Andrew Lass

This story has no beginning and may not be able to end. I would like to tell it, stuck as I am on one of its many tangents, if only it would sit still at least for a brief moment while it continues to expand. It is the story of chance meetings, some fortuitous, some foretold, and several others missed along the way. It was in 1941, in New York City, that the young French anthropologist Claude Lévi-Strauss first encountered the charismatic Russian linguist and onetime poet Roman Osipovich Jakobson. He attended his lectures on "Sound and Meaning" at the École Libre des Hautes Études in New York, and they spent endless hours in conversation sipping tea served by the distinguished folklorist Svatava-Pírková Jakobson, the Russian linguist's Czech wife. The friendship between the linguist and the anthropologist developed as their conversations continued on the campus of Mount Holyoke College and, I would assume, on the way there and back to the city. There were many other exchanges between them, at other times and places, but just as important were the conversations with other distinguished scholars and artists with equally convoluted life trajectories. In other words, in order to appreciate what it was that got sparked when their wires crossed—and I do intend the other possible meaning of this expression—one would need to know what other crossings they brought to this one and what impact their collaboration had on their future encounters. If God does not play dice, as Einstein insisted, how about billiards?

While theirs was not the first confluence of linguistics and anthropology—one could argue that the histories of both disciplines are from the beginning intimately linked—the impact of this particular encounter was decisive. On one side semiotics and on the other structural anthropology would hold center stage for a quarter of a century and rattle the foundations of a broad spectrum of knowledge for much longer. And then, like other fads, it slowly faded into the background as it gave way to a series of other hotly debated terms. There are many reasons why scientific paradigm shifts occur and plenty of other paradigms that try to address them. From the simple fact that ideas compete for their fifteen minutes of fame no less than Andy Warhol, to the seemingly more legitimate reason that they are subject to change like anything else and, vulnerable to critique, get replaced by a logic that seems to do better, at least for a time. And where intellectual history tends to follow the internal logic as well as the social, political, and economic background of the developmental changes, recent scholarship—perhaps itself reflecting a general concern with globalization and the postmodern—draws our attention to their movement through complex networks in which a variety of couriers and intersections play their decisive part. It is not just the individuals themselves, their ideas, and the social networks of their flow, but the letters, telegrams, and telephone calls, the radio broadcast and the printed word-image, trains, boats, and cars, even the occasional coffin, play their important part as the enablers and transporters, as do the places they mediate: the café or pub, classrooms, corridors, and, of course, the lawn chairs in front of Mount Holyoke's Porter Hall. The genealogy of influence demands a concern for the would-be trivia in order that we might better understand the play of chance, in the language of structuralism, the point of articulation where the contingent and the necessary meet. It's like the magic touch: it threatens to draw everyone who comes in contact with it into its fold, including the storyteller. It is the profound irony of crisis, of the devastating madness of the two world wars and what seems like an endless string of massacres that continue to this day, that it enables, so to speak, by force, new and productive encounters to emerge.

As with all of the individuals who attended the Pontigny seminars at Mount Holyoke College, the intellectual trajectories of these two formidable minds were certainly matched by the meandering paths of their lives. Between the complexity and wide range of topics that they covered and the equally extensive secondary literature, any attempt to do justice to their scholarship seems daunting to me. With that in mind, I have decided to explore here but a few loose ends in their work that I had not paid much attention to, years ago, when as a graduate student I was very much under the spell of their ideas. In hindsight, I am more aware and also more fascinated by the possibility that the many "elective affinities" that informed both their social and intellectual biographies had other potentialities that both men may or may not have been fully aware of but that were left mostly unexplored.[1] This, of course, is a truism that applies to anybody's and everybody's life, especially when considered after the fact. Nevertheless, taking a closer look at these "asides" and redrawing the contours of those features that are considered dominant may provide new insight into those features of an intellectual or artistic trend that are constant. My hope is to hold up a mirror to a particular past to better see the less obvious, precisely because I will see its image in reverse.

For example, we know that meeting Jakobson had a very decisive and identifiable impact on the development of Lévi-Strauss's theories and therefore on the future of anthropology. But how about the other encounters that were either ignored at the time or got to occupy a peripheral place in the literature? What if he had paid attention to what the French mathematician Jacques Hadamard was trying to tell him when approached (I picture them standing in the shade in front of the Mount Holyoke library) about the possibility of developing a mathematical model for the Australian kinship Lévi-Strauss was working on at the time? Hadamard declined the offer, saying that "mathematicians know only the four operations and marriage could not be included among any of them." But the anthropologist pursued the matter further with the young mathematician André Weil, one of the founders of the Bourbaki group and the brother of Simone Weil: "There is no need," he said, "to define marriage from a mathematical standpoint. Only relations between marriages are of interest," and got to work. This exchange, I decided, took place later that day, perhaps over tea and cookies in the cool shade of Porter Hall.[2] Anyway, the result is the concluding chapter in the groundbreaking *Elementary Structures of Kinship*.[3] This partially negative example helps me appreciate more fully the high status that mathematical modeling had at the time for those at the cutting edge of the humanities and social sciences. Lévi-Strauss's perseverance bore inspiring results, not least of which was a renewed interest in the study of kinship. And the book quite quickly settled in as the founding classic of structuralism in the social sciences.[4] The question, sixty years later, is, Why is this work considered his most controversial or, better, long forgotten? Did it get replaced by something more advanced? Not exactly. Just lost its fashionable glitter? Perhaps. Or was it actually a dead end road traveled? Perhaps we just move on to other things.

I think it is safe to say that some of the types of modeling that Lévi-Strauss engaged, while attractive and seemingly revolutionary, did not survive the test of time for good reason: they were flawed. But that's easy. More interesting is the question whether the specific fault could have been avoided had he pursued a different line of thought, one that was also available to him. The main objection often raised against his structuralist model is that it lacks the subject and could be described as just two-dimensional or flat, abstracted, and removed from the human agency it is intended to inform. Indeed, there were other possible ways of developing his model, and it would be interesting to try to imagine what it would look like if he had given more credence to Husserlian phenomenology rather than, for example, Hegelian dialectics and, later on, information theory. And this is where his friend and mentor Roman Jakobson comes into the story. According to Lévi-Strauss, his university training was in philosophy and his initial intention was to study law. One could assume, then, that his awareness of philosophical schools was anything but naïve. On several occasions in his publications he seems adamantly opposed to the work of Bergson or Sartre, and his reference to Merleau-Ponty appears to be more an expression of collegiality than of intellectual affinity. Yet Rousseau is the centerpiece of his beautifully meditative *Tristes Tropiques,* the semi-autobiographical work, written in the early 1950s, that recounts his coming of age as an anthropologist.[5] In this book, as in other publications, two defining moments stand out: his expedition into the Amazon rain forest in the 1930s, during his tenure as a teacher of sociology at the newly established University of São Paulo, and his stay in New York, as a refugee from Nazi-occupied France, when he taught at the École Libre and spent many hours sitting in the New York Public Library sifting through the vast collection of Native American mythology, the topic of his magnum opus, the four-volume *Mythologiques.*[6] It is also when he meets the giants of American anthropology (Boas, Kroaber, and Lowie, among others). But it is his meeting with Jakobson that stands out as the watershed in Lévi-Strauss's intellectual development. Kinship, "native" systems of thought or mythology, all sociocultural phenomena, he concludes, operate on the same principles as language. They are all meaning-making systems. They have underlying structures consisting of elementary principles governed by the rules of combination and transformation. Indeed, the meanings of cultural phenomena are not immanent; instead, they are built out of basic units, akin to the basic units of language (phonemes), and it is the *relationship* between them, their contrasting value, that makes the difference (meaning).[7]

Lévi-Strauss openly acknowledges his debt to structural linguistics, particularly to the work of Jakobson and that of the Swiss linguist Ferdinand de Saussure, to whose work Jakobson introduced him. But as we try to unravel the varied intellectual threads that inform the actual contact between these two thinkers, it is essential to keep in mind that, at the time of their meeting, they are at different points in their careers. Lévi-Strauss, on the one hand, is at the beginning, and Jakobson's is therefore a founding influence. For Jakobson, on the other hand, the exile to the United States marks an important turning point in his own trajectory. While his interest in linguistics was intimately tied to the artistic avant-gardes of east and Central Europe, in Sweden he had started to work on the relationship between children's speech and aphasia (speech loss), a clear expression of interest in the neurophysiological foundations of linguistic phenomena, an interest that became increasingly prominent in the years that followed. I think it is fair to say that Lévi-Strauss's apprenticeship with one of the founders of modern phonology was also an encounter with a mind itself increasingly drawn to the new sciences that seemed to provide a powerful model for a wide area of phenomena and, what is more, ground them in nature. And in so far as Jakobson saw himself at the forefront of establishing modern linguistics as an objective, empirical science, building conceptual bridges to other, well-established natural sciences made perfect sense. Lévi-Strauss's work, as it finds its true anthropological footing during his New York stay, is from its very outset following the very same goal, a belief in the efficacy of the mathematical and empirical sciences and the possibility of a scientific anthropology.

LET ME SHARE with you some highlights in the travels and tribulations of Roman Jakobson as a way of remembering one of the visitors to the Pontigny seminars at Mount Holyoke and also in order to place some of his key discoveries in the context of a life rich in friendships, creativity, and chronic exile.[8] My hope is that this brief excursion will also help us appreciate the linguistic foundations of Lévi-Strauss's structural anthropology.

Roman Osipovich Jakobson was born in Moscow on October 10, 1896. Considered by many to be among the major scholars of the twentieth century who could, and probably did, comment on just about anything that crossed his five senses, he is best known for his contributions to general linguistics, Slavic studies, poetics, and semiotics. His oeuvre—at last count—contains 650 titles, many of which were translated into at least as many languages as he claimed to speak: about fifteen. Needless to say, his work was very influential, and not only in his immediate area of research. The friendship with Lévi-Strauss is one of the most obvious examples. And he would be the first to acknowledge the influence that the scholars and artists he met or read as he traversed the physical and intellectual continents of Europe and the United States had on his work. In that sense, too, he reflects the whirlwind that was the twentieth century: the Russian Revolution of 1917, World War II, and the cold war. In the years preceding and following the revolution, he was an active member of the Futurists and friends with the poets Mayakovski, Kruchenykh, and the visual artists Khlebnikov and Malevich. He co-founded the Moscow linguistic circle and, later, the Opoyaz group (Society for the Study of Poetic Language) in St. Petersburg.[9] In 1920 he went to Prague—via Tallinn—as a translator for a Soviet diplomatic mission and decided to continue his studies there. He soon became deeply involved in the cultural life of Czechoslovakia. As a student and then professor he helped, in 1926, to found the Prague Linguistic Circle. He also become very close to the Czech artists, poets, and writers who formed the avant-garde movements of *Poetism* and *Devětsil*, in particular the Surrealists Teige and Nezval, as well as the Liberated Theater (Osvobozené divadlo) cabaret artists Voskovec, Werich, and Ježek, with whom he would reunite in New York during the war years.[10] The Nazis invaded Czechoslovakia on March 15, 1939. Well known to the Gestapo as a virulent anti-fascist (though being a Jew would have been bad enough), he managed to get out at the last minute. After having reduced his archive to "nine heaps of ashes," he moved from Brno, where he was teaching at Masaryk University, to Prague, where he hid in Svat'a's parents' wardrobe for a month while they tried to secure safe passage to another country. He finally succeeded in obtaining a visa to Denmark, and on April 22, 1939, traveled there by train via Berlin. Apparently, daredevil that he was, he spent time at the station during the change of trains writing to his friends, who were astonished when they received postcards from him posted in Berlin a couple of days after Hitler's fiftieth birthday celebration. In Denmark, where he lectured at the University of Copenhagen, he worked with the linguist Hjemslev; but, within a few months—anticipating the coming invasion—he fled to Norway and barely escaped death as the Nazis invaded on April 9, 1940. A Norwegian socialist from Oslo drove the couple to the far northern border with Sweden in a hearse; Jakobson lay in a coffin in the back while his wife sat in front with the driver, playing the role of the grieving widow. This was followed by another adventure on skis, as Svat'a nagged Roman along through the snowdrifts across the border into neutral Sweden. Whether all of this had any direct effect on his work is impossible to say, but he would recall his brief time in Sweden, where he researched the topics of child language and aphasia, as one of the most productive in his life. In May 1941 he was able to obtain a visa for the United States and traveled on the same ship as the philosopher Ernst Cassirer. It would be nice to know what they spoke about as the steamer made its way through the wreckage of the German battleship *Bismarck,* having narrowly missed the actual battle. As they approached New York Harbor he is said to have gasped, "Oh dear, I believe they speak English here." And he was right. In New York he found refuge at the École Libre des Haute Études, attached to the New School for Social Research, together with so many of the Jewish refugee scholars. He also managed to break his leg and had the good fortune to be rescued from the hospital by Franz Boas, who invited the Jakobsons to stay with him in New Jersey, which, I was told, made all the difference, and not only for his leg. In addition to Boas, he met the linguists Edward Sapir, Benjamin Whorf, and Leonard Bloomfield, and the young Lévi-Strauss was also invited to join what must have been quite a dinner party. The war period was, of course, rich with meetings in the city and outside it, including the Pontigny at Mount Holyoke seminars. From 1943 to 1949 Jakobson held a position at Columbia University. After that it was Harvard until 1967, with a simultaneous appointment at MIT. He managed to revisit Czechoslovakia twice during the cold war era. He continued to live in Cambridge, Massachusetts, and remained active, writing and lecturing until his death in 1982 at age eighty-five.

ACCORDING TO his own account, he was drawn to the topics of language and poetry early on, in high school, and that is what he pursued at the university in Moscow, where he studied Slavic philology. As mentioned earlier, he was an active member of the avant-garde, particularly the Futurists, and counted himself among the *zaumnyj* poets, who worked against the established modes of referentiality by exploring the poetics of sound, the sound of meaning. Those early interests are crucial for two reasons: one, they connect Jakobson with one of the founding principles of modernity and of modern art: the rupturing of referentiality and the recapturing of the sign. Jakobson recalls the impact that seeing the first Picasso and Braque paintings in Moscow had on his generation, but one could also mention the similarities between his own poetic experiments and the work of Gertrude Stein or James Joyce.[11] The second reason follows from the first: if one were to name the most important theoretical themes and contributions of his work, then most of them must be traced directly to these youthful years. There, for example, lies his lifelong interest in the relationship between sound and meaning (the title of the lecture series given in 1942 in New York and attended by Lévi-Strauss, in which Jakobson outlines the principles of modern phonology and, in particular, his theory of distinctive features). His identification of the poetic function and the aesthetic sign (a thesis advanced in the 1960s) can be traced to these beginnings as well.[12] To play with sound for the sake of sound is like playing with color for the sake of color. And to create objects from this play is to form sense that lies outside of meaning. While the young poet was playing, the mature scholar had the simple insight that to the classical typology of signs, all of which employ the mechanism of referentiality to point outside themselves—the way words refer to meanings, symptoms refer to maladies, and paintings depict the painted—a fourth type needed to be added: the sign that refers back to itself. Any artistic composition employs a battery of these stylistic devices (think, for example, of rhyme, meter, and assonance in poetry). Finally, one should add a third of the several theories associated with his name: his fascination with two poetic tropes, metonymy and metaphor, stem from his university days and link the interest in poetic language with general linguistics. Both tropes are types of associations of ideas: metonymy works with contiguity, while metaphor works with similarity (the same distinction is used by Freud in his theory of symptomatic displacement and by Frazer in his theories of magic). According to Jakobson, these two moves are the underlying principles of thought itself. By the time he arrives in New York, this dualistic principle will have matured into a general theory that will link child language acquisition and aphasia, the neurological disorder of language loss. But most important for my argument is the identification of the two principles of contiguity and similarity with the two axes of language, the two types of context that were first elaborated by Ferdinand de Saussure as the syntagmatic and paradigmatic contexts, the acts of selection and combination, which are determinative of the value and therefore also the meaning of any sign. It is this principle, together with the typology of signs (also organized around the axis of similarity and contiguity) and the theory of distinctive features, that would have the most immediate and direct impact on the work of Lévi-Strauss; they become the characteristic feature of his structural anthropology.

As ONE pursues the cross-currents of the French anthropologist's mind, several intellectual trends stand out. To name the most obvious, and from his own list of acknowledgments, we have American anthropology, Maussian exchange theory, Freudian psychoanalysis, Hegelian dialectics, and, of course, Jakobsonian linguistics. But there are many others—call them minor keys—and among them two that I find particularly interesting and, as far as I know, unexplored. First is the question of philosophy, specifically phenomenological philosophy, which seems to invite outright dismissal (several rather negative remarks are scattered throughout his writings). The second is his stated admiration for the avant-garde, particularly the French Surrealists, to which he devotes the occasional remark (especially in the published conversations) and essay. Neither has a strong presence in the actual development of his ideas, which, I contend, is both unfortunate and ironic. It could be argued that had he paid serious attention to the phenomenologist's analysis of intentionality or to the Surrealist's concern with the poetic as well as heuristic importance of irrationality and chance, the resulting theories would have been not only very different but also more dynamic. Instead, in the case of phenomenology, he found himself on the defensive when the philosopher Paul Ricoeur pointed out the flaws in his essentially neo-Kantian model.[13]

It is also ironic since both phenomenology and the avant-garde are prominent components of Jakobson's work—at least until his arrival in New York, and South Hadley, with Lévi-Strauss in tow. One could imagine saying that, whether or not Lévi-Strauss liked what he thought he saw of phenomenology or hung out with the Surrealists, the respective insights would get transferred to him via Jakobson anyway. But they didn't. Or, more exactly, while many of his stylistic devices are close to Jakobson's (e.g., arguments made by analogy across different domains) and in that sense typical of what passed for good thinking in the social sciences and humanities and worked its magic in the visual and verbal arts (analogy is one of Surrealism's principal keys), he did not incorporate any of the phenomenology that informs the linguist's work. If anything, he dropped the little that was there. One could even say that Jakobson was a "weak carrier." The opinion on this is divided, but I think that while Jakobson held the theories of Edmund Husserl, the founder of the phenomenological movement in philosophy, in great esteem,[14] his reading of the latter's work can nevertheless be argued to have been selective, for he does not seem to have explored fully the philosopher's model of consciousness and intentionality. Not that agency (the subject or speaker) is absent from Jakobson's work. On the contrary, he is to be credited for taking the issue of language into the pragmatics of communication. More specifically, his pioneering work on linguistic shifters is important in this regard. Nevertheless, the typical semiotic model of meaning and theory of linguistic context lacks the fuller exploration of the structure of experience (as different from linguistic structures) explored by the phenomenologists and which, if pursued, would, I imagine, force the development of a model of meaning-constitution that would be explicitly and fundamentally ego-centered. Just what the doctor would prescribe for Lévi-Strauss. For the most part, both authors tend to treat the subject rather schematically, using conceptual frameworks offered by Freudian psychoanalysis, Gestalt theory of perception, and, after the move to the United States, cybernetics or neurology.

What was it, then, that influenced these minds to reinforce their intellectual trajectories in one direction rather than another? In this context, it is important to remember that both authors, like the majority of scholars in the social sciences as well as the humanities of their generation and the generation before them, were working under the spell of a particular kind of scientific rationality which, I think it is fair to say, had a high exchange value and possessed a discernible look (I'll call it "a scientistic aesthetic" for now) in addition to a body of thought and methodology. We find it in Freud as well as in Marx, and Jakobson and Lévi-Strauss were no different. It is interesting to see, as one looks back, that this "scientistic aesthetic" was present regardless of whether the particular scholar's rigorous methodology passed the test of time or whether it was or was not actually reinforcing or subverting the received scientific order.

I sometimes think that the work of both Jakobson and Lévi-Strauss is interesting and even groundbreaking in reverse proportion to their attempts to anchor their work in scientific rationality, though, clearly, the "scientistic aesthetic" had a stronger draw than the alternatives to which, ironically, they were equally exposed. It is worth noting that Edmund Leach and Rodney Needham, two distinguished British anthropologists, contemporaries of Lévi-Strauss, and his ambivalent interpreters (and, in the case of Needham, translator), thought that he was a philosopher-poet rather than an anthropologist in pursuit of scientific truths. That was not meant as a compliment. I think it is, and a well-deserved one.

The ruptured sign is the defining moment of modernity; it is the brick and mortar of avant-garde art. It is also the object par excellence of the new sciences. From Freud to Crick and Watson, from Einstein to Shannon-Wiener, or from Husserl to Wittgenstein, the rational quest for truth was questioned, if not yet fully discarded, as the Cartesian call to "return to the things themselves" was reframed in new terms: the irrational unconscious, underlying structures, the relative positionality of the subject, and, perhaps most important, the problem of language and meaning. The work of Roman Jakobson is particularly revealing in this context, because he was both a scholar and an artist. I think it is only fair to say that while his intellectual quest followed the tenets of rationality and an unwavering trust in the heuristic value of modern science, his desire to bring exacting methods to the study of poetics, to unveil the enigmatic and beautiful as rule-governed acts of signification, would always retain his deep familiarity and taste for the artist's craft and, if I may be so bold, account for why his work was elegant, even poetic. He would always find what he was looking for; any object or field of knowledge would reveal its "subliminal verbal patterning" under his magic touch. His were artist's hands. And the very fundamentals that he discovered in the work of poetry and language were themselves the tools of his scientific method. His arguments were built and transformed by the artistic device of analogy, not by the scientific rule of identity.

THE PAST is always a matter of infinite regress. Especially if what we are after is truth of a particular kind—the truth of objective science that both Jakobson and Lévi-Strauss aspired to—and when, in this case at least, a history imagined and irrational should do equally well. After all, one's past is first and foremost enigmatic and often oneiric and lends itself well to the art of automatic writing. At least that is what I would like to hear from the grand master of Surrealism André Breton, and his Czech contemporaries Karel Teige and Vratislav Effenberger. In the end, people and ideas make very specific movements over very unpredictable paths, and in this particular case, it is the story of exile that has everything to say about why the creative juices flowed in one direction and not some other. If this sounds like a preamble to an explanation by reason of chaos, it is also one that celebrates the Surrealist insistence that one draws on the poetic power of irrationality and celebrates chance. If there is no creativity without crises, there is also no reality without poetry.

Is exile a destination, a sort of mirror image of the past? Anxiety-driven, impenetrable, and always on the move? It is also, as we are reminded by the Pontigny gatherings at Mount Holyoke, an opening move; that is, if you are unfortunate enough to be thrown in that direction and lucky enough to survive it. For so many it was a combination of pure chance and the right number of connections in place that helped them survive the often treacherous journey, over land and water, through prison camps and impenetrable bureaucracies and the paralyzing sickness of nostalgia. And then comes the offering: new contacts, different thoughts, and altered trajectories of the New World and the false promise that the hell the world had descended into was just temporary and that one day you would return home. You never do. There is no such thing.

NOTES

1. The allusion here is, of course, to Goethe's novel *Elective Affinities,* in which couples are drawn to each other and more for lots of pleasure, good conversation, and some troubling loose ends.

2. Jacques Hadamard did participate in the summer sessions at Mount Holyoke (see the essay by Donal O'Shea in this volume), but whether the exchange took place at that time or in New York City is not known. Lévi-Strauss recalls both this conversation and the one with Andre Weil in Claude Lévi-Strauss and Didier Eribon, *Conversation with Claude Lévi-Strauss* (Chicago: University of Chicago Press, 1991). I have applied a degree of poetic license in turning his phrasing into direct quotes.

3. Claude Lévi-Strauss's *Les structures élémentaires de la parenté* (Paris: Plon, 1949) did not appear in English until 1969 (Boston: Beacon Press).

4. The work provoked some strong reactions and a few heated exchanges, particularly among the British social anthropologists. Most notable among them is Rodney Needham's *Structure and Sentiment* (Chicago: University of Chicago Press, 1962).

5. Claude Lévi-Strauss, *Tristes Tropiques* (Paris: Plon, 1955). The authorized English translation retains the same title (New York: Atheneum, 1973).

6. Claude Lévi-Strauss, *Mythologiques,* 4 vols. (Paris: Plon, 1964–71).

7. Hence the significant difference recalled by Lévi-Strauss, which I have mentioned, between Hadamard's and Weil's response to the invitation to come up with a mathematical model of marriage. For the former, fundamentals are given, for the latter these givens are but a function of the relationship between them.

8. Jakobson's life has been the subject of several essays and interviews as well as his own writings. The present version is taken from Steven Rudy's fine introduction to Roman Jakobson, *My Futurist Years* (New York: Marsilio Publishers, 1997), ix–xi; and Roman Jakobson and Krystyna Pomorska, *Dialogues* (Cambridge: MIT and Cambridge University Presses, 1983). I have embellished it with a few vignettes that Svatava-Pírková Jakobson shared with me in the 1970s and elaborated on parts of his life relevant to the present discussion.

9. Together these two groups are referred to as the school of Russian Formalism. A thorough, though somewhat dated, discussion of the Russian context is provided by Victor Erlich, *Russian Formalism: History, Doctrine* (The Hague: Mouton, 1955).

10. In addition to works of scholarship and his own reminiscences mentioned earlier, Jakobson's close ties to the Czech avant-garde have been the subject of some research. For example, Vratislav Effenberger, "Roman Jakobson and the Czech Avant-Garde between the Wars," *American Journal of Semiotics* 2, no. 3 (1983): 13–21; Thomas Winner, "Roman Jakobson and Avant-garde Art," in *Roman Jakobson: Echoes of His Scholarship*, ed. Daniel Armstrong and C. H. van Schooneveld (Lisse: de Ridder, 1977), 503–14; Věra Linhartová, "La place de Roman Jakobson dans la vie littéraire et artistique," in Armstrong and Schooneveld, *Roman Jakobson*, 219–35. Jindřich Toman, *The Magic of a Common Language* (Cambridge: MIT Press, 1995), is an excellent, theoretically sophisticated history of the Prague Linguistic Circle.

11. In Jakobson's own words: "Such important experiments as nonobjective abstract painting and 'supraconscious' [*zaumnyj*] verbal art, by respectively canceling the represented or designated object, strikingly raised the problem of the nature and significance of the elements that exercise a semantic function in spatial figures on the one hand and in language on the other." Jakobson and Pomorska, *Dialogues, 7*.

12. Roman Jakobson, *Six Lectures on Sound and Meaning* (Cambridge: MIT Press, 1978). It is noteworthy that this collection of drafts of the original six lectures delivered in New York at the beginning of 1942, and first published in France in 1976, has a preface by Lévi-Strauss. The poetic function is discussed in "Closing Statement: Linguistics and Poetics," originally presented at a conference in 1958, then revised and published in *Style in Language*, ed. Thomas A. Sebeok (Cambridge: MIT Press, 1960), 350–77.

13. Paul Ricoeur, *The Conflict of Interpretations* (Evanston: Northwestern University Press, 1974). There is, of course, the infamous exchange between Lévi-Strauss and Sartre on the relevance, if not priority, of history, dialectics, and structure. In so far as Sartre could be identified as an existentialist (and therefore a phenomenologist by descent), this exchange could be seen as the one moment in which Lévi-Strauss's philosophical preferences are fully articulated. (See the final chapter of his *The Savage Mind* [Chicago: University of Chicago Press, 1966].) As for his interest in modern art, and with all due respect to Surrealism (see, e.g., his short essay on Max Ernst, "The Meditative Painter," in *The View from Afar* [New York: Basic Books, 1985], 243–47), Lévi-Strauss gets much more mileage out of a drawn-out parallel that he makes between the structure of myth and Wagner's *Ring* cycle in *Myth and Meaning* (New York: Schocken Books, 1979).

14. Jakobson is explicit about his admiration for Edmund Husserl's work. At his invitation, Husserl gave a lecture on the phenomenology of language to the Prague Linguistic Circle in November 1935. On the phenomenological, specifically Husserlian, foundations of Jakobson's linguistic theories, see Elmar Holenstein, *Roman Jakobsons phänomenologischer Strukturalismus* (Frankfurt am Main: Suhrkamp, 1975); and Toman, *Magic of a Common Language*.

Jacques Hadamard and Creativity in the Sciences

Donal O'Shea

WHEN HE checked in the first summer at Pontigny-en-Amérique in 1942, Jacques Hadamard was seventy-six years old. Revered in France as the intellectual heir to Henri Poincaré, he had been world famous among mathematicians since before the turn of the century. He held professorships at the Collège de France (from 1909), at the École polytechnique (from 1912), and at the École centrale (from 1920) until his retirement from all three at the age of seventy-one in 1937.

Those who knew him invariably mention his extraordinary memory and his equally spectacular absent-mindedness. He had a gift for creating community. He traveled widely: to the United States on at least five occasions, to Brazil, to Argentina, to Russia several times, to Japan, to China, to virtually every European country numerous times. He ran a famous seminar at the Collège de France covering every area of mathematics and physics. Visiting mathematicians invariably called. Einstein visited the Hadamards whenever he was in Paris.

Hadamard was highly cultured, loved music and the arts, and organized pick-up orchestras with visiting mathematicians at his home. He was insatiably curious about everything and, in addition to mathematics, had strong interests in physics, biology, chemistry, psychology, and philosophy. Despite his definition of a philosopher (someone who goes searching for a black cat in a dark room and, there being none, proceeds to find one), he joined the Société philosophique de France on its founding in 1901 and was a regular participant at the society's meetings.

A second cousin of Lucie Hadamard, wife of Albert Dreyfus, he held a position in Bordeaux at the time of Dreyfus's arrest. Although stunned, he originally did not suspect a miscarriage of justice. Albert's brother Mathieu convinced him of Dreyfus's innocence, and Hadamard became a vigorous Dreyfusard, even more so after it had been consistently misreported that some members of the Dreyfus family, and himself in particular, were certain of Dreyfus's guilt. The experience radicalized Hadamard, and he became a founding member of the Ligue des droits de l'homme, a group with which he remained connected all his life.

He married his childhood sweetheart, Louise-Anna Trénel, in 1892, a marriage that was, by all accounts, extraordinarily happy. They had five children, the first three boys, two of whom were killed in World War I (Verdun 1916) and the other in World War II (Tripolitaine 1944, as a member of the de Gaulle Free Force). His elder daughter joined the Resistance. The younger, Jacqueline, a physicist, also a Resistance courier, and a communist, escorted her parents out of France and accompanied them to the United States. The Hadamards, and Jacqueline especially, were very close friends of Mount Holyoke professor Helen Patch, who initiated Pontigny-en-Amérique.

This essay is a first attempt to reconstruct what Hadamard said and did at the Pontigny gatherings at Mount Holyoke College. Like any other mathematician, I know a fair amount about Hadamard and his work, and I was aware that he had spent time in the United States. But it came as a complete surprise to me to learn that he had ever been on the Mount Holyoke campus. What was he doing at an occasion like this? Despite his wide interests, he had, with the exception of a few papers on mathematical education and some antiwar pieces, never published anything other than mathematics prior to Pontigny. His little book *The Psychology of Invention in the Mathematical Field* is still in print and widely read. He must have gathered the materials for that book at Pontigny. Before turning to Pontigny, I wish, however, to describe why Hadamard was so well known.[1]

What Made Hadamard Famous

One of the things that have fascinated mathematicians for millennia are prime numbers: numbers like 2 or 3 or 5 or 17, which, unlike 18, say, are not divisible by any number other than 1 and themselves. Euclid had shown that there are infinitely many primes. They seem to get more and more scarce as numbers get bigger, however. There are four primes less than 10 (thus 40 percent), twenty-five primes less than 100 (25 percent), and 78,501 primes less than 1 million (fewer than 8 percent). In 1815, the German mathematician Johann Carl Friedrich Gauss, who could do massive computations by hand, conjectured that for larger and larger numbers, the proportion of primes tends toward zero. Actually, Gauss was much more precise: he conjectured that as numbers become larger and larger, the proportion of primes becomes closer and closer to 1 over the natural logarithm of the number (the natural logarithm of a number ranges between 2.3 times one less than the number of digits in the number and 2.3 times the number of digits). So, for example, a google is the number 1 followed by one hundred zeroes. About 1 in 230, or fewer than half of 1 percent, of numbers less than a google are primes: a lot of primes, but they are getting scarcer. Hadamard proved this result, as did almost simultaneously the Belgian mathematician Charles de la Vallée Poussin. Hadamard's proof, however, was to make him famous. Here is why.

Primes are the most primitive of numbers. A powerful trend in mathematics over the centuries had been to enlarge the class of numbers. The Greeks, and the Babylonians before them, accepted not just natural numbers (1, 2, 3, 4, 5...) but also fractions (one number divided by another, such as 2/3, 5/4...). They also dealt with roots of numbers, since the length of the diagonals of squares are square roots of the length of their sides. A crisis ensued when Pythagoras and his school discovered that the square root of 2, the quantity that when multiplied by itself gives 2 (and also the length in meters of the diagonal of a square with sides of one meter) was not a fraction and hence, in their view, not a number. In time, the ancients learned to accept that such quantities were in fact numbers, and they learned how to work with them. But a sense of opprobrium lingered: numbers that could be expressed as the quotient of two whole numbers were called rational numbers; others, such as the square root of 2, were called irrational. The Indian mathematician Brahmagupta (665 BC) accepted zero as a number and worked out the rules of arithmetic for negative numbers (such as -1, $-2/3$, $-\sqrt{2}$, -100), which were so convenient for financial and algebraic computations. With the enlarged number system and the spread of decimal notation from India to the Middle East to northern Africa to Europe, arithmetic became much simpler, and a good workable notion of a number emerged: a quantity, positive or negative, that could be expressed as a possibly infinite decimal. Such numbers were called real numbers, and seemed somehow god-given.

Over the centuries, the properties of real numbers were worked out: rational numbers were real numbers that had decimal expansions that either terminated or repeated. Irrational numbers were real numbers that had expansions that never repeated but could be approximated by a rational number by looking at a specified number of decimal places. The real numbers were shown to be in one-to-one correspondence with points on a line: any length corresponded to a number. Limits of real numbers were real numbers. Any square root, or for that matter cube root, or any root, of a positive real number was again a real number.

The only blemish was that negative numbers did not have square roots. Multiplying two positive numbers gives a positive number, and to have a consistent arithmetic, multiplying two negative numbers has to give a positive number. So, if you were looking for the square root of, -4, say, it couldn't be positive and it couldn't be negative. Thus, it couldn't be a real number. Whatever it was, it was easy to see that it had to be two times the square root of -1, whatever that is: $\sqrt{-4} = 2\sqrt{-1}$. In fact, if you forget to worry about whether or not $\sqrt{-1}$ exists, and just pretend that it does, you can do arithmetic with it, adding it to and multiplying it by other numbers to get lots of other numbers that behave well under arithmetic operations. To facilitate typesetting and forgetfulness, it is traditional to let $i = \sqrt{-1}$ (so $i^2 = -1$). So, for example, you could write $1 + \sqrt{-4} = 1 + 2i$. You could square this to get $-3 + 4i$, divide it by 2 to get $1/2 + i$. More generally, one gets a new class of numbers, called imaginary or, less pejoratively, complex numbers: numbers that are real numbers plus a possibly different real number times i. Limits of complex numbers are complex numbers, as is any sum, product, or quotient (except by zero) of complex numbers. Any root or power of a complex number is a complex number.

Complex numbers turned out to be just as easy to work with as real numbers. They obey the usual rules of arithmetic and algebra. The only thing lost is that given two complex numbers, you can't say that one is larger that the other. Given two different real numbers, one is always larger than the other, but it is meaningless to ask whether $2i$, say, is larger or smaller than 2. Despite this, complex numbers turn out to be useful for computations. Moreover, just as you can think of the real numbers as corresponding to points on a line, you can think of complex numbers as corresponding to points on a plane. Mathematicians had worked out the calculus of functions of such numbers (which was actually prettier and more regular that the calculus of functions of a real variable) by the mid-1800s. Nonetheless, through most of the nineteenth century there was a lingering feeling that complex numbers were a convenient shorthand, but that anything you could do with them, you could do with real numbers, and that their uses in physics were more for bookkeeping than real. There was a taint to them. They didn't seem quite right somehow.

Slowly, however, in the course of the nineteenth century it began to emerge that the complex numbers were deeply involved in understanding the real numbers and operations on them. At that time the modern notion of function as a mathematical device that converts numbers into other numbers crystallized. Functions could be defined by rules, or procedures, or formulas. A function might not be defined for a given number, but—and this is the important thing—if it was defined for a number, it converted that number into only one other number. It could happen that the same function could be defined in different ways that might look superficially rather different. The easiest way to describe a function was by a formula, so that, for example, the function which takes every number and returns it square could be denoted by the formula x^2 (which is shorthand for the function that assigns to the number x, the number x^2, where x^2 is in turn shorthand notation for x times x).

Among the most useful and computationally convenient formulas were series, which were just infinite sums of powers of x with coefficients.

An example of a series is

$$1-x^2 +x^4-x^6 +\dots$$

Like many series, this series doesn't make sense for every x. If you let $x = .1$, you get

$$1-.01+.0001-.000001+ \dots = .99009900\dots,$$

which is a perfectly good number. But if $x =2$, you get

$$1-4+16-64 +\dots,$$

and this is going to jump between ever larger negative and positive numbers. It is not hard, however, to show that, formally at least,

$$\frac{1}{1+x^2} = 1-x^2 + x^4-x^6 +\dots \tag{1}$$

Just multiply $1-x^2 + x^4-x^6 +\dots$ by $1 + x^2$ as follows

$$(1-x^2 + x^4-x^6 +\dots)(1+x^2) = 1(1+x^2)-x^2(1+x^2) + x^4(1+x^2)- x^6(1+x^2) +\dots$$

to get

$$1+x^2-x^2-x^4+x^4+x^6-x^6- \dots,$$

which equals 1.

One interprets equality (1) by saying that if both sides make sense, then the numbers are equal. So when $x = .1$, we have

$$\frac{1}{1+x^2}=\frac{1}{1+.1^2}=\frac{1}{1.01}= 1-.01+.0001-.000001+ \dots = .99009900\dots.$$

Both sides make sense if $-1 < x < 1$. For $x = 2$, however, the right-hand side

$$\frac{1}{1+x^2}=\frac{1}{1+2^2}=\frac{1}{5}= .2$$

makes sense (that is, is a number) while

$$1-x^2 + x^4 - x^6 +\dots = 1-4+16-64+ \dots$$

does not. In fact, the left-hand side makes sense for any real number. How could you have predicted that the series expansion for

$$\frac{1}{1+x^2} \tag{2}$$

would stop working when $x = 1$ or -1, when the expression (2) makes sense for every real number? Mysteriously, the reason turns out to be intimately connected with the fact that if you are allowed to plug in complex numbers for x, then

$$\frac{1}{1+x^2}$$

is not defined for $x = \sqrt{-1}$, because then $x^2 = -1$ and $1 + x^2 = 0$, and 1 divided by zero does not make sense. The number $\sqrt{-1}$ is of distance 1 from the origin in the complex plane. It turns out that once a series stops working for some number on the complex plane, it fails to work for any number whose distance to the origin is greater than that number. For some reason, to understand the behavior of functions of real numbers, you need to know how they behave for complex numbers. This was a hard truth to swallow—even the language (studying real numbers via imaginary numbers?) gets in the way—and was beginning to be appreciated, very slowly, by mathematicians in mid-nineteenth century.

Bernhard Riemann, one of the most original mathematicians who ever lived, pushed this nascent truth even further. Sickly, dirt poor, painfully shy, he finally obtained a full professorship, succeeding to the chair held by Gauss, at the age of twenty-eight at the university in Göttingen. In an eight-page paper that still surprises today, and that was like a thunderclap when published in 1859, he studies the function, which he denoted $\zeta(x)$, read zeta of x and now known as the Riemann zeta function, defined as

$$\zeta(x) = \frac{1}{2^x} + \frac{1}{3^x} + \frac{1}{4^x} + \frac{1}{5^x} + \cdots.$$

A century earlier Euler had shown that for every real number $x > 1$ this sum could be rewritten as an infinite product

$$\zeta(x) = \frac{1}{1-\frac{1}{2}^x} \cdot \frac{1}{1-\frac{1}{3}^x} \cdot \frac{1}{1-\frac{1}{5}^x} \cdot \frac{1}{1-\frac{1}{7}^x} \cdots$$

of terms of the form

$$\frac{1}{1-\frac{1}{p}^x},$$

one for each prime number p. This established a connection between the zeta function and prime numbers. When $x = 1$, the series defining $\zeta(x)$ becomes

$$1 + \tfrac{1}{2} + \tfrac{1}{3} + \tfrac{1}{4} + \ldots,$$

which was known to go to infinity as you keep adding the terms. In fact, Euler used this to give a new proof of Euclid's result that there were infinitely many prime numbers (if there were only finitely many, there would be only finitely many terms in the representation as a product, and the product of the terms would be a well-defined number that would have to equal $1 + \tfrac{1}{2} + \tfrac{1}{3} + \tfrac{1}{4} + \ldots$, contradicting the fact that the latter increases without bound).

Riemann considered $\zeta(x)$ where x could be any complex number. He shows that the series definition continues to make sense for all complex numbers $x = a + b\,i$ where b is any real number and a any real number greater than 1. More important, using the tools of complex analysis, he found several other expressions for this function, which, much in the same way that

$$\frac{1}{1+x^2}$$

shows that $1 - x^2 + x^4 - x^6 + \ldots$ is a function on the whole complex plane except at the points $x = -i$ and $x = i$, shows that $\zeta(x)$ is defined for every complex number except $x = 1$ where it goes to infinity. What completely shocked people, however, was Riemann's discovery that there was an intimate relationship between the values of x where the zeta function equaled zero (the so-called zeroes of the zeta function) and the way prime numbers were distributed among the integers. Riemann showed that $\zeta(x)$ is equal to zero when x is a negative even integer (that is, $x = -2, -4, -6, \ldots$) and that apart from these values (the so-called trivial zeroes), $\zeta(x)$ could not be zero if when you write $x = a + bi$ with a and b real, a is either larger than 1 or less than zero. Put differently, apart from the trivial zeroes, $\zeta(x)$ could be zero only for certain values of x in the so-called *critical strip*: the set of points $a + bi$ in the plane where a is greater than or equal to zero and less than or equal to 1. Riemann demonstrated that there were infinitely many zeroes in the critical strip, and that how they were distributed had profound consequences for the distribution of prime numbers. He conjectured that all of the nontrivial zeroes of $\zeta(x)$ not only were in the critical strip but also were of the form $x = \tfrac{1}{2} + bi$ where b is a real number: that is, they were on the single vertical line in the complex plane corresponding to numbers with real part equal to one half. He showed that if this conjecture, which has come to be known as the Riemann hypothesis, were true, then a much stronger result than the prime number theorem conjectured by Gauss was true: a result that not only easily implied the prime number theorem but also gave much more information with very sharp error estimates.

Riemann's paper was to have an enormous effect. As the years went on,

Riemann's methods, and the Riemann hypothesis in particular, drew the sustained attention of mathematicians, but a proof eluded everyone. Not only was it clear that the Riemann conjecture was more difficult than originally anticipated, but also there were many obscurities in the paper. Riemann had referred to his notes in the paper, and examination of them after his death showed that he had calculated the first few values of b for which ζ ($\frac{1}{2} + bi$) equals zero. Riemann's notes were almost as cryptic as his paper, and others were having trouble filling in details. In an effort to clarify this state of affairs, the French Academy of Sciences announced a Grand Prix competition in December 1890 for the best memoir on the distribution of prime numbers. The directions cited the desirability of clearing up the obscurities in Riemann's paper.

In his thesis,[2] which he defended in 1892, Hadamard studied the question of what happens when a series of the form

$$a_0 + a_1 x^1 + a_2 x^2 + a_3 x^3 + a_4 x^4 + \ldots$$

with arbitrary fixed complex coefficients a_0, a_1, a_2, ... begins to fail to converge (that is, begins to fail to make sense for some complex numbers x). This is a very delicate question, even when one has actually specified the coefficients, and Hadamard was interested in finding general conditions in terms of the coefficients a_i. His thesis was hard and very technical with lots of special cases. His examiners, the very well known mathematicians Picard, Hermite, and Joubert, could scarcely conceal their disappointment. Given Hadamard's talent and his exam scores, they were clearly hoping for more striking results. "This result is more theoretical than practical. At the level of generality at which the author chooses to operate, one cannot expect to obtain formulas of practical use," Picard wrote.[3] He went on to sum up, "It seems to me that the talent deployed is, no doubt, superior to the results obtained, but the fault may be ascribed to the question itself rather than to the author of the memoir."[4]

Between the time he had submitted the thesis and the time he defended it, Hadamard realized that his results were exactly what were needed to clarify many of Riemann's arguments, and he submitted a paper to the Academy. To everyone's astonishment, the paper won the grand prize. Partly as a result of the prize, Hadamard obtained a university position in Bordeaux in 1893. During the next three years he published sixteen papers, discovering many results and mathematical objects that still bear his name (Hadamard matrices, Hadamard determinants, the Hadamard three circles theorem), and then thirteen each in 1896 and 1897.

It was, however, Hadamard's proof of the Prime Number Theorem in a beautiful paper[5] in 1896 that made him world famous. Recall that Riemann had shown that all the nontrivial zeroes of the zeta function lay in the infinite vertical strip on the complex plane corresponding to all complex numbers whose real part is greater than or equal to zero and less than or equal to 1 (and he conjectured that all of them had real part equal to one half). Hadamard showed that none of the nontrivial zeroes had real part equal to 1 (so none of them lay on the right-hand edge of the strip), and he showed that this implied the prime number theorem conjectured by Gauss. The scientific world went crazy.

Riemann's paper suggested a deep link between prime numbers—the simplest, most basic of all numbers—and functions on the complex numbers, numbers that even mathematicians thought of as imaginary; between age-old objects that fascinated the Pythagoreans two and a half millennia ago and numbers whose existence everyone felt uneasy about. Nonetheless, there was a slight air of unreality to Riemann's paper. Before Hadamard, one could ignore it thinking that it recast the problem but didn't really say anything too different about the prime numbers that wasn't known before. Hadamard's result established a century-old result that was purely about prime numbers and that had nothing at all to do with complex numbers by proving a result that seemed to be only about complex numbers. It vindicated Riemann's approach. It was deeply counterintuitive, and it was impossible to ignore. Hadamard would go on to contribute to almost every area of mathematics, but this result, solving a long-standing problem relating to numbers that had fascinated persons since at least the time of the Pythagoreans two and half millennia earlier, and doing it using numbers that most individuals thought of as nonsensical, captured the world's imagination.

Hadamard's theorem upped the stakes on the Riemann hypothesis. David Hilbert, the well-known German mathematician, included it on his famous list of twenty-three problems that he hoped would be the work of the next century. When asked what he would do if he were to fall into a deep sleep and awake at the end of the century, he is reported to have said that the first thing he would ask is whether the Riemann hypothesis were true. In 2002, the Clay Mathematics Institute, a private institution devoted to the furtherance of mathematics, offered a $1 million reward to anyone who could solve any of seven problems, one of them the Riemann hypothesis.[6]

Hadamard and Pontigny

As the dean of science at the École Libre des Hautes Études, Hadamard played a large role in organizing Pontigny-en-Amérique. The general framework was the same each of the three summers: eight sections, two per week, one morning, one afternoon, each consisting of five daily two-hour *entretiens* (presentations and discussion). The third summer offered fewer sections, and the afternoon was reserved for more discussion and other presentations. Evenings were given over to concerts, films, and lighter lectures.

Hadamard attended each of the three summers, organizing the section relating to the sciences in the first two, and giving an *entretien* in the session on philosophy and science run by Jean Wahl in the third. The program for the first summer was put together rather late, and the titles, and in some cases the authors, of the individual *entretiens* have been lost. In particular, other than Hadamard himself, it is not at all clear who spoke in his section "Sur la science et son role dans la société moderne." Of the eight sections, it is the only one to have a compound title, and only one of two to have had just one name attached to it in a preliminary program mailed to Helen Patch by Gustave Cohen.[7]

Happily, the programs for the second and third summers still exist.[8] In the second summer, Hadamard's section was titled "Rapport entre les sciences," and he gave an *entretien* titled "Coopération des disciplines." The section also included another non-mathematical talk by the Armenian mathematician Edvard Kogbeliantz, best known today for his invention of three-dimensional chess. Hadamard's *entretien* in Wahl's section in the third summer was titled "La penseé et le langage." Kogbeliantz also presented an *entretien* in the same section.

Unfortunately, the notes for Hadamard's talks in the second and third summers seem to be lost.[9] He published two items, however, that can be attributed to Pontigny with reasonable certainty. The first is a paper in 1944 in *Renaissance*, the journal of the École Libre, titled "La science et le monde moderne." It seems to me very likely that this grew out of the notes for Hadamard's *entretien* in the first summer. The paper would have been appropriate to the title of the section. Moreover, Hadamard attributes a remark to Jean Perrin, who died later in 1942, without any mention of Perrin's death, which he would have been unlikely to overlook, given how close they were. The second is his book *The Psychology of Invention in the Mathematical Field.* He mailed the manuscript off to Princeton University Press just after returning from the third summer at Pontigny. He must have been working on the final stages of the book during the Pontigny symposium, and it is hard to imagine that he did not pass around the manuscript. In particular, the sixth chapter of the book, "Discovery as a Synthesis: The Help of Signs," contains a lengthy discussion of the role of words, language, and signs in thought. He cites Lévi-Strauss and Jakobson. This chapter must contain some, if not all, of the material he presented in "La penseé et le langage."

Jean Wahl and Jacques Hadamard during the Entretiens de Pontigny Conference, Mount Holyoke College, 1944. MS 0768, Entretiens de Pontigny records, 1942–45, Mount Holyoke College Archives and Special Collections.

"Science and the Modern World"

Hadamard's essay "La science et le monde moderne" begins by attacking head-on the notion that science has somehow played a role in Germany's military successes. "The crimes of Germany are not crimes of science," he writes, "but crimes of anti-science." [10] As an example of anti-science, he singles out a conference organized by the German mathematician Ludwig Bieberbach on the differences between German mathematics on the one hand and French and Jewish mathematics on the other. According to Hadamard, this sort of activity, and the Nazi devotion to ideology, resulted in the demise of Göttingen as one of the world's leading centers of mathematics and physics. "Germany has declared war on science, and war on the human spirit," he writes. [11]

Hadamard insists that metaphysical or moral problems lie outside the domain of science. He locates science instead in the constant questioning and willingness to reexamine received wisdom in the light of new observations and new thought without regard for consequences, and insists that the impulse that impels such investigation is deeply moral. So attacks on science decrying the inability of science to settle metaphysical or moral problems completely miss the point. He criticizes a discussion on possible partitions of Europe should the Allies win the war because it purported to draw its conclusions from scientific geopolitics. He points out that there can be no such thing as scientific geopolitics, and that science can never make normative statements. He ridicules a school text which asserts that a child's answer "A lizard is an animal that lives in the air while a fish lives in the water" to the question "What difference do you see between a lizard and a fish?" is somehow less scientific than, and therefore not as good as, saying that "a lizard is an aerial animal while a fish is aquatic." [12]

Hadamard builds a strong, and careful, case that science is based on constant questioning of one's preconceptions and assumptions, constant interrogation of the conditions under which something has been observed, and a willingness to look unflinchingly at what results. He attacks the Baconian notion of science being built one fact on another, pointing out that the difficulties begin with the architecture and interpretation of the facts. It does not suffice to multiply experiences; one also needs to vary experiences. And this takes imagination, disciplined by facts and the outcomes of what one observes, and above all prudence. Being constantly open to, and on guard for, error is a struggle. "I speak not of simple journalistic honesty, but of the higher honesty that is scientific prudence. One meets individuals who possess, without doubt, the first, but who do not know how to begin to understand the second. Others secretly detest it and for them ... the true crime of science is that it is deserving of being called honest." [13] He agrees with Poincaré that this systematic doubt, what he calls scientific prudence, is moral.

In many respects the article is vintage Hadamard. He presents many examples, some quite unusual, which are examined carefully. Except for mathematics, which had Euclid, and for the scientific work of Archimedes, he dismisses, quite convincingly, Greek science as nonexistent. The Greeks manage to find some facts accessible to direct observation, but get nothing deeper. For example, they fail to draw anything of significance from the observation that striking a piece of amber makes it attract ashes and other light objects. Hadamard contrasts Gilbert's search (1600) two thousand years later for analogous phenomena in objects close at hand, under a variety of conditions, with the obsession of Thales and subsequent Greek thinkers with the rarity of amber and their search for other rare materials that might also exhibit the same phenomena. The identical failure to capitalize on observation happened with magnets. He speculates that one reason why the Greeks seem to have been unable to conceive of fecund questions and sound experiments may have had to do with their detachment from things at hand fostered by their reliance on slavery and the subsequent valorization of liberal (or free) learning, in distinction to servile learning. For him, Leonardo da Vinci is the father of modern thought and of the modern world. He contrasts the unschooled, direct investigations of Leonardo, who knew neither Latin nor Greek, with the sterile scholarly investigations of Leonardo's contemporaries who sought wisdom in rediscovered works of the ancients and spent their time learning Latin conjugations. He quotes from Leonardo's introduction to his treatise on painting, calling it "a turning point in the history of the human spirit."

The article ends with an extensive, almost lyrical quote from Poincaré: "And yet I can not separate [scientific truth and moral truth], and whosoever loves the one cannot help loving the other.... It must be added that those who fear the one will also fear the other, for they are the ones who in everything are concerned above all with consequences. I liken the two truths, because the same reasons make us love them and because the same reasons make us fear them." [14]

There is an odd irony in the choice of the two mathematicians, Bieberbach and Poincaré, with whom Hadamard opens and closes his article, and I am not at all sure that it is unintentional. Twentieth-century mathematics begins with a new field of mathematics, topology, invented by Poincaré and a new set of problems and worlds to consider. The most famous of these problems, at the time of Pontigny and now, is the so-called Poincaré conjecture: a conjectural characterization of the simplest higher-dimensional manifold, the three-dimensional sphere. Up to the time of Pontigny, the nicest advance on this problem was made by Bieberbach. Today, at the beginning of the new century, the Poincaré conjecture is one of the seven millennial prize problems singled out by the Clay Institute, and there is an announced, but as of this writing unverified, proof of it.

Hadamard's view of science is quite nuanced and curiously modern. For him, the essence of science is located not in its results, which he sees as open to revision and interpretation, but in its methods. What takes center stage is not truth but the search for truth, and the willingness to reject that which cannot be rigorously established. For Hadamard, everything is on the table, all the time. Nothing is certain; there is nothing that cannot, and should not, be questioned.

The Psychology of Invention in the Mathematical Field

Hadamard's lovely little book *The Psychology of Invention in the Mathematical Field* is certainly his most widely read book and is still in print. Just as certainly, it owes a great deal to Pontigny-en-Amérique. Hadamard's longtime interest in exploring how individuals discovered or created new ideas dated back at least as far as Poincaré's lecture on the subject in 1908, which Hadamard frequently cites. He had attended a symposium organized by the French psychologist Claparède in 1937 on invention in various fields, and he lectured on mathematical invention at Columbia University and at the École Libre.

It is not hard to see why the topic attracted Hadamard. He must have pondered how Riemann could have seen what he did. Hadamard was the first to fill in the details in Riemann's 1859 paper, and no one would have appreciated more the leaps that Riemann made. Hadamard must have wondered how it was that his thesis work, work that struck his examiners and others as hypertechnical and that only he found interesting and significant for reasons that he could not have explained, was exactly what was necessary to clarify and advance Riemann's work.

Poincaré and Riemann were two of the most intuitive thinkers that mathematics has ever known. They invented whole new fields. They were way out in front of their contemporaries. They knew what was important, saw much further, and invented what they needed when confronted with an impasse. They moved ahead so quickly that they created gaps behind them. They worked entirely differently from Hadamard, who worked by boring in, by framing, and by making things absolutely precise. Hadamard made major discoveries in almost every area of mathematics by worrying about anomalies and a telling example or two, and bringing extraordinary analytic skills to bear. In most people's hands, the results would have been of mere technical interest. In Hadamard's, they were the key to much more. Hadamard burrowed, finding gaps that no one, himself included, had previously recognized and filled them with rich, fertile soil.

These differences must have driven anyone as curious as Hadamard crazy. His approach to invention mirrors the way he works on mathematics. After a brief survey touching on work in the area, he first looks at the unconscious, arguing convincingly that several different mental functions are performed unconsciously. The book was written before the advent of computer science, much less neuroscience and the interactions of computer science and cognitive psychology, so that he does not have access to imagery borrowed from computer science, and the book seems a little dated as a result. As in his mathematical work, Hadamard focuses on a relatively small number of cases, and pushes hard. He discerns four stages of invention: preparation (largely conscious), incubation (unconscious putting together of ideas and half-conscious selection), illumination (discovery), and verification and making precise the results (conscious). This first part deals with a matter that Hadamard had considered for a long time. He uses various writings of other mathematicians and recounts exchanges that he had had in Europe.

He then goes on to consider the way different individuals represent mathematical (and other scientific) ideas. He surveys several mathematicians, regretting that he does not have a number of French mathematicians at hand to ask, and taking care to ask only mathematicians who are truly first-rate: Jesse Douglas, Garrett Birkhoff, Norbert Weiner. He does not ask Edvard Kogbeliantz (who is perfectly capable), or even Antoni Zygmund, who attended in 1942 and who is a very fine mathematician.[15] Like himself, Claude Lévi-Strauss and Roman Jakobson use schematic pictures to represent ideas. Unlike Hadamard's, however, Lévi-Strauss's schemata are three-dimensional. Hadamard convincingly makes the case that for some individuals, words are not necessary for thought; indeed, finding the words to express what has been discovered can be difficult. He approvingly quotes a letter from Jakobson saying that signs are necessary for thought, but that while language is the most usual system of signs, there can be others. What is refreshing here is Hadamard's openness: while he, and most others to whom he talks, do not need words to think (and find, in fact, that words inhibit thought), he notes that there are those who think primarily using words. We learn that both Locke and John Stuart Mill believe words are essential for complex thought. He spends a lot of time on Max Müller, with whom he sharply disagrees, clearly bothered by how someone he obviously respects could believe that words are necessary for thinking. He quotes the psychologist Ribot, who identifies a "topographical visual type" of thinking that uses words as intermediaries, and who observes that those who use it often cannot conceive of how others can think differently.

With his preliminary conclusions on the unconscious and on representations of thoughts in hand, Hadamard is able to shed more light on the distinction between intuitive thinkers such as Riemann or Poincaré and logical thinkers, such as Weierstrass. (He does not classify himself here, but if one were to accept this dichotomy, one would most likely put him on the logical side.) He notes that the dichotomy is ultimately a false one, no thinker being a pure type. There are parts in the writings of so-called logical thinkers where one can follow the details but have no idea how the result was found in the first place. Hadamard also rejects the attempt, common at the time, to politicize the distinction, pointing out that assertions that the Teutonic race is more intuitive, and the French and Hebrew more logical, are false to the extent that they have any meaning whatsoever. He proposes that there are at least three different ways in which what is called intuitive thought can differ from logical: more or less depth in the unconscious, more or less direction of thought, and the differences in auxiliary representations.

The influence of Pontigny-en-Amérique reappears in the last part of the book, where Hadamard considers some other psychological issues raised by Raymond de Saussure relating to the effect of emotional factors on discovery and motivation. Although Hadamard was not successful in getting Einstein to attend Pontigny, he did get him to send in a note describing his thought processes.

FURTHER RESEARCH and the discovery of some still unidentified archive may yet uncover the schedule of the 1942 Pontigny-en-Amérique proceedings, the actual notes from Hadamard's talks, or, even better, accounts, biographical or autobiographical, of Hadamard's interactions with the other participants. Pending that, we are left with some largely unanswerable questions. We know that Hadamard was highly respected, but we do not know the nature of his interactions with the other participants.[16] Did they defer to him? Patronize him? Some of the remarks in the works that I have cited suggest that he must have had sharp intellectual differences with several other participants. The Pontigny participants had widely divergent political views, and Hadamard must have entered into the exchanges. In his political views he was to the left of most Gaullists, and although very patriotic and French to the core, he was strongly international in outlook. It is hard to imagine him being comfortable with most Gaullists. In his later years, Hadamard seems to have become more aware of the fact of anti-Semitism, and its consequences. Was this perhaps a result of discussions at Pontigny?

Preparation for Pontigny seems to have elicited two very strong pieces of non-mathematical work from Hadamard, both of which deserve to be more widely known. The book on the psychology of mathematical invention is known to mathematicians, but no one seems to know the *Renaissance* piece. The character of Hadamard's publications changes markedly after Pontigny. Prior to Pontigny, Hadamard did not stray too far in print from mathematics. Afterwards, he contributes to a wider variety of fields, and elaborates on some of the themes that he raises at Pontigny. He also publishes two short papers on the Dreyfus affair. Perhaps the shift was natural as Hadamard aged, but it is tempting, albeit highly speculative and quite probably overreaching, to ascribe some of the change to Hadamard's experiences at Pontigny. Without additional material, we will never know.

NOTES

1. References for this essay include Jacques Hadamard, "La science et le monde moderne," *Renaissance (Revue trimestrielle publiée par l'École Libre des Hautes Études, New York)* 1, no. 4 (1943): 523–58; Hadamard, *The Psychology of Invention in the Mathematical Field* (Princeton: Princeton University Press, 1945), republished (1996) by Princeton University Press under the title *The Mathematician's Mind: The Psychology of Invention in the Mathematical Field;* and Vladimir Maz'ya and Tatyana Shaposhnikov, *Jacques Hadamard: A Universal Mathematician* (Providence: American Mathematical Society, 1999). This last is to date the only full-length biography of Hadamard that has been published. The authors have done an invaluable service stitching together all primary source materials that they could find. Unhappily, the book underscores the paucity of primary, archival material on Hadamard.

2. Jacques Hadamard, "Essai sur l'étude des functions donneés par leur development de Taylor" (Paris: Collège de France, 1892).

3. Archives nationales, Paris, Archives personelles des professeurs du Collège de France, F17/24600.

4. Ibid.

5. Jacques Hadamard, "Sur la distribution des zeros de la fonction $\zeta(s)$ et ses conséquences arithmétiques," *Bulletin de la Société Mathématique de France* 24 (1896): 199–220.

6. See http://www.claymath.org/Millennium_Prize_Problems/.

7. Gustave Cohen to Helen Patch, May 26, 1942, Mount Holyoke College Archives, MS 0768.

8. Ibid.

9. There can be no doubt that such notes existed. In *The Psychology of Invention in the Mathematical Field,* Hadamard writes that he cannot give a talk on a subject that is not mathematics without copious notes.

10. Hadamard, "La science et le monde moderne," 525.

11. Ibid., 524.

12. Ibid., 527ff.

13. Ibid., 556.

14. Ibid., 557. Quoted from the introduction to *La valeur de la science* (1905); English translation by G. B. Halsted.

15. That Hadamard did not ask Zygmund leads me to believe that Hadamard had not started working on this section of the book in 1942.

16. One of the Mount Holyoke participants reports that Hadamard spent a good deal of time, presumably in year two, with the filmmaker Jean Benoît-Lévy and the physician Camille Dreyfus.

V

Conversations in Exile

What has Helen to hope for? Nothing short of the death of the Immortals would restore her freedom, since it is the gods, not her fellow men, who have dared to put her in bondage. Her fate does not depend on the outcome of the war; Paris or Menelaus may get her, but for her nothing can really change. She is the prisoner of the passions her beauty excited, and her passivity is, so to speak, their underside. . . . Homer is as implacable toward Helen as Tolstoy is toward Anna. Both women have run away from home thinking that they could abolish the past and capture the future in some unchanging essence of love. They awake in exile and feel nothing but a dull disgust for the shriveled ecstasy that has outlived their hope. The promise of freedom has been sloughed off in servitude; love does not obey the rules of love but yields to some more ancient and ruder law. Beauty and death have become neighbors and from their alliance springs a necessity akin to that of force.

Rachel Bespaloff, *On the Iliad* (1947)

In a dissolving society which blindly follows the natural course of ruin, catastrophe can be foreseen. Only salvation, not ruin, comes unexpectedly, for salvation, not ruin, depends upon the liberty and the will of men. Kafka's so-called prophecies were but a sober analysis of underlying structures which today have come into the open.

Hannah Arendt, "Franz Kafka: A Reevaluation" (1944)

As many of the contributors to this volume have argued, the face-to-face encounters at Pontigny-en-Amérique engendered fruitful, if subtle, shifts in the poetic, philosophical, and artistic exchanges between American and European culture. The formal and informal conversations that took place then may not have led to immediate or discernible outcomes. Nevertheless, more than sixty years later, their afterlife continues to occupy us. The contributions in this section embody the very essence of conversation as a form of action and of response to injustice and to imagining a world not prone to war and violence.

First, in "A Tale of Two Iliads," Christopher Benfey considers the imaginary dialogue between the French Jewish philosophers Simone Weil and Rachel Bespaloff. His close reading of their respective essays on the *Iliad*, "L'*Iliade*, ou, le poème de la force," and *De L'Iliade*, investigates the converging and diverging understanding of force within the context of Nazi-occupied France and the impact of the war on these two contemporaries and their mutual friend Jean Wahl.

The second essay documents an actual dialogue that took place at the Pontigny symposium in 2003. In the form of a conversation, Elisabeth Young-Bruehl, Arendt's biographer, and Jerome Kohn, the director of the Hannah Arendt Center in New York, consider Arendt's understanding of violence. Their long-standing conversation about ideas, politics, and action dates back to their first encounter in 1968 in Arendt's seminar "Political Experiences in the Twentieth Century." In the true spirit of the Pontigny conversations of 1942–44, Young-Bruehl and Kohn take on the task of rereading Arendt's understanding of the philosophical and political uses and abuses of force, violence, and power. Building on Arendt's Pontigny talk in 1944 and subsequent essay "Franz Kafka: A Revaluation" (*Partisan Review*, 1944), and taking the two essays on the *Iliad* by Rachel Bespaloff and Simone Weil as points of reference, they place Arendt's judgment of violence during the Vietnam War within the context of the aftermath of the terrorist attacks on September 11, 2001, the Iraq war, and curtailment of rights in the wake of the Patriot Act. In order to preserve the immediacy and fluidity of the conversation, the two interlocutors' responses to each other are identified as "installments" and their direct address preserved. The timeliness and continued relevance of this conversation stand as a reminder of the urgent necessity for conversing face-to-face with others in dark times.

And finally, Holger Teschke, a German writer and former dramaturge and director at the Berliner Ensemble Theater in Berlin, describes in his notes to a short excerpt from Brecht's little-known play *Conversations in Exile* (1940) the actual conversations between Brecht and Benjamin that took place in Denmark in 1934 and 1938. Their legacy embodies the multifaceted experience of refugees under German fascism. Brecht began the play while in exile in Finland, on his way to California via the Soviet Union. The play, a dialogue between two German refugees at a railroad station pub, a space of limbo for those on the run across borders in times of war and totalitarian regimes, was performed as a staged reading at the symposium at Mount Holyoke College as a tribute to participants in Pontigny-en-Amérique.

A Tale of Two Iliads

CHRISTOPHER BENFEY

THE CRITIC Kenneth Burke once suggested that classic literary works could serve as "equipment for living" by revealing familiar narrative patterns in new and chaotic circumstances.[1] If so, it should not surprise us that European readers in times of war should look to their first poem for guidance. As early as the fall of 1935, Jean Giraudoux's popular play *La guerre de Troie n'aura pas lieu* encouraged his French audience to think of their country as vulnerable Troy while an armed and menacing Hitler was the "Tiger at the Gates" (as the play was titled in English). Truth was the first casualty of war, Giraudoux warned. "Everyone, when there's war in the air," as his Andromache puts it, "learns to live in a new element: falsehood." Giraudoux's suggestion that the Trojan War was an absurd contest over empty abstractions such as honor, courage, and heroism had an absurd real-life sequel when Giraudoux himself was named minister of wartime propaganda in 1939. In the wake of Munich, Minister Giraudoux announced that the most pressing danger to French security was not the Nazis but "one hundred thousand Ashkenasis, escaped from the ghettoes of Poland or Rumania."[2]

After September 1939, the analogy between the crisis in Europe and the *Iliad*—which opens with broken truces and failed attempts to appease Achilles' wrath—seemed altogether too apt. During the fraught early months of the war, two young French writers of Jewish background, Simone Weil and Rachel Bespaloff, apparently unaware of the coincidence, wrote arresting and still fresh responses to the *Iliad*. During the winter of 1940, Weil published in the Marseilles-based journal *Cahiers du Sud* her famous essay "L'*Iliade, ou, le poème de la force.*" Three years later—after both Weil and Bespaloff had fled France for New York—Jacques Schiffrin, a childhood friend of Bespaloff's, published *De L'Iliade* in New York under the Brentano's imprint. Mary McCarthy translated both essays into English, and plans were made to publish them in a single volume.[3] When rights to Weil's essay proved unavailable, Bespaloff's *On the Iliad* appeared separately in 1947, as the ninth volume in the Bollingen series, with a long introduction—nearly half as long as Bespaloff's own essay—by the Austrian novelist Hermann Broch, author of *The Death of Virgil.* In their respective essays, Weil and Bespaloff adopt some of the same themes while diverging sharply in their approach and interpretation. One sees the rightness of the idea, first pursued by Schiffrin and Bollingen editor John Barrett, of bringing these two complementary essays under one roof—the one condemning force outright while the other argues for resistance in defense of life's "perishable joys."

MOST OF human life, Simone Weil wrote in her essay on the *Iliad,* "takes place far from hot baths," but her own discomforts were mainly self-inflicted. She was born in Paris in 1909 into an assimilated Jewish family of means. Her father was a kindly internist and her mother a forceful woman who looked after the children. Simone Weil was a gifted child, graduating first in her class in philosophy—Simone de Beauvoir was second—at the École normale supérieure in 1931. Her mentor was the philosopher Émile Chartier, known as "Alain," under whose guidance Weil's political convictions began to surface. Beauvoir recounts her first—and last—conversation with Simone Weil: "She intrigued me because of her great reputation for intelligence and her bizarre outfits....I don't know how the conversation got started. She said in piercing tones that only one thing mattered these days: the revolution that would feed all the starving people on the earth. I retorted, no less adamantly, that the problem was not to make men happy, but to help them find a meaning in their existence. She glared at me and said, 'It's clear you've never gone hungry.' Our relations ended right there."[4]

Simone Weil had never gone hungry either, but during the mid-1930s she began to seek opportunities to experience the suffering of others. During 1934–35 she took a break from her teaching to work on the assembly line at a Renault factory. Two years later she was in Spain, enlisting in a workers' brigade against Franco's forces. The physical frailty and clumsiness that had made factory work such a trial for her brought near disaster when she stepped into a pot of boiling oil, severely burning herself, and necessitating a return to the world of bourgeois safety she so despised.

Weil's experiences in the Renault factory and in Spain confirmed her growing convictions regarding the dehumanizing effects of modern industrialism and war. She traced these tendencies back to the ancient Romans, who, in her view, established a mechanistic regime based on brute force. In several powerful essays written during the mid-1930s, she condemned the Romans and their imperial successors, Napoleon and Hitler. A staunch pacifist, Weil argued for negotiations with Hitler and endorsed Neville Chamberlain's policy of appeasement. Alluding to Giraudoux's caustic play, she wrote an essay, published in 1937, titled *Let Us Not Begin Again the Trojan War,* in which she railed against the debasement of civic language. "At the center of the Trojan War, there was at least a woman," she wrote. "For our contemporaries, words adorned with capital letters play the role of Helen."[5]

During the spring of 1937, in fragile health and suffering from severe migraines, Simone Weil checked into a clinic at Montana in Switzerland, as a way station on a long-planned trip to Italy. At Montana she befriended a young medical student named Jean Posternak and, finding him an eager pupil, suggested that he "learn Greek, it's an easy language." She copied out for him a few hundred lines from the *Iliad* in her own translation. On her return from Italy, she announced to Posternak that she had developed "two new loves." One was T. E. Lawrence's *Seven Pillars of Wisdom,* of which she wrote, "Never since the *Iliad,* so far as I know, has a war been described with such sincerity and such complete absence of rhetoric, either heroic or hair-raising." "The other love," she wrote, "is Goya." Weil was deeply moved by a new edition of Goya's series of etchings *The Disasters of War.* "It arouses," she wrote Posternak, "an equal degree of horror and admiration." It is easy to see why Weil would be drawn to Lawrence and the Arab resistance fighters. In a letter to propaganda minister Giraudoux, she protested his defense of French colonial policy: "And how can it be said that we brought culture to the Arabs, when it was they who preserved the traditions of Greece for us through the Middle Ages?"[6] But Goya's depiction of war, I believe, had a more important bearing on Weil's interpretation of the *Iliad.* During the summer of 1939, she renewed her admiration for the artist with repeated visits to the great Goya exhibition at the Museum of Art in Geneva, where the treasures of the Prado had been moved for safekeeping during the Spanish civil war. The exhibition closed on August 31, the day before Germany invaded Poland.

The "disasters" Goya depicted—graphic scenes of torture, rape, mutilated corpses, firing squads, mass burials—were perpetrated by Napoleon's troops in their invasion and occupation of Spain between 1808 and 1814. Goya claimed to have witnessed many of these atrocities and portrayed them with dispassionate objectivity. And yet, there are no names attached, no recognizable officers or victims, and, perhaps most important—as Susan Sontag points out in her discussion of the series in *Regarding the Pain of Others*—no narrative. "Each image, captioned with a brief phrase lamenting the wickedness of the invaders and the monstrousness of the suffering they inflicted, stands independently of the others."[7] Goya's anonymous scenes of mayhem are meant to be representative, the "products"—as Stephen Crane expressed it in *The Red Badge of Courage*—of the machinery of war. And this—as becomes immediately clear from the opening sentences of her extraordinary essay—is how Simone Weil (whether drawing inspiration or confirmation from Goya) read the *Iliad,* as a disconnected series of "disasters of war," outside of any narrative or comprehensive meaning beyond the dehumanizing operations of force.

* * *

Weil's "The *Iliad,* or the Poem of Force" has a single argument, stated clearly in the first sentence and shown to hold true for the entire *Iliad.* "The true hero, the true subject, the center of the *Iliad* is force," which she defines as "that *x* that turns anybody who is subjected to it into a *thing.*" Instead of showing how force plays on the various characters of the *Iliad* (Achilles, Hector, Helen, and the rest), Weil examines a procession of human types—the suppliant, the slave, and the soldier—and shows how force reduces each of them to the status of a soulless thing. If force itself is the hero, it hardly matters who is wielding it or why. Weil's essay opens with a barrage of brief quotations from the *Iliad.* Here is the first passage she quotes:

> …the horses
> Rattled the empty chariots through the files of battle,
> Longing for their noble drivers. But they on the ground
> Lay, dearer to the vultures than to their wives.

And the second:

> All around, his black hair
> Was spread; in the dust his whole head lay,
> That once-charming head; now Zeus had let his enemies
> Defile it on his native soil.[8]

Weil gives no context for these extracts, nor does she identify the victims; reduced to "things," they are, properly speaking, nameless anyway. It's not that she expects us to recognize these passages—Agamemnon slaughtering Trojans in book 11, Hector's outstretched corpse in book 22; she wants us to look instead at the "spectacle the *Iliad* never tires of showing us," the transformation of men into things. "The bitterness of such a spectacle is offered us absolutely undiluted," she writes. The passive voice conceals Weil's own strategy: it is she, not Homer, who "offers" these spectacles undiluted.

It is striking how few aspects of the *Iliad* Weil dwells on in an essay of forty pages or so, and how much she leaves out: the whole "comedy of the gods" (as Rachel Bespaloff called it), Helen's ambiguous role, the embassies and negotiations. Even her detailed analyses of two scenes of supplication, which ought to interrupt the battle, merely confirm for Weil that the *Iliad*—in Christopher Logue's memorable phrase—is "all day permanent red."[9] In both scenes, however, Weil modifies Homer's version in slight but telling ways. Weil introduces the first passage, characteristically, without names or encompassing narrative: "A man stands disarmed and naked with a weapon pointing at him; this person becomes a corpse before anybody or anything touches him." Then she quotes a few lines from book 21:

> Motionless, he pondered. And the other drew near,
> Terrified, anxious to touch his knees, hoping in his heart
> To escape evil death and black destiny…
> With one hand he clasped, suppliant, his knees,
> While the other clung to the sharp spear, not letting go.

We have the image clearly in mind: a callous soldier points his spear at a naked man begging for his life, who realizes "that the weapon which is pointing at him will not be diverted."

But it turns out that this vivid image owes more to Goya's menacing bayonets than to Homer. Lycaon, one of Priam's sons and a half-brother to Hector, has just dragged himself from the rapids of the Scamander River, unarmed, it is true, but not "naked." Achilles, who captured and enslaved Lycaon on a previous raid, is determined not to let him get away this time. He throws his heavy spear but misses: "the spear shot past his back and stuck in the earth, still starved for human flesh" (I quote the Robert Fagles translation).[10] It is at this point that Lycaon "clung to the sharp spear, not letting go." Weil tells us, twice, that there is "a weapon pointing at" Lycaon, when in fact Achilles' spear is stuck in the ground.

Weil also manipulates for her own purposes the culminating encounter in book 24 when Priam comes to Achilles' tent to beg for the corpse of his son Hector:

> No one saw great Priam enter. He stopped,
> Clasped the knees of Achilles, kissed his hands,
> Those terrible man-killing hands that had slaughtered so many of his sons.

As John Gould, in his authoritative analysis of rituals of supplication in Greek literature, notes, Homer's "concentration on the hands as independent agents focusses the emotional tension on the central gesture"—clasping Achilles' knees—"of Priam's supplication."[11] When Homer's attention shifts to Achilles' hands, according to Weil, "the very presence of the suffering creature is forgotten." In her translation, Achilles, "remembering his own father, longed to weep; / Taking the old man's arm, he pushed him away."

For Weil, Achilles' harsh gesture is yet another example of force turning a person into a thing: "It was not insensibility that made Achilles with a single movement of his hand push away the old man who had been clinging to his knees....It was merely a question of his being as free in his attitudes and movements as if, clasping his knees, there were not a suppliant but an inert object." This analysis would be convincing if Achilles had indeed "with a single movement of his hand pushed away the old man." But Weil has suppressed a key word from the passage, and this suppression undercuts her interpretation of the entire scene. That word is "gently." Here is Robert Fagles's translation:

> Those words stirred within Achilles a deep desire
> to grieve for his own father. Taking the old man's hand
> he gently moved him back. And overpowered by memory
> both men gave way to grief....
> Then, when brilliant Achilles had had his fill of tears
> and the longing for it had left his mind and body,
> he rose from his seat, raised the old man by the hand.[12]

The point is not that Simone Weil misreads Homer but *why* she does so—namely, to isolate and intensify scenes of horror as Goya did in his *Disasters*. By inviting us to imagine Achilles' spear pointed menacingly at a naked suppliant rather than stuck in the ground, and by suppressing Achilles' "gentleness," Weil has extracted from the complicated weave of Homer's narrative two sharply etched "disasters of war."

Weil had hoped to publish her essay on the *Iliad* in the *Nouvelle Revue Française*, the most prominent French literary journal. Jean Paulhan, the editor, admired the essay but requested substantial cuts, adding that of the members of his editorial board only the philosopher Jean Wahl thought the essay should be published in its original form.[13] With the Nazi occupation of Paris during the summer of 1940, Paulhan was replaced by the collaborationist Drieu la Rochelle, and Weil submitted the revised essay instead to *Cahiers du Sud*, based in Marseilles, where Weil and her parents had fled with the intention of emigrating to the United States.

During the months of waiting for an exit visa, Simone Weil had her most productive period as a writer. Armed with a copy of the *Iliad* and a rucksack of clothes in case she was arrested, Weil haunted the offices of *Cahiers du Sud*, secretly distributed Resistance tracts, and filled the notebooks from which were culled the posthumous collections, *Gravity and Grace* and *Waiting on God*, for which she is best known. Still seeking a life "far from hot baths," she lodged for a few weeks with a farmer-priest in rural Provence, sleeping on the barn floor and joining in the daily work of the farm. Meanwhile, with the help of several priests with whom she was in contact, Weil continued to try to reconcile the religion of slaves she discerned in the Gospels (though not in the Roman church) with the compassion for suffering humanity she gleaned from the *Iliad*. In May 1942 she boarded a ship bound for Casablanca, and eventually sailed for New York with her parents on June 7.

AMONG THE refugees waiting for an exit visa in Marseilles during that same late spring of 1942 were the writer Rachel Bespaloff and her traveling companion, the philosopher Jean Wahl. Fired from his post at the Sorbonne, where he was one of the first to introduce Kierkegaard and Heidegger to French audiences, Wahl had been tortured and interrogated by the Gestapo at the prison of La Sante before being interned at the French concentration camp at Drancy outside Paris. A cholera epidemic and the intervention of a sympathetic doctor led to Wahl's temporary release, and he escaped to Vichy in the back of a butcher truck. Bespaloff, with funds and connections in New York, was eager to help Wahl (who had an invitation to teach at the New School) get out of France. Three weeks after Weil's departure from Marseilles, Wahl and Bespaloff boarded a cargo ship bound for New York; it was one of the last refugee ships to leave France.

During these tense months, Rachel Bespaloff, with Jean Wahl's strong encouragement, was working on her own essay on the *Iliad*—"my method of facing the war," as she put it.[14] Editors and commentators continue to accept the view, propagated by Bespaloff herself and her associates, that the almost simultaneous writing of the two essays on the *Iliad* was, as Hermann Broch put it, "coincidentally parallel." One would like to know more about Jean Wahl's role in these proceedings, however, and Monique Jutrin's edition of Bespaloff's letters to Wahl clarifies the uncertainties without entirely dispelling them.

As an editor at the *NRF*, Wahl had read and admired Weil's essay; a native of Marseilles, he also had close ties to *Cahiers du Sud*, where it was eventually published. He was a friend of Weil's (they had first met in 1937, when together they attended the opening night of Giraudoux's *Electra*) and an even closer friend to Bespaloff, and eagerly followed the progress of Bespaloff's essay on the *Iliad*. In March 1942 she asked him where she might publish it, and conceded that *Cahiers du Sud* seemed doubtful since the journal had just published the "très belle étude de Simone Weil." What an "amusing coincidence," she remarked, adding (to diminish rather than augment the coincidence) that the writer André Rousseaux had also recently written "something on Homer."

"Who is Rachel Bespaloff?" Camus asked Jean Grenier, his former philosophy teacher in Algiers, after reading and admiring Bespaloff's impressive collection of essays *Cheminements et carrefours* in August 1939. Bespaloff deliberately cultivated an aura of mystery, and much about her life and tragic death remains in shadow. Born in 1895, she spent her early years in Kiev in a cultivated Jewish family. Her father, Daniel Pasmanik, was a doctor and leader in Zionist circles, and her mother, Debora Perlmutter, had a doctorate in philosophy; by 1900 they had moved the family to the more religiously tolerant city of Geneva. There, Rachel studied dance and music—her professor of composition was Ernest Bloch—and received her diploma in piano performance from the Conservatory of Geneva in 1914. By 1919 she was in Paris teaching music at the Opéra; three years later she married a Ukrainian businessman and associate of her father, Shraga Nissim Bespaloff—they had a daughter, Naomi, in 1927—and that was the end of her musical career.

It was the beginning, however, of her career as a philosopher and writer. Dr. Pasmanik and Nissim Bespaloff were both admirers of the Russian philosopher and religious thinker Lev Shestov, and were eager to bring out a French edition of the master's works. Rachel Bespaloff met Shestov in 1925, and developed friendships with many of the liberal-minded thinkers in his circle: Daniel Halévy (the associate of Péguy and friend of Degas), Gabriel Marcel, her childhood friend from Kiev Jacques Schiffrin, and Jean Wahl. After Dr. Pasmanik's death in 1930, Nissim Bespaloff moved his family to the Villa Madonna in Saint-Raphael and began cultivating a cherry orchard. This *vie de province* with echoes of Chekhov did not appeal to Rachel, who felt cut off from Parisian intellectual life and complained of the dangers of "Bovary-ism." She composed voluminous letters on her reading to Halévy and others. One of these meditations, an intense engagement with Heidegger's recently published *Being and Time,* so impressed Gabriel Marcel that he recommended publication; "Lettre à M. Daniel Halévy sur Heidegger" appeared in *La Revue Philosophique* in 1933, and was among the very first discussions of Heidegger in French.[15] Other essays followed, on Marcel, on Julien Green and Malraux, on Shestov, collected in *Cheminements et carrefours* and published, in 1938, with a dedication to Shestov, who died the same year.

During the spring of 1938, Bespaloff began rereading the *Iliad* with her daughter. That fall, suffering from "nervous depression," she checked into the same clinic at Montana in which Weil had spent a few months the previous year. Like Weil, Bespaloff spent many hours in the Goya exhibition in Geneva—"for me," she wrote Jean Wahl in August 1939, "that was one of the greatest things this year." Meanwhile, she continued to work on what she called her "Notes on the *Iliad,*" completing several pages "two or three months before the catastrophe of 40," and was unnerved when Jean Grenier sent her a copy of Simone Weil's essay on the *Iliad.* "There are entire pages of my notes," she wrote Grenier, "that might seem to be plagiarized." What seems clear in retrospect is that Bespaloff had written much of her essay while unaware of Simone Weil's work, but that she made revisions after learning of the "amusing coincidence." After the "strange defeat" of the French in 1940, and the subsequent occupation of Paris, aspects of Weil's essay, especially its dogmatic pacifism regarding the baneful consequences of any use of force, were bound to trouble readers like Wahl and Bespaloff, who were eager to marshal resistance against Hitler. "It is hopeless to look in the *Iliad* for a condemnation of war as such," Bespaloff wrote, and with Wahl's encouragement, her *On the Iliad* became an eloquent answer to Simone Weil's "poem of force."

THE MOST striking overlap between the two essays, perhaps prompting Bespaloff's fears of apparent plagiarism, concerns Homer's evenhandedness toward Greeks and Trojans. Weil had called the *Iliad* as "impartial as sunlight.... [O]ne is barely aware that the poet is a Greek and not a Trojan," while Bespaloff writes: "Who is good in the *Iliad*? Who is bad? Such distinctions do not exist; there are only men suffering, warriors fighting, some winning, some losing." Homer's equity fits Weil's overarching argument far better than Bespaloff's, however. If Homer refuses to take sides, Bespaloff does not hesitate to do so. The hero of the *Iliad* in her view is neither "force," as it was for Weil, nor its embodiment in Achilles. Her hero is Hector, to whom she devotes her opening chapter: "Suffering and loss have stripped Hector bare; he has nothing left but himself. In the crowd of mediocrities that are Priam's sons, he stands alone, a prince, born to rule. Neither superman, nor demigod, nor godlike, he is a man and among men a prince.... Loaded as he is with favors, he has much to lose.... Apollo's protégé, Ilion's protector, defender of a city, a wife, a child, Hector is the guardian of the perishable joys." Bespaloff's hero, then, is not force but resistance, and Hector is the "resistance-hero": "Not the wrath of Achilles, but the duel between Achilles and Hector, the tragic confrontation of the revenge-hero and the resistance-hero, is what forms the *Iliad*'s true center, and governs its unity and its development."

The impression left by Simone Weil's essay is that of battle and the horrors of battle. In Bespaloff's essay, by contrast, battle is almost entirely missing. Hector is her hero because he is the guardian of noncombatants. Unlike Weil, Bespaloff is particularly attentive to Homer's women; her compassionate portrait of Helen in exile is a permanent contribution to Homeric criticism. For Bespaloff, Helen will lose no matter who wins the Trojan War: "Paris or Menelaus may get her, but for her nothing can really change. She is the prisoner of the passions her beauty created." One senses a personal, even autobiographical investment in Bespaloff's comparison of Helen to Tolstoy's Anna Karenina: "Homer is as implacable toward Helen as Tolstoy is toward Anna. Both women have run away from home thinking that they could abolish the past and capture the future in some unchanging essence of love. They awake in exile and feel nothing but a dull disgust for the shriveled ecstasy that has outlived their hope." Bespaloff lingers on the moment, "a scene of starry serenity," when Priam from his perch on the ramparts asks Helen to name the Greek heroes in the enemy camp set to besiege Troy. "Here, at the very peak of the *Iliad*, is one of those pauses, those moments of contemplation, when the spell of Becoming is broken, and the world of action, with all its fury, dips into peace."

SIMONE WEIL and Rachel Bespaloff arrived in New York within weeks of each other, during the summer of 1942. Weil joined her parents in an apartment on Riverside Drive, desperate to find a way to join de Gaulle's Free French in some capacity in London, and finding respite from her impatience with both Americans and French émigrés only in the Harlem church services she loved to attend.[16] Her final letter from New York before leaving for London in the fall of 1942 is a long and passionate self-defense addressed to Jean Wahl. Wahl, who had accepted a position teaching philosophy at Mount Holyoke, had evidently conveyed to Weil rumors concerning her alleged sympathies toward Vichy. "What may have given rise to such rumors," she told Wahl, "is the fact that I don't much like to hear perfectly comfortable people here using words like coward and traitor about people in France who are managing as best they can in a terrible situation." She took the occasion to repudiate her earlier pacifism, which she had so eloquently expressed in her essay on the *Iliad*: "Ever since the day when I decided, after a very painful inner struggle, that in spite of my pacifist inclinations it had become an overriding obligation in my eyes to work for Hitler's destruction...my resolve has not altered; and that day was the one on which Hitler entered Prague—in May 1939, if I remember right. My decision was tardy, perhaps...and I bitterly reproach myself for it." [17]

Simone Weil died on August 24, 1943, in a sanatorium in Kent, having deliberately restricted her intake of food to the rations inflicted on her compatriots in occupied France. The Italian writer and critic Nicola Chiaromonte, who had read Weil's essay on the *Iliad* in Marseilles during his own flight from Paris, encouraged his friend Dwight MacDonald to publish it in the journal *Politics*, where it appeared, in Mary McCarthy's superb translation, in November 1945. (Later, in recognition of its pacifist argument, it was reprinted by the Quaker publishing house at Pendle Hill in Philadelphia.)

Rachel Bespaloff worked on French-language broadcasts for the Voice of America before accepting a teaching position, at Jean Wahl's recommendation, at Mount Holyoke, where she taught French for six years, beginning in 1943. In 1945, Wahl returned to France to resume teaching at the Sorbonne, leaving Bespaloff, as she put it, "even more alone." She complained of the uncertainty of her temporary contract at Mount Holyoke, and described the feeling of being cut off from friends and cultural life in New York and Paris as "like an amputation." Mary McCarthy met Bespaloff only once, at a dinner party in 1947 hosted by Shiffrin with Hannah Arendt and Hermann Broch in attendance. McCarthy described her as "a small, dark lady who wore white gloves and who talked a good deal about Jean Wahl." [18] That same year, Bespaloff's husband, from whom she was separated, died in New York. Her last essay,

Rachel Bespaloff, Marcelle de Manziarly, unidentified woman, and Henry and Lotte Rox at the Entretiens de Pontigny Conference, Mount Holyoke College, 1944. MS 0768, Entretiens de Pontigny records, 1942–45, Mount Holyoke College Archives and Special Collections.

an eloquent meditation on Camus's work titled "The Man Condemned to Death," was published in French in *Esprit* in 1949.[19] Camus, she wrote, "belongs to a generation"—her own—"which history forced to live in a climate of violent death," amid "the smoke of crematories." During the spring break of that year at Mount Holyoke, Rachel Bespaloff sealed her kitchen doors with towels and turned on the gas. She died on April 6, 1949.[20]

NOTES

1. Earlier versions of this essay appeared in the September 25, 2003, issue of *New York Review of Books* and as the introduction to *War and the Iliad* (New York: New York Review Books, 2005), which reprints the essays by Bespaloff and Weil, as well as Hermann Broch's essay on Bespaloff. Quotations from the essays are from this edition.

2. See Jeffrey Mehlman, "A Future for Andromaque: Aryan and Jew in Giraudoux's France," in *Legacies of Anti-Semitism in France* (Minneapolis: University of Minnesota Press, 1983), 47.

3. See William McGuire, *Bollingen: An Adventure in Collecting the Past* (Princeton: Bollingen/Princeton University Press, 1982), 104–5.

4. Quoted in Francine du Plessix Gray, *Simone Weil* (New York: Viking Penguin, 2001), 35.

5. Simone Weil, *Écrits historiques et politiques* (Paris: Gallimard, 1960), 258.

6. Quotations are from Simone Weil, *Seventy Letters*, trans. Richard Rees (London: Oxford University Press, 1965).

7. Susan Sontag, *Regarding the Pain of Others* (New York: Farrar, Straus and Giroux, 2003), 44.

8. All translations from the *Iliad*, unless otherwise indicated, are Weil's, from Mary McCarthy's English version in *Politics* (November 1945).

9. Christopher Logue, *All Day Permanent Red: The First Battle Scenes of Homer's Iliad* (New York: Farrar, Straus and Giroux, 2003). A striking feature of Logue's creatively "rewritten" passages from the *Iliad* is that, like Weil and Bespaloff, he draws parallels between the Trojan War and World War II, most explicitly in borrowings from Céline and in vivid lines juxtaposing the Russian advance on Berlin with sulking Achilles.

10. Homer, *The Iliad*, trans. Robert Fagles (New York: Penguin, 2003), 522.

11. John Gould, "Hiketeia," *Journal of Hellenic Studies* 93 (1973): 96.

12. Homer, *The Iliad*, 605. The Greek word in question is *eka*.

13. On Paulhan, Wahl, Weil, and the *NRF*, see Simone Weil, *Écrits historiques et politiques*, vol. 2 of *Oeuvres complètes*, ed. Simone Fraisse (Paris: Gallimard, 1989), 309. This volume also includes the annotated text of Weil's "L'*Iliade*, ou, le poème de la force."

14. All quotations are from Rachel Bespaloff, *Lettres à Jean Wahl, 1937–1947*, ed. Monique Jutrin (Paris: Éditions Claire Paulhan, 2003).

15. The essay is reprinted in *Revue Conférence*, no. 6 (1998): 452–79, along with a helpful sketch of Bespaloff's life by Jean-Pierre Halévy (on which I have drawn).

16. On Weil's interest in African American culture in New York, see Jeffrey Mehlman, *Émigré New York: French Intellectuals in Wartime Manhattan, 1940–1944* (Baltimore: Johns Hopkins University Press, 2000), chap. 5.

17. Weil, *Seventy Letters*, 158.

18. Mary McCarthy to William McGuire, March 3, 1970, Manuscript Division, Bollingen Foundation, Library of Congress, Washington, D.C.

19. Rachel Bespaloff, "The World of the Man Condemned to Death," in *Camus: A Collection of Critical Essays,* ed. Germaine Brée (Englewood Cliffs, N.J.: Prentice-Hall, 1962), 93.

20. Bespaloff's invalid mother, yet another burden to her during her final years, was in an adjacent room and also died of gas inhalation.

Hannah Arendt on Action and Violence with Reference to Simone Weil and Rachel Bespaloff on Homer's *Iliad*

A Conversation

JEROME KOHN AND ELISABETH YOUNG-BRUEHL

Installment I: J. K.

IN 1968 ELISABETH and I met for the first time in Hannah Arendt's seminar "Political Experiences in the Twentieth Century," and we have been talking ever since. We have often wondered why, in 1968, just as her students were protesting America's aggression in Vietnam, which she also opposed, Arendt chose to evoke the wars, revolutions, and unprecedented terror that had destroyed so many millions of lives in the first half of the twentieth century. Just five years earlier, in her book *On Revolution,* she had affirmed the political and legal principles of the Constitution of the United States, which inspired students from Berkeley to Columbia to rebel against what appeared to them as the betrayal of those principles.[1] But in her seminar, which she said might just as well have been called "Exercises in Imagination," Arendt was intent that her students vicariously experience what her generation had known immediately: a time in the not distant past when politics had played itself out in a concatenation of actions and reactions of extreme violence. If she meant to caution us, I'm afraid that in our enthusiasm we were not much inclined toward caution of any kind. On the contrary, we were equally enthused by what we were learning and what we were doing, for what we read and talked about in the seminar determined us to resist, sometimes with force, the violence that had been devastating the world in an almost continuous process of escalation since 1914, the year in which "the real twentieth century" (as the Russian poet Anna Akhmatova called it) had begun.

Surely we were not entirely wrong; but what then was Arendt thinking? She did not believe in progress and was not an optimist, but she was not a pessimist either. She never thought that merely knowing what had happened in the past could prevent catastrophes from occurring in the future, which followed directly from her conviction that the course of human affairs, shot through with contingencies, is never entirely predictable; yet she did not counsel resignation. I believe that for Arendt the importance of elucidating the past lay in showing that the present has *become* what in reality it is, a world in which a new beginning is always possible but also is always conditional on taking not personal but political responsibility for the circumstances (unforeseen though they may have been) from which the present world emerged. The reality of the realm of politics and action, in her view, is precisely its *responsible freedom*, which is ignored when that realm is envisioned as a stage on which the successive acts of a drama are resolved according to a plan, regardless whether it is viewed with favor or disfavor, and no matter how scientifically it may be calculated or thought out. For Arendt such a resolution, like the notion of a fate inflicted, stands opposed to freedom, and for that reason has never yet and probably never will be realized in historical time. On a philosophical level it is the ideal that lurks behind visions of an ultimate "end" to the so-called forces of history, whether that end be conceived as history's conclusion or telos, or both. It is likely, I believe, that the pitfalls of supplanting responsible action with an irresponsible faith in history were part of the caution that was lost on us in 1968. But however that may be, Elisabeth's and my fortuitous meeting that year developed into a deep and abiding friendship, the living roots of which are still nourished by the conversation that began in Arendt's seminar.

A good deal more might be said about that seminar, but first it should be noted that Elisabeth and I, while discussing how we might contribute to the celebration of the Pontigny-en-Amérique *entretiens* convened at Mount Holyoke during World War II, came up with the idea that instead of writing two conventional papers, we would attempt to convey something of the spirit of our conversation. The conversation that has engaged us for many years is, to quote Michael Oakeshott, "not an enterprise designed to yield an extrinsic profit," nor, it may be added, is it one in which the predominance of one voice over another is either feasible or desirable.[2] It is not, in short, a preparation for some other activity, as if its aim were to find a location beyond its own where its lessons might be applied. In that respect it is analogous to Arendt's understanding of political activity: how it will develop and where it will lead are not discernable in advance of its undertaking, and its only lasting lessons (like those of political action) arise from the experience of freely taking part in an unrehearsed adventure, which may and inevitably will be interrupted, but within which no conclusion is potential.

There is nothing that prohibits a conversation from reflecting on itself, and four related benefits that Elisabeth and I have found in doing so may be briefly mentioned. First, to participate spontaneously in endlessly resumed talk provides a sense of continuity for those who are aware of a break in traditional ways of thinking and, which is much the same, a loss of meaning in the beliefs that have been handed down to them. Second, to be willing to enter and entertain the thoughts and articulated feelings of another is one way of approaching what Immanuel Kant called an "enlarged mentality," which for him was the condition apart from which the faculty of human judgment cannot be exercised. Third, a mentality sufficiently enlarged to treat with consideration viewpoints and interests distinct from one's own, which may amount to fundamental differences of opinion, issues in a degree of self-knowledge, that is, in recognizing oneself as a shareholder, but no more than a shareholder, in a common world. And fourth, to be active as an equal member of a mutually responsive co-partnership—even if it be only of two—is to have arrived in a situation in which one's character submits to formation and can gradually grow firm. Since these beneficial claims of conversation are first glimpsed and then brought to clarity only in the activity of conversing, it would be premature, at this point, to elaborate or attempt to substantiate them.

The expression of spontaneous thoughts, which constitutes a large part of the delight of conversation, is not constrained by the rules of argumentation, not even when the conversation contains arguments. But a conversation can and often does have a topic, and ours is the general urgency of the widespread acceptance of the principle of political violence. This presents not only a many-faceted but also an ironic problem, since it is manifest in direct proportion to the increase in awareness that the contemporary world has become, as never before, one world, hailed precipitately as the emergence of a global community. We cannot solve the problem of global violence by talking about it, but we can try to understand it, and we have agreed by and large to limit what we say to that endeavor. In doing so we have not sacrificed spontaneity altogether, for we are not constructing an argument but simply responding to what the other has written, deeply concerned and wondering where, if anywhere, these conversational installments—or, if you prefer, this essay in conversability—may lead.

Installment II: E. Y. B.

When we have a political talk, when we share an analysis of the political situation and take responsibility for understanding, we both come away from it fortified, even happy—the kind of happiness that we feel when we read something or hear something from the larger forum that seems honest and full of good judgment. I know one of the reasons why our conversations have focused so often on the nature of judgment is that we both sense that Arendt in her effort to explore the nature of thinking and judgment had in her mind the key problem of our national politics. As you said, we came of political age, as her students, in the middle of the Vietnam War, a war that our leaders hoped would solve the perceived political problem of communist domination in Southeast Asia. And that meant that we were citizens at a time when our country, through the bad judgment of its leaders and a consequent near breakdown of our country's democratic processes, was involved in a war that all can see now, in retrospect, was a disaster for our country, for Vietnam and Southeast Asia, and for the world.

At that time, I think we learned from Arendt how crucial it is in "dark times" that there be people who do not get swept up in the moment-to-moment, day-to-day, year-to-year cascade of events, or in the feelings that cascading events, out-of-control events, induce: feelings of helplessness and desperation; feelings that lead people to want a quick solution, a remedy, and a rule to follow, an explanation and a command deduced from the explanation. We learned how hard it is to do the thing Arendt named very simply "stop and think." When we talked politics, then as now, we would produce for ourselves, at least, the space and time to "stop and think," and it would bring us happiness—that peculiar happiness of citizens, which our Constitution invokes.

Those conversations then, like the ones now, also took place under the influence of Arendt's example. She was our model for stopping and thinking, and our model for trying to get a view on the cascade of events, to be able to look below the chaotic and confusing surface into the deeper patterns and meanings. She taught us, in those lectures on the nature of thinking and judgment, that thinking deals with meanings and that judgment needs particular examples to focus on, that judgment is guided by individual and particular examples and not by rules, norms, theories, visions of History or Nature. Judgment focuses on examples, and judgment also needs examples of people thinking and judging

I remember how forcefully we were struck by that "Political Experiences in the Twentieth Century" course Arendt gave at the New School. Her idea was to imagine a particular person—an exemplary person—living through the events in Europe in the early to mid-twentieth century, experiencing that cascade of events and trying to make sense of it. It was, in effect, a literary enterprise, an imaginative enterprise. I think it was rather like Kafka putting his K. in the Castle and showing how he tried to make sense of it, without any companion to rely on, that is, in the complete unsafety and disorientation of isolation.

She brought her reading of Kafka's imaginative creation to the Pontigny at Mount Holyoke in 1944, toward the end of the war, as news came crashing in from Europe of novel political events initiated by the novel form of government that was then beginning to be called "totalitarianism," of which she would herself give the monumental analysis in *The Origins of Totalitarianism*.[3] It is very striking that the two other women whose efforts to understand totalitarianism come to mind in connection with this revisiting of Pontigny—Simone Weil and Rachel Bespaloff—also turned to a literary source, Homer's *Iliad* (and, in Bespaloff's case, also to Tolstoy's *War and Peace),* to stimulate and guide their thinking. They, too, were looking for a deeper meaning in the cascade of wartime events. They both turned to great examples of stories of war in order to meditate on force. Arendt turned to Kafka—and I think she did so because she felt that, although she was writing in the middle of a war, it was not the war per se, not the battles, and not even the novelties of the types of battles, the means for waging war, that needed understanding; it was the form of government in Nazi Germany that presented the greatest challenge to understanding.

At that Pontigny meeting, Arendt made a case for reading Kafka as a political thinker, studying a form of government unknown to Montesquieu—the one that she herself was witnessing in its mature totalitarian form. (In 1944 she could read reports on the concentration camps, which she later viewed as the defining result of totalitarianism.) Kafka's fictions were like experiential maps that pointed to the essence of rule by bureaucracy. No one before had seen bureaucracy as a form of government (despite the "-cracy" in the word itself); on the contrary, bureaucracy was understood as a means toward the end of ruling, as a means that could be exported to colonies in order to bring order to people who were considered primitive, pre-political. Kafka, Arendt argued, could really, deeply, understand his world as one in which this means had become an end in itself. She could see bureaucracy dedicated to the vast extension of bureaucracy—bureaucratic imperialism. And the means for this extension was violence.

Arendt was arguing that Kafka did not just understand his world, but understood it so well that he ended up understanding the mid-twentieth-century world, and it can certainly be argued that he understood ours, now, as well. He was a seer as well as a sage. And this has to do with the way in which he imagined the future—and captured his vision of temporal experience in that figure which Arendt explored in *Between Past and Future,* the figure which gave that collection of essays its name.[4] The future does not—so that figure shows—stretch out before us, but comes to us, comes at us, as the past comes from behind us. And Kafka understood that that future is never the one we plan; it is more likely to be, indeed, the one we do not plan, even the one that mocks the arrogance of human planning

All the journalists who have dared to be critical of our war in Iraq since hostilities were officially declared ended have remarked that much more planning went into the war than into the peace. That is true enough, but not really to the point. It is certainly the case that an interim Iraqi government could have been organized before the bombs began to fall, from among the Iraqi dissidents and political exiles (not the businessmen living in safety abroad, but the political exiles). There did not have to be an American occupation government proving the well-known fact that military training is not for governance and the equally well known fact that occupation governments are not popular among people who wanted liberation. It is also certainly the case that a tremendous opportunity was missed to find a model for bringing United Nations (not just American) support to the opponents of authoritarian regimes before the possibilities of "regime change" are even discussed much less planned by governments preparing to declare war. But the more important point is that the American conquerors of Iraq do not seem to have had any cognizance that the aftermath of the military victory, which was virtually assured, was a complete unknown; that the postwar future was not plannable as the war was.

A problem of means and ends was at play here, too. The American administration really seems to have thought that the means for dealing with Saddam Hussein—war, violence—were equivalent to "regime change." The assumption seems to have been that if the war was won decisively enough, that would constitute regime change; that violence is a political process. What was operating was a kind of notion that those who have overwhelming means, overwhelming force, have the end: rule.

This has never been a reasonable assumption—even when it has resulted eventually in a new regime, as it did, say, in Japan or Germany after the saturation bombings and atomic bombings during World War II. Violence is not a political process. And the matter is, now, vastly complicated by the conditions of violence in the world. There is a worldwide acceptance of violence now that makes for conditions quite different from those apparent in any previous historical moment—an unprecedented condition. Violence is still commanded by nation-states, of course, but the novelty is that groups of all sorts can command it not just for local purposes such as civil wars and national liberation movements, but for potentially limitless enterprises—for global terrorism. Any kind of group can lay hold of "weapons of mass destruction"; any kind of group can make its own members into bombs—and a continually recruiting and regenerating group composed of suicide bombers is unstoppable. Any kind of group can use modern technologies of communication and violence anywhere, anytime, to any extent.

We can see the beginnings of what this unprecedented type and level of violence stimulates in the existing nation-states, particularly our own. It stimulates the desire to create a police state, to turn bureaucracies into police agencies. In our country, the erosion of our legal system and our constitutional protections that began with the Patriot Act after the September 11 terrorist attack signals the allure of the idea of transforming bureaucracies into police agencies. What we have to fear is the idea that the only protection possible against global terrorism is a totalitarian fortress, a fortress that would have to be worldwide. A castle beyond even Kafka's nightmare.

Installment III: J. K.

To begin with, I would like to try to see how the work, or at least some of it, of three writers you mentioned, Weil, Bespaloff, and Kafka, bears on Arendt's political thought. In doing so, my overall concern is with what you intimated: the widespread tendency to accept virtually as a given the reliance on the means and implements of violence to achieve political ends. From there it is only a short step to the belief that maintaining political power depends on continuing to command the ever more ingenious, ever more deadly techniques of violence. Not only militarists believe this, but also liberal and conservative pundits, as well as politicians from left of center, right of center, and center. The belief in the efficacy of violent implements has, moreover, a time-honored philosophical history stretching back to antiquity's definition of political power, or dominion, as the rule of one or few over many others. From the sixteenth-century notion of the absolute power of sovereign states, to the twentieth century's proclamation that "power grows out of the barrel of a gun" (Mao Zedong), to the immensity of America's current military budget, this belief has hardly been questioned. Indeed, it has received a sort of scientific justification in biological, physiological, ethological, zoological, and polemological hypotheses advanced in the study of the violent proclivities embedded, supposedly, in the very nature of humans and other animals.

An acute aspect of the problem of violence today lies, as you noted, in the existence of individuals who are literally dying to kill. As you said, they may but need not be state-sponsored terrorists, willing to destroy themselves to destroy those perceived as persecutors and exploiters. The difference of ideas about how to eliminate, or at any rate mitigate, this not entirely new but technologically enhanced threat of violence is usually, if not explicitly, voiced within the assumed equation of power with the means of violence. To anyone familiar with Arendt's conceptual analyses of power and violence, that equation is, to put it mildly, highly questionable. What is the relevance to this aspect of Arendt's thought of Weil's and Bespaloff's essays on Homer's *Iliad*, and of Arendt's reading of Kafka, which she first presented here at Mount Holyoke, presumably at the invitation of Jean Wahl (whom she had known in

Paris in the 1930s), shortly after arriving in America as an uprooted and state-less refugee from her native Germany?

I cannot imagine any more concrete illustrations of that part of Kafka's elu-sive time parable you referred to, Elisabeth, in which "he" experiences the fu-ture as a force driving "him" backward into the past, than Weil's "The *Iliad* or the Poem of Force" and Bespaloff's "On the *Iliad*."[5] In the parable, "he" is not a determinate "somebody," with either gender or age, but an "X ray" of the "inner structure" of "his" mental processes. Neither Weil nor Bespaloff, I think, read the *Iliad* as an allegory of her times, or not only or chiefly that; rather these two extraordinarily impressive women of Jewish heritage found what might have been their way into the future impassable, blocked by the intolerable pressure of the circumstances—*la force des choses*—that, unbidden and unanticipated, plummeted about them. Perhaps it was no mere coincidence that they were driven as far back as possible, to the epic each regarded as the fount of Western civilization. It may be that nothing else would have sufficed. In very different ways Weil and Bespaloff sought in the origin, the self-contained perfection of the *Iliad,* about which both wrote brilliantly, to escape from "the mangled, slashed ground of history" and "the rage, violence, and fury" of the "catastro-phe" that engulfed them (as Bespaloff put it in her essay).

But this is a far cry from what Kafka's parable meant to Arendt, which she likened to a "parabola," surrounding and casting pure light directly on "him" who, inserted by "his" birth into the continuum of time, is the beginning of a *now,* the beginning of a beginning, the actualization of a potentiality concealed in the *mundus,* or human world. This now, utterly unlike the im-movable or eternal present, the *nunc stans* or *nunc aeternitatis* of medieval meditative and other philosophies, is, on the contrary, the mentally experi-enced battleground of the ever-accumulating, mutually annihilating, forward-pushing force of the "no longer" clashing against the backward-driving force of the "not yet." Kafka's parable is a counterintuitive understanding of time, in which "he" stands "his" ground by fighting on both fronts at once; in Arendt's interpretation of the parable, "he" opens a gap that determines a track in "space-time" where, if anywhere, "he" can go on fighting by judging both forces, the past and the future. This meaning of the parable provides the key that unlocked Kafka's novels, *The Trial* and *The Castle,* in Arendt's singular reading of them. It seems appropriate to add that Kafka's great loneliness haunted Arendt, in the sense that he was able to imagine and draw, as she said, a "blueprint" of a different world where he "could have been at home." While the unreality of that world kept it "at a certain distance" from her, at the same time she knew that it "is our future, too—if we are to have any future at all."

Although Weil and Bespaloff found no refuge from their world by returning to its origin, their essays on the *Iliad* were immensely significant to Arendt.
To give an example, Weil's essay begins with the startling statement that the
"hero," the "subject," the "center" of the *Iliad* is "force," which she defines as
"that x that turns anybody who is subjected to it into a thing." Force or violence is a question not only of killing, of extinguishing life, but also of transforming "a human being into a thing while he is still alive," "a thing that has a
soul," as Weil put it. And these living corpses, these animate things, are not
limited to those who suffer violence but include those who inflict it, for the
merciless conquerors, benighted by what they mistake for omnipotence, are
as insensate as stones. Anyone familiar with Arendt's account of Nazi death
camps cannot but be struck by its uncanny similarity to what Weil wrote before the camps existed. In other words, Arendt recognized in Weil's depiction
of violence, and at times expressed in almost the same words, the systematic
dehumanization of both the persecuted and their persecutors that occurred,
not in the *Iliad,* but in the "laboratories" of totalitarian terror. Needless to say,
Weil's emphasis on the necessity of retribution or Nemesis, and her conclusion that the essence of epic genius is "that there is no refuge from fate," are
just about the opposite of the power generated by free human action that
Arendt saw instantiated in the *Iliad.*

Bespaloff's essay differs from Weil's not only in length and complexity, but
also in presenting a more judicious reading of the *Iliad* in which the epic's
principal characters, including three women, Andromache, Thetis, and Helen,
are psychologically differentiated. For Arendt, Bespaloff's distinction between
power and violence must have been eye-opening. Speaking of Achilles,
Bespaloff wrote that loss of power appears "at the very height of force." What
Bespaloff meant was that, for example, when Achilles encounters an unarmed
boy "in the way" of his will to omnipotence, he "can only reply to the mute de-
fiance of his defenseless adversary with an ever-growing violence," which,
in its "cruelty," is incapable of "total destruction." The boy is savagely killed
but lives on forever in Homer's song of Achilles' wrath. One can almost see
Arendt's wry smile at the notion of an "aesthetic" immortality "outside and
beyond history." For Arendt, as for Pericles and those few who through the
ages have merited the name "statesman" or understood its meaning, there
is indeed an immortality, an *earthly* immortality, which lies at the heart of
the political. Its source is the generation of power that appears as words and
deeds "paying back" violence; all of which, again, Arendt saw instantiated in
the *Iliad.* She certainly did not believe in human omnipotence or even self-
sufficiency, or in the sovereignty of individuals or states; what she knew all

too well is that violence can destroy power, without ever being able to reproduce it.

The first word of Bespaloff's essay is "suffering," and her entire essay is based on "suffering and loss." If suffering becomes articulate in poetry, it is despair that issues in the choice and responsibility of individual mortals. Hector, "guardian of the perishable joys," suffers complete loss—his wife, his child, his home, his city, his life—but he transforms despair into "courage" in his final "act of self-mastery," the act that makes him "worthy" and the equal of Achilles, who kills him. Achilles is mortal and immortal and causes more suffering and at once suffers more misery than any other hero, which are the two inseparable sides of his mixed nature. The freedom of his self-assertion against destiny is his choice, for which he alone is responsible, not to live out the course of his mortal life but to die in his youth as a glorious immortal. Hector and Achilles encapsulate (in a nutshell, Arendt would say), the "equity" or "equality" that Bespaloff and, to a lesser extent, Weil perceived as Homer's astonishing ability to look with impartiality on Trojans and Achaeans, both of whom were what we today would call Greeks, a concept unknown to Homer.

This impartiality, the hallmark of Kant's "enlarged mentality," has crucial repercussions in Arendt's thought. Recognizing the "equity" of the other is, for Bespaloff, the ground of justice, and for Arendt justice, first and foremost, is a matter of judging right from wrong and good from evil in particular cases as they arise. Bespaloff comes close to this when she says that "ethical experience lives only in the acts that embody it," thereby distinguishing ethics from divisive moral and religious beliefs that subsume particular cases under doctrinal rules and standards. If Homer's blindness is the emblem of his impartiality toward the prejudices or prejudgments of Trojans and Achaeans, today, provided the idea of humanity is realized as it was by Arendt in her fundamental conception of human plurality, its consequences are grave—no longer for different Greeks, but for different "everyones" who willy-nilly share the earth as long as they live. The problem confronting all of us is twofold. On the one hand, violence against human plurality is ongoing if not increasing, and on the other, human plurality is, as Arendt says, *"the* condition…*sine qua non"* and *"per quam,"* that is, the necessary and sufficient condition "of all political life." The epitome of political life is not violence but action, acting in concert with one's peers, which at one and the same time establishes the equality of distinct, even unique, beings, and releases the power, revolutionary or otherwise, required to move the human world.

Installment IV: E. Y. B.

I am prompted to continue our discussion in the direction pointed by your clear distinctions among the ways in which Weil, Bespaloff, and Arendt faced the dehumanization wrought by the war: with Weil resigning herself to suffering and awaiting Nemesis, Bespaloff emphasizing how poetry can redeem suffering, and Arendt pushing herself to understand how violence dehumanizes and how violence destroys power. The religious thinker, the artist, and the political theorist, seeing the same reality, responded in their characteristic (and, I would say, characterologically) distinct ways.

Power, Arendt argued, comes from people acting in concert. It cannot come from using violence, although violence can—to a point—serve it. Always, though, there comes that point, the point at which violence destroys power. This is why Kant counseled so wisely, "Conduct the war so as not to make the peace impossible." One of the essential political abilities—political judgment abilities—is to know how to use violence only to achieve a limited end and only in such a way as to preserve to the maximal extent the humanity of those who wield it and those who are declared the enemies. Gradually, over the course of the twentieth century, and then very dramatically in World War II, this ability became rarer and rarer. The totalitarian concentration camps are the exemplum of violent dehumanization in an institution; the bombings of Hiroshima and Nagasaki are the exemplum of violent dehumanization in an episode. Both involved turning civil spaces into war zones and noncombatants into war victims in unprecedented ways. Since those novelties, despite valiant efforts in the forms of international laws and conventions, destruction of spaces where violence should not occur has only continued. We live in an era of genocides; we witness the "violentization" of the world—and see its corollaries in the domestic violence wrought by people who live in violentized societies.

This violentization phenomenon, which is so fundamentally determinative of the world as we know it now, is not something that can be measured in the social-scientific manner—with incidence studies, tabulations of lives lost or of weapons manufactured. It is, as you imply, most clearly manifest in the acceptance of violence as a solution for political problems (and by some, for all problems), and, more fundamentally, in the mistaken concept that violence that is not strictly limited and used only to restore nonviolence can produce anything other than more violence. I noted before that the kind of terror existing now, which governments hope a "war on terror" will defeat, is a novelty, and you suggest that acceptance of violence as a solution is the crucial feature of both the terror and the "war on terror." This is the dehumanization we face:

terrorized, people accept that only violence can protect them from terror; and even the terrorists accept this, viewing themselves as the victims of the terror wrought by those they attack.

Weil, Bespaloff, and Arendt all recognized that in the Trojan War, as in the war they were facing, dehumanization was the fate of everyone. Force touched Achaeans and Trojans alike. Their responses—each in its own way—arose from their impartiality. And I want to reflect on this impartiality—but beginning from the fact that of the three, only Arendt focused her attention on how the dehumanization they all described was novel in the history of the world.

One of the hardest things to grasp, I think, about Arendt's *Origins of Totalitarianism,* which she was beginning to write in 1944, when she spoke at the Mount Holyoke Pontigny, is that she wrote as a historian but not as a historian looking for the cause of totalitarianism or of World War II. She wrote about multiple "elements" crystallizing into totalitarianism, and her goal was to delineate how, in the future, elements—the ones she had described or variants on them—might crystallize again in a world in which totalitarianism, this novel form of government, had itself become an element. Her deepest concern was with the future. Her goal was not to lay blame, but to ask how people who had survived totalitarianism's crystallization could see the future coming at them.

Key to this seeing, this judging, was a capacity, in an unprecedented world situation, to expect the unexpected, the unprecedented. And I think that she was saying that those who are obsessed with causes do not have this freedom of mind. That is, impartiality of political judgment requires both a deep inquiry into the past as it presses upon us all—an inquiry into its elements, not the causes of events—and a sense for how the future may do the same, that is, press upon us all.

Arendt came to realize—to make the political judgment—that one of the consequences of the crimes peculiar to totalitarianism was that they presented all who survived the emergence of totalitarianism with a novel situation for legal judgment. As she concluded in her *Eichmann in Jerusalem,* "The court here was confronted with a crime it could not find in the law books and with a criminal whose like was unknown in any court, at least prior to the Nuremberg Trials."[6] This was the political judgment that should, she felt, have preceded any legal judgment, for it would have informed the judges that they could not just apply the law.

Impartiality, seeing things from many angles, all sides, which depends on a capacity to be free from merely searching for causes—and trying to assign blame—is almost impossible to attain under threat of violence, or in conditions of terror. Or, to put the matter the other way around, if you want to destroy people's capacity for impartiality, and for not being obsessed with blaming, the surest means is to create an atmosphere of acceptance of violence.

Installment V: J. K.

I want to pick up on the generally accepted use of violent means to serve political ends. What is inherently wrong with that acceptance is not that violence lacks justification—in the short run it may be justifiable, as in the self-defense of an individual or a nation—but that in the long run it is never legitimate. This entails a further distinction between violence and the power that "springs up" when people "act in concert," whose legitimacy *is* "the initial getting together" of those willing to put aside and transcend their private interests to care for what concerns them in common. This way of distinguishing between private and public realms of activity brings to the fore the issue of sovereignty, a term bandied about by one and all, in and outside the United Nations and the European Union, with a remarkable absence of thought as to what it implies. Arendt thought a lot about the concept of sovereignty, and her great, and greatly respected, adversary in this matter is Thomas Hobbes. Hobbes was the first modern political philosopher, and perhaps the most farsighted.

The measure of how much the United Stares has changed in recent years can be taken by reconsidering Hobbes, who had little if any influence on our very well read Founding Fathers. Those revolutionaries knew that political power is generated through the public expression of diverse opinions, which more than any other factor united the colonists by forging their will to be free and independent from Great Britain. The expression of opinions was integral to what they called "public happiness," and their diversity was incorporated in the Constitution by its framers' insistence on a multiplicity of powers in both the federal government and the constituent states, as well as in the addition of a Bill of Rights that in principle is never to be contravened by a higher authority than the Constitution, of which there is none. Thus Madison saw clearly that citizens' "private rights and public happiness" are inseparably linked, and that these powers and rights, checking and balancing each other, would provide the dynamic architectonic within which the power of the people of the United States could expand as they acted together into an open and unknown future.[7] Hobbes had nothing to do with this. But what he wrote 350 years ago has become all too relevant to the situation of Americans today.

First, Hobbes saw that in terms of violence, all men are equal, for "the weakest has strength enough to kill the strongest, either by secret machination, or by confederacy with others, that are in the same danger with himself" (*Leviathan,* 13).[8] Since they live in "continual fear, and danger of violent death," men in their natural state "have no pleasure, but on the contrary a great deal of grief, in keeping company." The fear of violent death flows seamlessly into the commonwealth Hobbes proceeds to describe. Second, Hobbes's commonwealth or Leviathan is an "artificial man," a "mortal God," that "overawes" its subjects, who forfeit to it all rights except the "natural" right to preserve their lives by any means in the case of prosecution or war. What Hobbes called "mixed government" or "diversity of opinions" can only weaken the "absolute power" of Leviathan (29), an artifact made by men who desire security to pursue their private, mainly economic, interests in exchange for the public freedom to express their opinions and join together in action. Third, the "absolute" or "sovereign" power of Hobbes's commonwealth means that justice and law are what it decrees them to be. With his relentless logic Hobbes does not shy away from the fact that Leviathan is a tyranny, for "tyranny, signifieth nothing more, nor less, than the name of sovereignty." It follows that "the toleration of a professed hatred of tyranny" is identical to "a toleration of hatred to commonwealth in general" (*Leviathan,* "A Review and Conclusion"). Finally, Leviathan does not pretend to permanence, which in part is akin to what Arendt meant by "earthly immortality." Without political freedom, "the obligation of subjects," according to Hobbes, lasts only as long as the sovereign power "is able to protect them." Because their subjects cannot themselves act, sovereign states or tyrannies "live in the condition of perpetual war, and upon the confines of battle, with their frontiers armed, and cannons planted against their neighbors round about" (21). If in war "the enemies get a final victory," then "there is no further protection of subjects in their loyalty" to Leviathan; "then is the commonwealth *dissolved*" (29).

In its Constitution the American republic stands in the sharpest contrast to Hobbes's Leviathan, but today we have so far diverged from our foundation that our republic has come to resemble it. Indeed, the United States goes beyond Hobbes insofar as it is considered and considers itself as the world's sole "superpower." The idea of a single superpower, one super-Leviathan, recognizes power as Hobbes understood it, that is, as overwhelming force through the possession and control of the ultimate means of violence, only now on a worldwide scale. Madison, when he spoke of the people as the "fountain of power" (255), understood power in its literal sense, that is, as potentiality, the unquantifiable potential of a people acting together in accord with the principles of their constituted freedom. Hobbes knew that the stability of Leviathan was provisional, but today, in the deafening light of the events of September 11, 2001, and the ongoing debacle in Iraq, his notion of the weak being equal to the strong in their ability to inflict violent death has taken on a whole new meaning. It is not the superior force of the United States but its power to inspire freedom—our own let alone that of others—that has been thrown into question.

To Arendt "perhaps the greatest American innovation in politics...was the consistent abolition of sovereignty within the body politic of the Republic, the insight [shared with Hobbes] that in the realm of human affairs sovereignty and tyranny are the same."[9] The non-sovereignty of the republic meant that it was not a national state in the European sense, but that its power really did arise from the people, from the increasing diversity of the people and opinions it incorporated. The republic was not only a federation of states but also a confederation—an agreement, *foedus,* and trust, *fides*—among these people in their equality as citizens. The weakness of individuals that Hobbes saw overcome by Leviathan's sovereignty Arendt saw overcome by their plurality, a plurality "bound by promises," which enormously enhances their potential for power. The word "sovereignty" nowhere appears in the Constitution, which moreover contradicts the concept of sovereignty in its sixth article, an article that appears in no document comparable to the one that constitutes the people of the United States. As far as the stability of the world is concerned, Article 6 states explicitly that "all Treaties made, or which shall be made, under the Authority of the United States, shall be the supreme Law of the Land." And if treaties are not "but words" enforced by the means of violence, as Hobbes thought, what else can they be but promises stamped with golden seals?

Political freedom is freedom not only from tyranny but also from violence, insofar as the potential to make and keep promises is realized as *action* creating "islands of predictability" within a future that is never wholly calculable. Arendt knew that the substitution of "violence for power can bring victory, but the price is very high," paid not only "by the vanquished" but also by "the victor in terms of his own power."[10] How tragically ironic it is that this republic's potential to increase freedom in the world by its example has turned into a breeding ground of violence, almost as if what Hobbes most feared, a "war of all against all," were finally realized, not as a pre-political "state of nature," but as post-political apathy, a sort of thoughtless Stoicism. Is it possible that thinking what we ourselves are doing and allowing to be done in our name, the precondition of judgment, is the last resource we have? As important as it is to reflect that, apart from our Constitution, we are not a people, not a political entity at all, it is something else entirely to wonder and imagine how public spirit, which today surely encompasses the common humanity of all peoples, might be revived. Our technologically shrunken world is not yet a global community, though it might become one if human plurality were recognized as power's end-in-itself, its condition *and* result. Instruments of violence can never be a means to that end, for the doctrine of sovereignty, coupled with the notion of a single superpower, reveals violence in its "extreme form" of "one against all" and mocks the relation of means and ends. The only end violence determines is the destruction of power, which, unless we have become deaf as stones, must be fully manifest when our president says, "We will export death and violence to the four corners of the earth in defense of our great nation."[11]

Installment VI: E. Y. B.

I want to draw out explicitly the conclusion for our present situation that, in my mind, follows from your reflections. To put it briefly: I think that assertion of American sovereignty is the key ingredient—in practice and in ideology—of what our government is contributing to the deteriorating international situation. During the months before the American invasion of Iraq and in the months since, there has been a great deal of discussion in the newspapers and on television talk shows about whether this war marks the dawning of an era of American empire. Our political discourse has, in the whole post-Vietnam period, been predictably imprecise, but this discussion of empire has raised imprecision to a new level. And I think you are implying that it would be much clearer what the new "imperialists" are really doing and thinking if we called this not imperialism but assertion of American sovereignty and saw it as crucially aimed at justifying the use of violence not for specific limited ends but for the open-ended assertion of sovereignty.

Long before the current administration was first elected in 2000 (in an election that deeply threatened the independence of our judiciary, and thus the national principle of governmental checks and balances), American governments had made it very clear that our participation in international treaties and United Nations conventions was tied to assertions of American sovereignty. Provisions in United Nations conventions that required just what Article 6 of our Constitution states explicitly, namely, that "all Treaties made, or which shall be made, under the Authority of the United States, shall be the supreme Law of the Land," have been consistently rejected. Our governments have refused to ratify UN conventions because they have been said to compromise our sovereignty. In the years of this administration, there has been a remarkable pattern of withdrawal from international treaties—the Kyoto accords, for example—and violation of them, in the treatment of prisoners at Guantanamo Bay, for example. And generally, as everyone is aware, there is a preference for unilateral rather than multilateral action and a repudiation of the United Nations as source of resolutions and of international inspectors and peacekeepers. But it was with the doctrine of "preemptive strike" that this administration took the step that crucially links this growing assertion of sovereignty, this super-Leviathan ideology, to the justification of violence.

I want to step back from this description for a moment and consider historically why this assertion of sovereignty seems to me to be not a mode of imperialism but something else. Arendt drew very important distinctions in *The Origins of Totalitarianism* between European empires prior to the second half of the nineteenth century—or prior to the discovery of diamonds in South Africa in the 1870s—and the ones typical of that period of imperialism. The European empire builders from the Caesars to the Hapsburgs had aimed to bring territories under their political control, to make them part of an enlarging body politic—the Romans, of course, doing that with much more inclination to let the peoples they assimilated to their empire govern themselves than the nineteenth-century Europeans. The political aim of the late-nineteenth-century European imperialists was to establish monopoly control over natural resources and to keep on in pursuit of those natural resources wherever they were known to be or were discovered. The imperialists were the bourgeoisie, who backed the installation of colonial regimes that could be used to promote economic control; their aim was power for power's sake, not for the sake of expanded political institutions. Thus a tremendous competition among imperialist states was set off—and World War I followed.

The situation now is entirely different. Since the end of World War II, there has been an American bourgeoisie that has wanted to expand American corporations across the globe—to globalize. But there has been no aspiration to rule directly in the developing world, to expand the reach of our political institutions—to make more states, for example, on the pre-nineteenth-century model; and there has been no aspiration on the nineteenth-century model to install colonial administrators and train colonial troops. Rather, the aim of making the entire world as favorable to American economic enterprise as possible has been served by trade agreements, and by promoting, aiding, and arming those existing regimes that supported American enterprise—and undermining, more or less actively, more or less overtly, those that did not. Rhetoric about democracy to the contrary notwithstanding, it has been not their political forms that have recommended the regimes America has supported—they have been sometimes autocratic, sometimes somewhat democratic—but their cooperativeness and their allegiance to American enterprise, which, until 1989, meant as well their hostility to Soviet or Chinese enterprise. This has been imperialism without direct political involvement either by absorption of a territory or by installation of a colonial regime.

The novelty of what has happened in Iraq is that the American purpose of getting a regime in place that supports American enterprise—which, in this case, means primarily acquisition of cheap oil—has involved a massive "preemptive strike," not an operation on the scale of Grenada or Panama. The preemptive strike was preceded by an argument that if America did not strike preemptively it would be struck, and a second argument that Iraq was linked to the terrorists of the al-Qaeda network so that this preemptive strike was part of the "war on terrorism." There was, before the first argument was made, no indication whatsoever that Saddam Hussein was poised to strike the United States. That regime had struck Kuwait, precipitating the Gulf war, and it had struck, during that war, America's ally Israel, but since the Gulf war it had been turned inward, controlling in a hideously authoritarian manner its own ethic and religious groups. The second argument seems now to have been based on a series of fabrications and supports a "war on terrorism" that has no definable limits to it.

When Arendt wrote "Lying in Politics," her reflection on the Pentagon Papers, in 1972, she was returning to the theme of bureaucracy that she had focused on in 1944 with Kafka's guidance and then written about extensively in *The Origins of Totalitarianism.* Her reflection, as was her standard procedure, was designed to pull out of a familiar theme its novel aspect, and in this case the novel aspect was that the United States government bureaucracies conducting the war in Vietnam were receiving from their own intelligence services all the information they needed to make an accurate assessment of the situation in Vietnam before the war and during the steady escalation of the war, and they were ignoring it. As Arendt noted, the remoteness from reality of the bureaucrats, the "non-relation between facts and decision, between the intelligence community and the civilian and military services, is perhaps the most momentous, and certainly the best guarded, secret that the Pentagon Papers revealed." Summarily, Arendt concluded: "One sometimes has the impression that a computer, rather than 'decision makers,' had been let loose in Southeast Asia. The problem solvers did not *judge;* they calculated."[12]

In the historical background of the tendency of the Vietnam War–era bureaucrats to think in theories and to calculate rather than judge was the influence on American administrations during the cold war of an anticommunist ideology. Arendt distinguished clearly between the traditional American prejudice against and hostility to socialism and communism of the 1920s and 1930s and the ideology of anticommunism that grew up after World War II and was the work of former communists—or former Stalinists—who needed a new object of belief after their god, communism, had failed. An ideology, by definition, is a total explanation for the course of history, for how the world has come to be as it is and where it is inevitably going. It relieves the mind of any need to judge, and eventually, if believed in long and deeply enough, of any capacity to judge.

Arendt noted that it is people who have suffered a great trauma of disillusionment who reach for an ideology, an explanation that assures them of their eventual triumph. She also noted that the ideologist's key mental move is to find an analogy in the past for each and every event, which means that the trauma once suffered can be seen if it threatens again and be, the second time around, avoided or mastered. I think that the ideology that is being reached for now is the assertion of sovereignty, and not just on the long-familiar "my country right or wrong" patriotic model.

This is, rather, worship of the European-style nation-state and a kind of "mystical nationhood" (to use the phrase Gustave Cohen used at Pontigny, as an exponent of French sovereignty). And this is just the nation-state the American republic, with its critique of sovereignty, was meant to repudiate. Assertion of sovereignty—we might call it the sole-superpower doctrine—has been building as an ideology for some time, but certainly the attack of September 11—so frequently analogized to the attack on Pearl Harbor—galvanized it, unleashing a huge surge of traumatized patriotic rhetoric and the "Patriot Act," with its unconstitutional provisions.

As far as capacity to judge is concerned, the manifestation of this ideology at work is different from the "lying in politics" Arendt studied in the Pentagon Papers. It is becoming clear that over the last several years the intelligence supplied by the intelligence community in this country, and, it seems, among our allies, became less and less pure. Intelligence was put in the service of the bureaucrats who wanted to invade Iraq. There was no simple remoteness from the facts involved here, but rather a manipulation of the facts. There was no split between the intelligence communities operating in relative isolation from executive order and an executive ignoring intelligence in its pursuit of its goals. This was not a case of an administration wanting to deceive its citizens and then eventually becoming caught up in its own deception, becoming self-deceived and unable to see the reality it had once simply ignored. This was an administration manipulating intelligence, intending to prevent from becoming public any intelligence that might refute its claims or disrupt its plans. The very foundation for good judgment—connection and closeness to reality—was undermined. This is a kind of assertion of the sovereignty of a view of the world, an ideology, that accompanies assertion of political sovereignty, and it actively precludes political judgment. This is really violence against the conditions of political judgment itself.

NOTES

1. Hannah Arendt, *On Revolution* (New York: Viking Press, 1968).

2. Michael Oakeshott, *Rationalism in Politics* (New York: Basic Books, 1962), 198.

3. Arendt's talk in 1944 appears as "Franz Kafka: A Reevaluation," in *Essays in Understanding, 1930–1954* (New York: Harcourt Brace & Co., 1993), 69–80. It was first published in *Partisan Review* (Fall 1944). See also Arendt, *The Origins of Totalitarianism* (1951; reprint, New York: Schocken Books, 2004).

4. Hannah Arendt, *Between Past and Present* (New York: Viking Press, 1968).

5. Simone Weil, "The *Iliad*, or, The Poem of Force," and Rachel Bespaloff, "On the *Iliad*," in *War and the Iliad*, with an essay by Hermann Broch, trans. Mary McCarthy, intro. Christopher Benfey (New York: New York Review Books, 2005), 1–37, 39–100.

6. Hannah Arendt, *Eichmann in Jerusalem: A Report on the Banality of Evil* (New York: Viking Press, 1964), 298.

7. Alexander Hamilton, James Madison, and John Jay, *The Federalist Papers*, ed. Garry Wills (New York: Bantam Books, 1982), 67.

8. Thomas Hobbes, *Leviathan*, ed. and intro. C. B. Macpherson (Harmondsworth: Penguin, 1986). Quotations are cited by section.

9. Hannah Arendt, *On Violence* (New York: Harvest Books, 1970), 53.

10. Arendt, *On Revolution*, 152.

11. This is attributed to President George W. Bush by Bob Woodward in his book *Bush at War* (New York: Simon & Schuster, 2002).

12. Hannah Arendt, *Crises of the Republic* (New York: Harcourt Brace Jovanovich, 1972), 37.

Concerning the Label Emigrant

Brecht's Conversations in Exile *and the Century of Refugees*

HOLGER TESCHKE

> In the dark times
> Will there also be singing?
> Yes, there will also be singing
> About the dark times.
>
> Bertolt Brecht

PONTIGNY-EN-AMÉRIQUE provided a space for French refugees to gather and continue their conversation about art, ideas, and politics in the dark time of World War II. Other refugees, particularly those lucky enough to escape from Nazi Germany, were equally eager to create spaces for exchanging ideas and forging resistance, even as they found themselves in constant flight. The dark times in Europe between 1933 and 1942 are the topic of Bertolt Brecht's conversational play about the situation of two German refugees in Scandinavian exile.[1] Brecht's play offers both a complementary account of similar "conversations in exile" as well as some probing questions about the historical significance of such momentary and "fugitive" exchanges.

In 1940, Brecht wrote the first version of *Conversations in Exile* in Finland, where he found refuge at the estate of the poet and playwright Hella Wuolijoki, after his flight from Denmark and Sweden. Prior to his stay in Finland, Brecht had two long conversations, one in 1934 and another in 1938, with the German Jewish thinker Walter Benjamin, who visited him from his own exile in Paris. Benjamin, himself a participant in the Pontigny *entretiens* at the abbey in Burgundy in 1938, was working on an essay on Kafka. In the center of these "Svendborg Conversations," which are documented by Benjamin in his diary, was the phenomenon of the man of the masses, *der Massenmensch,* who appears at the beginning of the age of industrialization in Europe and North America and populates the metropolises. Two of these "city dwellers" driven into exile by Hitler, the physicist Ziffel and the worker Kalle, appear in Brecht's *Conversations in Exile.* In late-night conversations at a railway station pub in the Finnish town of Helsingførs, they share ideas about their visions for Europe's future—ideas that no doubt were also discussed among the participants of the Pontigny-en-Amérique encounters at Mount Holyoke in the summers from 1942 to 1944.

"The best school for dialectics is emigration" notes Ziffel in their conversation about humor and Hegel. "The sharpest dialectical philosophers are the refugees. They've been made refugees by great changes and all they study is changes. They sit amongst the rubbish in their camps, under the stars, plotting victory [over] the catastrophe all around them" (13).

The political catastrophes in Europe between 1933 and 1945 provided more than ample studies in change. With Hitler's election as Germany's *Reichskanzler* in 1933 and after his treaty with Stalin in 1939, the hope for a peaceful democratic Germany and for a socialism beyond dictatorship in the Soviet Union disappeared. This insight was particularly bitter for those left-wing intellectuals like Brecht and Benjamin who had hoped for so long for a revolutionary change in the world. They imagined a step toward a democratic socialism, distinct from Stalin's dictatorship. Through a synthesis of civil rights, modernity, and a planned economy, they envisioned a fair and equal distribution of the earth's wealth. Instead of this utopia, Hitler's Brown Revolution created National Socialism, which not only banished all the achievements of civil rights and modernity, but also developed a planned economy toward war with the aim to conquer and rule all of Europe. It is no coincidence that Brecht's protagonists end up in the northernmost corner of the continent, surrounded by the Wehrmacht and the Red Army. The only tightrope over the abyss of despair is the dialectical wit of their philosophical conversations. The refugees study the world map and find only one small door of escape:

> Fleeing from my fellow-countrymen
> I have now reached Finland. Friends
> Whom yesterday I didn't know, put up some beds
> In clean rooms. Over the radio
> I hear the victory bulletins of the scum of the earth. Curiously
> I examine a map of the continent. High up in Lapland
> Towards the Arctic Ocean
> I can still see a small door. (Brecht, *Poems,* 349)

This small door, still open at the Finnish border, was a small town, from where Brecht embarked on the Trans-Siberian Railway through the Soviet Union, always aware that he and his family might be arrested at any stop and disappear in one of the countless camps of the Gulag Archipelago.

A similar small door that Benjamin spotted for himself became a deadly trap. Caught by the Spanish border police in the Pyrenees after an exhausting trek on his way to Portugal and passage to the United States, Benjamin and the small group of refugees with him were ordered back to France. Fearing the fangs of the Gestapo, Benjamin committed suicide in Port Bou. After he learned about the death of his friend, Brecht wrote:

> Empires collapse. Gang leaders
> Are strutting about like statesman. The peoples
> Can no longer be seen under all those armaments.
>
> So the future lies in darkness and the forces of right
> Are weak. All this was plain to you
> When you destroyed a torturable body. ("On the Suicide of the Refugee
>   W.B.," *Poems*, 363)

The "Conversations in Exile," therefore, are also conversations among the dead. Theater must set the inertia of the dead against the statistics of politics: instead of making comparisons between Auschwitz and the Gulag as a political divertissement for an evening, theater must expose the roots of these tragedies.

Benjamin's "Theses on the Philosophy of History," the clearest political text in German literature since the revolutionary pamphlet *The Hessian Messenger (Hessische Landbote)* by the nineteenth-century playwright Georg Büchner, exposes precisely *the* danger that threatens the survival of tradition and that of the human species through the repression of the dead.[2] This danger emerges when thought becomes an instrument of the ruling classes. As long as literature and theater shy away from describing the peace (and the tragedy) of their own corruption in irreconcilable language, their work will remain without consequence. "Peace to the palaces," the slogan of Büchner's challenge to the masses more than two centuries ago, holds true on both sides of the disappearing front. But the "war to the huts" has long since returned to the metropolises from the Third World. Today, as the dark vision of a "Civil World War" has long become everyday reality—millions of refugees are fleeing across the world, and politicians, sixty years after Hiroshima, are talking openly about "limited nuclear strikes"—Brecht's "Conversations in Exile" appear in an even more unbearable light on stage. In this light, his protagonists seem more to play a Beckettian endgame than engage in a philosophical play about a future, more worthy of human beings.

Instead of Brecht's utopia of a socialist alternative, today one might end the play with Ziffel's outburst, excerpted here, and thus hand over to the audience the task of thinking about a peaceful and just future for our species in the twenty-first century. What theater *can* do is to give the dead, the murdered, and the forgotten their voice back: "Where can we go, when everywhere they expect the superhuman from us? It's not just one or two nations, who are going through a Great Era, it's becoming inevitable for all nations.... [One] needs Homeric bravery just to walk in the street, the self-denial of a Buddha just so they'll tolerate your existence. You can only stop yourself [from] becom[ing] a murderer if you can summon up the humanity of a St. Francis. The world is becoming a home for heroes. Where can we go?" (*Conversations*, 17). Perhaps we can find the answer in the last line of Brecht's famous poem "Concerning the Label Emigrant" from 1938:

> Everyone of us
> Who with torn shoes walks through the crowd
> Bears witness to the shame which now defiles our land.
> But none of us
> Will stay here. The final word
> Is yet unspoken. (*Poems*, 301)

Excerpt from *Conversations in Exile*

The following excerpt of Brecht's rarely performed play illustrates the precariousness of conversations that take place during times of war. Whereas some refugees escape successfully to places of refuge and re-ground themselves temporarily, the figures in Brecht's play epitomize that permanent liminal status of those without passports.

PASSPORTS AND THE NOBILITY OF MAN

ZIFFEL: But—we are men and man is noble.

KALLE: Huh. Man is obsolete, living is obsolete, eating is obsolete, having opinions is obsolete.

ZIFFEL: I don't agree—

KALLE: No? This word "nobility." What in your view is the noblest part of man?

ZIFFEL: As a business man I'd say "A love of order"?

KALLE: Wrong. The noblest part of a man is his passport.

ZIFFEL: Yes, passports are a great wonder of the world—

KALLE: A man can come into existence anywhere, any time, in the most stupid way, by accident. But not a passport. That's why it's accepted if it's good, but a man can be as good as he wants and no one will accept him.

ZIFFEL: So you could say, a passport is more important than the man who carries it. The man is just a kind of mechanical device for carrying the passport from country to country.

KALLE: The passport is the thing. But the man is necessary to the passport, in a sense: in the same way that a surgeon needs a patient to operate on. It's the same in a modern country. The important thing is the Führer or the Duce:

Scene from staged reading of Brecht's *Conversations in Exile,* November 7, 2003, Pontigny symposium, Mount Holyoke College. Photograph by Fred LeBlanc.

but they need people to lead. They're great men, but then someone has to be the little man, otherwise it doesn't work.

ZIFFEL: Yes, great men need us. The great men who have surfaced in various parts of the world display a great interest in mankind. It's not like it used to be, when they just let you rot. Now the state cares. For example, people couldn't understand why the Führer was so keen on collecting men from the border zones and moving them in cattle trucks to the middle of Germany. Only since the war has the reason become clear: there's a lot of wear and tear and he needs replacements. That's why passports are so important these days, you need them to keep order. Imagine if you and I were running around without papers saying who we are, why, they wouldn't be able to find us when our turn came to be deported. You were talking about surgeons. Surgery is only possible because the surgeon knows, say, where the appendix is located in the body. If it could move around without the knowledge of the surgeon, in the shoulder blade, or your head, or your knee, think of the chaos. Everything would get cut to bits. Every lover of order knows what I'm talking about.

NOTES

1. Bertolt Brecht, *Conversations in Exile (Flüchtlingsgespräche),* trans. David Dollenmayer, adapted by Howard Brenton, *Theater* 17, no. 2 (Spring 1986): 8–18, cited by page in the text. Brecht's poems are quoted from *Poems, 1913–1956: Bertolt Brecht,* ed. John Willett and Ralph Manheim, with the cooperation of Erich Fried (New York: Methuen, 1976), and are cited by page in the text.

2. The "Theses" appear in English in Walter Benjamin, *Illuminations,* ed. and with an introduction by Hannah Arendt, trans. Harry Zohn (New York: Harcourt, Brace & World, 1968). See Georg Büchner, *Complete Works and Letters,* trans. Henry J. Schmidt, ed. Walter Hinderer and Henry J. Schmidt (New York: Continuum, 1986).

VI

Remembering Rachel Bespaloff

There follows a scene of starry serenity in which the human accent, however, is still audible. Priam asks Helen to tell him the names of the most famous of the Achaian warriors that he can see in the enemy camp. The battlefield is quiet; a few steps away from each other, the two armies stand face-to-face awaiting the single combat that will decide the outcome of the war. Here, at the very peak of the *Iliad,* is one of those pauses, those moments of contemplation, when the spell of Becoming is broken, and the world of action, with all its fury, dips into peace. The plain where the warrior herd was raging is no more than a tranquil mirage to Helen and the old king.

Rachel Bespaloff, *On the Iliad* (1947)

Rachel Bespaloff had an affinity for despair, and she may well have found kinship in Hannah Arendt's talk on Kafka at Pontigny-en-Amérique in 1944. We have no record of her response to Arendt's talk. We may never know the extent of the friendship between these two extraordinary thinkers, but it seems fitting to begin our remembrance of Bespaloff by recalling the constellation that includes Arendt, Kafka, and Benjamin, and, by extension, Bespaloff herself.

In her collection of essays *Men in Dark Times,* Arendt reprinted some of her previous writings on the illuminations of men and women whose "uncertain, flickering, and often weak light" would kindle hope even to those whose eyes were used to darkness. Arendt's collection, which includes essays on Benjamin and Brecht, echoes the conversations in exile between those two thinkers, who talked, among other things, about Kafka's stance toward modernity and the uncanny portrayal of alienation and powerlessness in his writing. Both refugees may have been on Arendt's mind when, in her essay on Benjamin, she quoted Kafka's entry in his diary of October 19, 1921: "Anyone who cannot cope with life while he is alive needs one hand to ward off a little his despair over his fate…but with his other hand he can jot down what he sees among the ruins, for he sees different and more things than the others; after all, he is dead in his own lifetime and the real survivor." Directly following this quote, Arendt inserts an excerpt from a letter Benjamin wrote to his friend Gershom Scholem on April 17, 1931: "Like one who keeps afloat on a shipwreck by climbing to the top of a mast that is already crumbling. But from there he has a chance to give a signal leading to his rescue."

At the Pontigny-en-Amérique gathering at Mount Holyoke, Arendt introduced her listeners to Kafka in an essay later published in *Partisan Review* in the fall of 1944. Again, she echoed Brecht's and Benjamin's conversation about Kafka's understanding of modernity. Kafka, she suggested, "wanted to build up a world in accordance with human needs and human dignities, a world where man's actions are determined by himself and which is ruled by his laws and not by mysterious forces emanating from above or from below."

At the time Arendt wrote these words, Bespaloff considered the attachment to the world in Albert Camus's *The Stranger* and *The Plague* in light of the "naked death, in a storm of cold violence" that had become the norm. We conclude this volume with a tribute to Rachel Bespaloff, whose life embodies not just the physical and mental experience of exile "in the storm of cold violence," but also that desire for opening a space for those conversations and encounters that make hope possible in times of war and its aftermath. Bespaloff was not reconciled to the world in which she lived. This inability to reconcile the terror with the vision for a better world manifested itself in Bespaloff's thinking and writing about transcendence as a possible potential for mending the rupture caused as much by historical circumstances as by existential angst. The relation between terror and a vision for a better world, which is at the heart of Arendt's reading of Kafka, surfaced again during a roundtable on November 9, 2003, at the Pontigny symposium at Mount Holyoke College.

Different generations of students and scholars spoke of Bespaloff's intellectually sharp and elegant prose and her demanding demeanor as a teacher and as a mother. We present here a collection of texts and reminiscences that rekindle not just the memories of Bespaloff as an enduring thinker, but also the relevance of her writing for present and future generations of thinkers. Olivier Salazar-Ferrer captures the essence of Bespaloff's conflicted personal and philosophical experiences in his essay "Rachel Bespaloff and the Nostalgia for the Instant." Monique Jutrin, the editor of the recently published correspondence between Bespaloff and Jean Wahl, traces her initial encounter with Bespaloff's voice—"the voice of a sensitive, intelligent, lucid woman." Alyssa Danigelis offers a moving account of her similar discovery of Bespaloff in the college archive at Mount Holyoke. And three of Bespaloff's students in the 1940s, Renee Scialom Cary, Barbara Levin Amster, and Bespaloff's own daughter, Naomi Bespaloff Levinson, remember how their lives were changed through their encounters with Bespaloff as teacher. They movingly tell their stories of coming of age through French literature and the strict kindness Bespaloff bestowed upon them.

Rachel Bespaloff and the Nostalgia for the Instant

Olivier Salazar-Ferrer

A woman of great classical intelligence, both impulsive and fragile, Rachel Bespaloff gave in to misfortune and despair by committing suicide in exile, in the United States, in 1949. And yet, she had always shown a remarkable lucidity in the midst of her suffering, and was ready to recommend to her best friends (Gabriel Marcel, Jean Grenier, Jean Wahl) the torment of doubt as a means of sharpening one's thinking. Like Simone Weil, Hannah Arendt, or Milena Jesenká, Franz Kafka's friend, she was one of those Jewish women passionately attached to the truth as justice of knowledge. Her sense of decency prevented her from revealing her personal hell, so she turned to the historical hell that reflected her own. The Jewish genocide amplified her own tragedy. She developed an even deeper form of despair, in which her indignation rebelled against the impossible played out as historical fact.

Her friendship with Leon Shestov had taught her to dislike idleness of mind. Her intellectual exchanges with Daniel Halévy, Julien Green, Jean Grenier, Gabriel Marcel, Boris de Schloezer, Jean Wahl, Albert Camus, and Jean-Paul Sartre brought out her inflexible and vigilant consciousness in her questioning of Judaism and Christianity.[1] Her contemporaries, however, reacted to her essays with condescension. A woman philosopher in 1930 was a bit like a woman in the nineteenth century wearing men's clothes. Philosophical societies at the time were still a male preserve. Yet, she was a remarkable commentator who thought of her critical approach as both an invigorating in-depth analysis and a manner of putting the analyzed work to a spiritual test. In her writing, the dialectical method, which she mastered to perfection, was not weighed down by the slightest introspective remark, inasmuch as she did not submit to any philosophical dogmas, to any kind of politics, aesthetics, or any moral code. Her glimpses of happiness were to be found in music. As a virtuoso pianist, capable of conducting an orchestra, she found a kindred spirit in Shestov's translator, de Schloezer, who was also a musicologist. Before 1940, she was a woman of wit and learning, haughty and passionate, whose essays on Heidegger and Kierkegaard made such a powerful impression on Gabriel Marcel and Jean Wahl that they decided to publish them immediately in the *Revue Philosophique*.[2] This led to the publication of a book, *Cheminements et carrefours* (1938), an assessment of existential philosophy and literature.

During her exile at Mount Holyoke, Bespaloff continued to publish a series of remarkable articles in magazines such as *Fontaine, Esprit,* and *Renaissance,* based in New York, as well as in *Les Lettres Françaises,* Roger Caillois's magazine, which was published in Argentina. Her last book, *On the Iliad,* the English version of which followed shortly after the first French edition, seemed to echo Simone Weil's essay *"The Iliad,* or, The Poem of Force." [3] Oblivion then

Roundtable honoring Rachel Bespaloff: *(front to back)* Naomi Bespaloff Levinson, Olivier Salazar-Ferrer, Renee Scialom Cary, Barbara Levin Amster. Mount Holyoke College, 2003. Photograph courtesy Mount Holyoke College Office of Communications.

effaced the memory of this woman, who died in the remote United States, leaving her friends a few scattered manuscripts written in a sparkling style, together with the image of an unfulfilled life. Taking Shestov's despair regarding time as her starting point, Bespaloff searched for a reconciliation with one's existence through analogy with the harmony of the musical instant. What could one expect from the instant other than the intuition of eternity? Was such a wisdom of the instant attainable during such a tragic period of history? This was the question that guided her interpretations of Heidegger's work, of Charles Péguy's, of D. H. Lawrence's, of Jean Grenier's, and of Montaigne's.

Two Antithetical Disciples: Benjamin Fondane and Bespaloff

Benjamin Fondane (1898–1944) and Rachel Bespaloff represent two antithetical but equally tragic disciples of Leon Shestov (1866–1938). Fondane adopted the master's irrationalism without reservation, while Bespaloff raised a number of doubts against him in order to take the path of classical wisdom that had been invigorated by Shestov's disquieting interrogations. Bespaloff's handwritten dedication on the copy of *Cheminements et carrefours* addressed to Shestov is clear: "You must be asking yourself: 'Why has she dedicated this volume to me if she didn't want to or couldn't hear me?' But what is a master if not someone who teaches us to think, even against him, and who reveals to us our own possibilities and our limitations?"

She did not share Fondane's battle against rationality, either: "We never agreed!" she confided in a letter to de Schloezer, shattered by the news of Fondane's tragic end in Auschwitz in 1944.[4] To her, Shestov's philosophy was only an exercise in anxiety, and starting with *Cheminements et carrefours* the disagreement deepened. In her view, the source of the unhappiness of the human condition was to be found not in reason, but rather in self-conscious existence and in some obscure rupture of the primordial unity.

In her letter to Daniel Halévy about Heidegger, which dates back to the same period as Fondane's essay, Bespaloff addresses this unhappiness.[5] In her letters to Fondane, in 1932, she immediately challenged his Shestovian interpretation of Heidegger. Fondane accepted her criticism, and four years later, without mentioning Bespaloff's name, he completely changed his position in *La conscience malheureuse* (1936), in which his chapter on Heidegger adopts Bespaloff's argument that contrasted the two philosophers' conceptions of time.[6]

For Shestov, anxiety is an opening to the absurd, a springboard for the leap into the impossible. For Heidegger, anxiety is not at all the premonition of a storm in which time is smashed to pieces during the flash-instant of an incommensurable freedom. On the contrary, anxiety is the sign of our finite duration.[7] Bespaloff shared Vladimir Jankelevitch's intuition that musical experience can reconcile the contradictions between subjectivity and reality, "in so far as this is a modality of creation in which thought and human sensibility hand over what is incommensurable in them to the categories of pure understanding and to the common affectivity."[8]

Let us follow Bespaloff's slowly developing resistance to Shestov's philosophy. We must imagine the evening when Fondane, Bespaloff, Shestov, and Husserl met, in February 1929, in Paris. She was already starting to distance herself from Shestov at that moment. She nevertheless defended him "by attacking Husserl in a sharp and brilliant manner" that evening.[9] In 1933, in an essay on the notion of repetition in Kierkegaard, she observed that in Nietzsche's and Kierkegaard's case, "the destructive passion irresistibly comes to light in them, and is each time more demanding, more thirsty for holocausts. Kierkegaard's immutable god, during the last years of his life, Nietzsche's Dionysian divinity, before his madness, are nothing but the incarnation of the all-powerful instinct of cruelty."[10]

In 1934 she provided a analysis of Kierkegaard's *Fear and Trembling* in the *Revue Philosophique de la France et de l'Étranger,* in which she severely criticized him from a Nietzschean point of view. She observed that he had "the appetite for absolute domination, the resentment against life, the desire to make life expiate the humiliation that it inflicts upon him—and to put it bluntly, an impotence of the heart."[11] In 1935 Fondane replied to her by placing her on Jean Wahl's side in his article "Héraclite le pauvre" (Poor Heraclitus); and he is right: "I don't know whether, like me, you recognize in these phrases an armed attack against the Shestovian position of the 'fight against self-evidence.' "[12] He noted that Bespaloff's insightful essay is in many ways similar to Wahl's: only Kierkegaard's tragedy moves her and the mechanism through which he managed to explain himself through dialectics: "From now on, when reading *Fear and Trembling* we are exempt from fearing and from trembling."[13] Bespaloff, as well as Wahl, "avoid calling themselves into question."[14]

The dialectical duel continued. Having received *La conscience malheureuse* in 1936, Bespaloff wanted, above all, to express her interest in the chapters on Bergson, Freud, and Husserl and her profound disagreement with the idea that the development of rationality has apparently engendered the unhappiness of human consciousness while at the same time taken us away from the reality of primitive mentalities. Far from being original, the conflict between reason and magical thinking refers to a "deeper lesion" of existence, in so far as existence "is always conscious of itself."[15]

Subjectivity and Reality

In 1937 Boris de Schloezer confided to Shestov that Bespaloff "resisted" Shestov. She argued that it was existence rather than knowledge that was marred by some original "rupture."[16] In fact, when she submitted her manuscript of *Cheminements et carrefours* to Shestov, he was terribly disappointed. This work is, in many ways, a declaration of war against Shestov's thought. The sharp confrontation between Shestov and Nietzsche, in the chapter titled "Shestov Facing Nietzsche," shatters the plausibility of Shestov's Nietzscheanism. In 1938 Bespaloff disproved the Shestovization of Nietzsche, as she had disproved, in 1932, Fondane's Shestovization of Heidegger. Their disagreements concerning the indictment of knowledge, the acceptance of necessity, the creation of universal values, the acknowledgment of the value of faith and of original sin, the question of the absurd, and the idea of the metaphysical miracle all deconstruct Shestov's Nietzscheanism. Moreover, this debate signals the profound rift between existential thought and Shestov's lived ethical position: "There is a silence in him, an abstention that dissimulates a fundamental question: he accuses morality of providing us only with values that help us tolerate existence and he refuses to create values that would enable us to change it."[17]

Was the doctrine of the overcoming of ethical values tenable during the years when fascist movements were rising to power? "Doesn't the stubborn manner in which Shestov avoids this problem hide an inner disagreement between his ethical sensibility and his metaphysical aspiration?" asked Bespaloff.[18] This question was at the heart of their discord. Like Wahl, like Marcel, like Karl Jaspers, she remained attached to critical and wakeful reason, and she refused what she called the "infinite un-knowing of innocence."[19] "I admit I feel no urge to go back to stupidity," she remarked ironically in her letter to Fondane.[20] The only thing she chose to keep from her former master was a lesson in philosophical anxiety and uncertainty, or what she called the "nakedness of the 'no.'" Shortly before Camus published *Le mythe de Sisyphe* (1940), Bespaloff mounted a radical attack against Shestov's existential thought: "His doubting opens up the possible for us, his negation walls us in," she said.[21] Camus will argue in *Le mythe de Sisyphe*, "Negation is the god of existential thinkers." But beneath this disagreement lies another, more fundamental conflict. Whereas Shestov aims to shatter the boundaries of time under the pressure of an overcoming of rationality through faith, Bespaloff tries to define the plenitude of the instant that is the site of the manifestation of freedom. In D. H. Lawrence, in Péguy, in Green, in Proust, and, ultimately, in

Montaigne, she strives, in the manner of a classical philosopher, to maintain the play of tensions without attempting to suppress the permanent confrontation of human contradictions. Her final way was that of Stoic wisdom. Wasn't it possible to regain a satisfying sense of joy in the finitude of the instant?

Wisdom in Hell

What was Bespaloff's response to this question? "The events in Germany have fully expressed the feelings of indignation, fury, and shamefulness. Once again, this miserable people bows down to the great law of the Exodus,"[22] she wrote in 1938 in a letter to Wahl. After 1944, the Jewish genocide completely altered her idea of classical wisdom: How can a witness still lay any claims to a happy recapturing of the instant? Historical tragedy caught up with existential tragedy. Was she thinking of Fondane when she wrote:

> Blessing life in the cattle wagons, heading for the death factories, is something different. The wise man does not get into these wagons, or if he finds himself thrown in one of them, he does not take his wisdom with him. He has even lost the possibility of committing suicide. What kind of wisdom can there be for the person who suddenly, as Kafka showed it in *Metamorphosis,* finds himself banned from the world of human beings, transformed into a cockroach? Wisdom is too close to aesthetics to stand the test of ugliness. Is wisdom available to a human being who has been transformed into vermin? It is no longer enough to bring the wisdom of heaven down to earth, as Montaigne did; one has to drag wisdom into the human hell.[23]

In her conclusion, she further stresses: "He [Montaigne] did not descend into hell. He modestly teaches how not to turn life into hell. And this is already difficult enough."[24] One must read between the lines of her last article on Camus, "The World of the Man Condemned to Death." This eloquent and insightful meditation on the world of *L'étranger* and *La peste* also bears witness to how profoundly the Jewish genocide wounded her sensibility. "What does the ethic of rebellious acceptance bring the man who is rotting in the concentration camps of life?" she asked.[25]

In focusing her investigation on the idea of revolt, Bespaloff brought into view the major ethical problem. Revolt, she argued, does not make one exempt from ethics; revolt does not provide any value in itself. Nevertheless, she turned to Shestov's lesson of anxiety in order to warn Camus of the dangers of moral preaching: "He is among those who search through groaning, although he carefully avoids the groans—and he is the sincere disciple of the great existential thinkers who formed him," but he risks forgetting Pascal's lesson and lapsing into the edifying morality of heroic humanism. Doesn't Bespaloff speak to us here with Shestov's voice? "Conversely, the danger he risks is to go from the existential to existentialism.... Job is not satisfied with the 'certainties of history.' He asks for, he demands a completely different answer. It so happens that the walls are too thick for the voices of the *We* to reach a victim of plague.... He should therefore stick to his vocation of an 'absurd' thinker, which is to restlessly bring everything into question, to take up in his characters the inner dispute which opposes Montaigne and Pascal."[26]

Although her article dealt mainly with the numerous tensions in *Le malentendu* and *La peste*, it was no doubt with reference to Fondane's article "Le lundi existentiel" that she remarked, "One can imagine Sisyphus happy, but joy is forever out of his reach." Indeed, Fondane had written: "But this is precisely what is difficult! and it is even out of this difficulty that existential thought emerged. That Sisyphus imagine himself happy, this is exactly what the Platonic, Stoic, and Hegelian systems of thought are asking for ... but what is left of Sisyphus' myth in all this"?[27]

Having argued that Camus managed to maintain opposite sides of his personality in existence, Bespaloff concluded that Camus possessed "the remarkable coexistence ... of the gift of fusion and of contradiction," so that "there is nothing he need disavow in order to reconcile within himself the teachings of the classics and those of Kierkegaard, Dostoevski, and Shestov."[28] A much-sought-after, and possibly desperate, reconciliation. Isn't this what she seeks to manifest in her writing? The literary work, as she said, "is situated at the crossroads of the intuition of the eternal and the experience of this world here, or rather it is the testimony of their fusion."[29] From this point of view, she mounted a fierce attack on Sartre's conception of engaged literature, and of the manner in which he brought contemplation into disrepute, precisely in the name of a freedom in the instant.

Classicism, in Bespaloff's view, is inseparable from an acceptance of finitude; she will reassert this idea in *On the Iliad*: "It is on an acceptance of powerlessness, on the summit of the powers and of the passion of thought, that the understanding of truth as religious feeling in the prophets and the tragic writers rests."[30] Wahl later wrote in this respect: "Shestov opposes to Hellenism, whether Dionysian or Apollonian, something else which he calls Jerusalem. But ... Rachel Bespaloff sees it [i.e., Jerusalem] in agreement with the Greek spirit.... [W]here her masters divided, she learned from them, and from Tolstoy, to reconcile and to unite."[31] "Where her masters divided"—that is to say, Kierkegaard, Nietzsche, Shestov—one should reconcile. Many of those who followed Wahl's example, such as Camus, Grenier, and Jacques

Maritain, were similarly careful to avoid creating an unbridgeable rift between Athens and Jerusalem, between reason and faith, and to make possible the plenitude of the instant, which Shestov's philosophy resolutely placed beyond our reach.

NOTES

1. Her correspondence with Gabriel Marcel, Daniel Halévy, Boris de Schloezer, Jean-Paul Sartre, and Jean Wahl has been published as follows: *Lettres à Jean Wahl, 1937–1947. Sur le fond le plus déchiqueté de l'histoire: édition établie, introduite et annotée par Monique Jutrin* (Paris: Éditions Claire Paulhan, 2003); "Lettres à Gabriel Marcel (1935–1946)," *Conférence* (Meaux) 18 (2004): 549–612 ; "Lettre à Daniel Halévy [on Heidegger]," *Conférence* 6 (1998): 435–79; "Lettres à Boris de Schloezer, I: 1942–1946," *Conférence* 16 (2003): 413–59, and "II: 1947–1949," *Conférence* 17 (2003): 521–65; "Sur la question juive [Rachel Bespaloff–Daniel Halévy]," *Conférence* 13 (2001): 623–67; "Lettre inédite à Jean-Paul Sartre," in *Lettres à Jean Wahl*, 162–63; "Lettre à Benjamin Fondane," in *Voyageur n'a pas fini de voyager*, ed. Patrice Beray and Michel Carassou (Paris: Paris Méditerranée, 1996), 118–20; and "Lettres au Père Fessard," *Deucalion* (Neuchâtel) 5 (1955): 141–68.

2. Compare Rachel Bespaloff, *Lettres à Jean Wahl*.

3. Simone Weil, *L'Iliade, ou, le poème de la force* (Paris: Gallimard, 1953).

4. Rachel Bespaloff to Boris de Schloezer, Monaco Library, Paris.

5. Bespaloff, "Lettre à Daniel Halévy."

6. Benjamin Fondane, *La conscience malheureuse* (Paris: Denoël et Steele, 1936), 169–70.

7. Rachel Bespaloff, *Cheminements et carrefours* (Paris: Vrin, 1938), 52.

8. Ibid.

9. Benjamin Fondane, *Rencontres avec Léon Chestov, Sur les rives de l'Ilissus* (Paris: Plasma, 1982), 45.

10. Rachel Bespaloff, "Sur la répétition chez Kierkegaard," *Revue Philosophique de la France et de l'Étranger* (May–June 1934).

11. Ibid., 180.

12. Benjamin Fondane, "Héraclite le pauvre ou nécessité de Kierkegaard," *Cahiers du Sud* 13, no. 177 (November 1935): 758.

13. Ibid., 767.

14. Ibid.

15. Bespaloff, "Lettre à Benjamin Fondane," 120.

16. Fondane, *Rencontres avec Léon Chestov*, 134.

17. Bespaloff, *Cheminements et carrefours*, 239–40.

18. Ibid., 239–40.

19. Ibid., 192.

20. Bespaloff, "Lettre à Benjamin Fondane," 120.

21. Bespaloff, *Cheminements*, 195.

22. Rachel Bespaloff to Jean Wahl, December 2, 1938, in *Lettres à Jean Wahl*, 61.

23. Rachel Bespaloff, "L'instant chez Montaigne," *Deucalion*, no. 3 (1950): 107.

24. Ibid.

25. Rachel Bespaloff, "The World of the Man Condemned to Death," trans. Eric Schoenfeld,

in *Camus: A Collection of Critical Essays*, ed. Germaine Brée (Englewood Cliffs, N.J.: Prentice-Hall, 1962), 101.

26. Rachel Bespaloff, "Le monde du condamné à mort," *Esprit* (January 1950): 13.

27. Benjamin Fondane, *Le lundi existentiel et le dimanche de l'histoire, suivi de la Philosophique vivante* (Paris: Éditions du Rocher, 1990), 20, 61.

28. Bespaloff, "The World of the Man Condemned to Death," 106.

29. Rachel Bespaloff, "À propos de 'Qu'est-ce que la littérature' de Sartre," *Fontaine* (November 1947): 706.

30. Rachel Bespaloff, "De l'*Iliade*," *Conférence* 10–11 (2000): 660.

31. Jean Wahl, *Poésie, pensée, perception* (Paris: Calman-Lévy, 1948), 274.

Rediscovering Rachel Bespaloff

Monique Jutrin

For many years I have been studying the work of Benjamin Fondane, a poet, philosopher, critic, and playwright, who was a contemporary of Rachel Bespaloff. In a diary of Fondane's encounters and discussions with Shestov I came across the name of Rachel Bespaloff for the first time.[1] She appeared an irritating woman who never agreed with Shestov. Bespaloff's father, Daniel Pasmanik, a friend of Shestov's, introduced his daughter to him. At first, she was very impressed by Shestov. He awakened her to philosophical thought, and she is still considered a disciple of Shestov, though she later became opposed to certain aspects of his philosophy.

So, I can situate my first encounter in the context of my research on existential thinkers like Shestov, Fondane, and Jean Wahl who preceded the existentialism of Sartre. But it was during my work on the Wahl papers at the Library of the IMEC (Institut mémoires de l'édition contemporaine) in Paris that I discovered Bespaloff's letters to Wahl. There for the first time I "heard" her voice—the voice of a sensitive, intelligent, lucid woman. I was deeply struck by her sharp reflections on literature, philosophy, and art, but also on the political events of that period (1938–48). Her correspondence with Jean Wahl begins in 1938, a year of terrible events. including the Munich accord in September and Kristallnacht in November. Bespaloff was immediately aware of their gravity and understood that France was no longer a safe place for her.

When I spoke about these letters to Claire Paulhan, who is responsible for the Wahl papers, I expressed my enthusiasm, and she proposed that we publish them with her own publishing house. She insisted that I find Bespaloff's daughter in order to obtain her agreement. At that moment, in August 1999, we didn't even know where her daughter, Naomi Levinson, was living. This was the beginning of an adventure that took a few years. Little by little, I discovered Bespaloff's writings and manuscripts. I was not alone in that research: Olivier Salazar-Ferrer, whom I met through our Benjamin Fondane Society, discovered Bespaloff at the same time and we collaborated.

My book was published in the spring of 2003. I chose the subtitle *Sur le fond le plus déchiqueté de l'Histoire* (Against the Most Shattered Background of History), which is a quotation from Bespaloff's article on Wahl's poetry.[2] In addition to publishing Bespaloff's letters to Wahl, I also delivered two papers. The first one was at the Shestov-Fondane Conference in Paris in 2000: I spoke about the differences and similarities among Bespaloff, Shestov, and Fondane.[3] The second one, in Orléans, was on Bespaloff's reading of Charles Péguy.[4] Afterwards, her article on Péguy's humanism was republished in the review *Amitié Charles Péguy*.[5] More recently, I wrote a text for a collective publication in Germany on engagement and am editing Bespaloff's work in France and Italy.[6]

Bespaloff's Intellectual Relationship with Jean Wahl

Rachel Bespaloff met Jean Wahl after she turned away from Shestov in search of her own philosophy. She appreciated Wahl's way of thinking, full of incertitude and doubt, not hurrying toward a conclusion. They agreed on many points and discussed liberty, transcendence, and destiny. Both shared the same conception of existential philosophy and were fascinated by Kierkegaard; their views on Shestov and Gabriel Marcel were similar. She wrote a long article about Wahl's book on Kierkegaard.[7] Bespaloff was also interested in Wahl's poetry. She told him that she felt him entirely present in his poems, and wrote a long article about them, saying, "Wahl's poetry is not philosophical, it is the writing of a poet who annexes his explorations and perplexities as a philosopher."[8]

As for my own engagement with Bespaloff, I was taken by her lucid grasp of the period in which she was living. She understood deeply all its implications for the human being. After the war she wrote to her Christian friend Gaston Fessard, in 1949: "Pas une seule valeur, chrétienne ou juive, qui soit périmée, mais pas une seule qui ne doive être jetée dans le creuset de nos souffrances, pour être fondue à nouveau [No one value, Christian or Jewish, is out of date, but they all must be reconsidered through the crucible of our sufferings in order to be renewed]."[9]

The "Ethical Experience"

In her last writings, Bespaloff judges literature and philosophy by their capacity to measure themselves against the experience of the Shoah and to face tragedy: "When the last choice disappears, in the gas chamber or under torture, does the human being find a supreme resource that permits him to affirm his being beyond his own destruction?"[10] Thus we understand why her last writings are mostly about tragedy and liberty. She was also obsessed by the question of God, the silence or absence of God during those years. Did he abandon us? Did we abandon him? She was deeply concerned by the tragedy of the Jewish people. She felt angry and humiliated. And when the state of Israel was created, she considered that this was "the only possible answer to the genocide."[11]

Bespaloff never separated literature and philosophy from real life and experience. Through the authors she was studying, Bespaloff was in search of a very special experience, "l'instant de vérité" (the instant of truth). Her first book, *Cheminements et carrefours,* contains five essays on existential writers: Julien Green, André Malraux, Kierkegaard, Gabriel Marcel, and Shestov.[12] Her reading is focused on what she calls "l'expérience éthique" (the ethical experience), which she defines clearly in her second book, *On the Iliad.* As we know, she was reading the *Iliad* again, in order to confront the experience of war and violence. She tried to understand contemporary events through Greek and biblical sources. There she finds a form of thinking that she calls "ethical." I quote from Mary McCarthy's translation: "a form of thought essentially ethical, if this word is used merely to designate the experience of total distress where the very absence of choice compels us to choose. 'Inwardness lasts only an instant,' says Kierkegaard. The thought of the Bible and of Homer feeds on these instants, even when it seems to plunge downward into history."[13]

I appreciate Bespaloff's courage, her confronting of others, even friends such as Leon Shestov, Benjamin Fondane, Gabriel Marcel. To be right or wrong was not important for her. To agree was not satisfying. She wanted to continue the debate far beyond the agreement.

She wanted peace, but was not able to find it. Marked by tragedy, living life as a tragedy, she looked for an escape. She found it in art, in literature, music, philosophy, for a while, for an "instant." When she was no longer able to find that outlet, tired and depressed, she put an end to her life.

NOTES

1. Benjamin Fondane, *Rencontres avec Léon Chestov* (Paris: Plasma, 1982). Born in Romania in 1898, Fondane arrived in Paris in 1923 and was murdered in Auschwitz in 1944. He was a friend and a disciple of the Russian existential philosopher Leon Shestov. For more information, see *www.fondane.org.*

2. Rachel Bespaloff, "La poésie de Jean Wahl," first published in Bespaloff, *Lettres à Jean Wahl (1937–1947). Sur le fond le plus déchiqueté de l'histoire,* ed. Monique Jutrin (Paris: Éditions Claire Paulhan, 2003), 129–36.

3. Monique Jutrin, "Rachel Bespaloff, Léon Chestov, Benjamin Fondane: différends et convergences," unpublished paper.

4. Monique Jutrin, "Une lectrice de Péguy: Rachel Bespaloff," *Le Porche* 8 (December 2001): 32–36.

5. Rachel Bespaloff, "L'humanisme de Péguy" *L'Amitié Charles Péguy* 96 (October–December 2001): 511–27.

6. Monique Jutrin, "Rachel Bespaloff: lecture et expérience éthique," in *Esprit civique und*

Engagement (Tübingen: Stauffenburg Verlag, 2003). Bespaloff's works are *De l'Iliade* (Paris: Allia, 2004), and *Cheminements et carrefours* (Paris: Vrin, 2004).

7. Rachel Bespaloff, "Notes sur les *Études kierkegaardiennes* de Jean Wahl," *Revue Philosophique de la France et de l'Étranger* (June–July 1939): 301–23.

8. See Jutrin, "Rachel Bespaloff."

9. Rachel Bespaloff, "Lettres au R. P. Gaston Fessard," *Deucalion* 5 (1955): 140–69.

10. Rachel Bespaloff, "L'instant et la liberté chez Montaigne," *Deucalion* 3 (1950): 65–107.

11. Like her parents, Rachel Bespaloff was a Zionist. This is confirmed in her correspondence and in her article "The Twofold Relationship," *Contemporary Jewish Record* 6, no. 3 (June 1943): 244–53.

12. Rachel Bespaloff, *Cheminements et carrefours: Julien Green, André Malraux, Gabriel Marcel, Kierkegaard, Chestov devant Nietzsche* (1938), preface by Monique Jutrin (Paris: J. Vrin, 2004).

13. Rachel Bespaloff, *On the Iliad,* trans. Mary McCarthy, intro. Hermann Broch (Princeton: Princeton University Press, 1947).

Searching for Rachel Bespaloff

Alyssa Danigelis

Rachel Bespaloff's books were the only ones I ever considered stealing. I held the old copies in my hands at the Mount Holyoke College library in the spring of 2001 and seriously contemplated breaking the law and the honor code. Not having these copies would make a post-graduation attempt to write her biography nearly impossible. Right? But I couldn't do it, not only because I have never stolen anything in my life, but also because my mother is a librarian. All books must be returned.

So I opted instead to hunt down rare copies in other countries and awaited the arrival of their foreign, smoky-smelling pages. I sliced the pages open with a Swiss Army knife, reveling in the fact that I was the first to read them. But Rachel Bespaloff felt further away than ever.

The library was the first place where I ever heard of her. Peter Carini, then director of the Mount Holyoke College Archives, approached me in the reading room at the beginning of the 2000–2001 school year. In a hushed voice he said that the archives had a collection in French that needed processing, but it was potentially very sensitive because the professor whose letters it contained had committed suicide. Would I take it on? I spent many hours examining Rachel's tight handwriting, even bringing in French professor Catherine LeGouis to help me decipher words. I attempted to transcribe and then roughly translate all of her letters.

All I had to do was process the collection, but I gradually dug up every article Rachel ever published, searched out places where she could have been mentioned, tracked down the biographies and works of people who knew her best. Who were these people she wrote about? I wanted to find her, and if it meant unearthing dusty books, running around libraries, calling a hotel in France, e-mailing tons of people, and even sending a friend to the Bibliothèque nationale in Paris to copy passages out of books by hand, well, I would do it.

My goal eventually became to write about Rachel Bespaloff, but I felt that I was constantly writing an introduction to a book that didn't exist. Where to begin? With her journey from France to New York City? With Pontigny? With her death? With her birth? Her books? Her experience at Mount Holyoke? So I turned to other sources for inspiration. In 1848 Emily Dickinson wrote a letter from Mount Holyoke Female Seminary: "Home was always dear to me, &

dearer still the friends around it, but never did it seem so dear as now. All, all are kind to me but their tones fall strangely on my ear & their countenances meet mine not like home faces, I can assure you, most sincerely." [1]

"Why?" Naomi Levinson, Rachel's daughter, asked me more than once. "Why did my mother kill herself?" Some days I thought I knew why. It was springtime when she did it. Around spring break. She had a pile of papers to correct. Her husband had died only two years before. Her daughter was away at school. Adding to the loneliness was the burden of a severely ailing mother. South Hadley is a far cry from Paris. Survivor's guilt. Fear. Anger. Terrible fatigue. But at a certain point I have no idea why. My theories just disintegrate. She certainly isn't the only brilliant, beautiful woman to have killed herself. Literary history is full of them. One could argue that she always grappled with dark demons and in 1949 she lost.

Stone Reader, a filmmaker's journey to find the author of an out-of-print book, brings Rachel to mind, connecting her to my quest to understand her work and capture her life in a biography. I, too, felt the seasons change on me and wondered if I could ever truly unlock the secrets. A severe form of writer's block overtook me. Occasionally I could not write because I was afraid of wading through the piles of articles, notes, books, photocopies, and letters only to come up empty again. Rachel became my Dora Bruder, the elusive Holocaust runaway whose life the author Patrick Modiano tries to imagine.

In her second book, *On the Iliad,* Rachel writes about Helen, describing her beauty in a passage that speaks a great truth, perhaps about Rachel herself:

> The most beautiful of women seemed born for a radiant destiny; everything pointed that way; everything appeared to contribute to it. But, as it turns out, the gods only chose her to work misfortune on herself and on the two nations. Beauty is not a promise of happiness here; it is a burden and a curse. At the same time, it isolates and elevates; it has something preservative in it that wards off outrage and shame. Hence its sacred character—to use the word in its original, ambiguous sense—on the one hand, life-giving, exalting; on the other, accursed and dread. [2]

Reading Rachel Bespaloff's other philosophical work, especially her articles on existentialism and her critiques of the philosophers of her day, is like reading Marx for the first time. Initially it feels like a language—be it French or English—I have yet to master. Then it reveals its fascinating turns of the mind.

There are several themes that are present in her work. One is the existence of multiple identities, a theme she actually lived. In her article "The Twofold Relationship," published in the *Contemporary Jewish Record* in 1943, she analyzes what it means to be Jewish and to live in France. A dedicated Zionist, she writes: "The Frenchman has a right to make mistakes: in back of him there is always France. The Jew has no privilege: when disaster strikes he stands alone before a dismembered people."[3] Her final assessment in 1943 doesn't offer any answer (or solution) to this struggle. She writes, referring to the mission of the Jewish people, "Today it is misfortune which gathers this people, too unhappy to despair, and urges it to go to meet itself on the road to its unity."[4]

According to Monique Jutrin, in her introduction to Claire Paulhan's edition of Bespaloff's *Lettres à Jean Wahl,* Nissim Bespaloff once told his wife, "Ta Sion à toi, c'est Paris [Your Zion, it's Paris]." Bespaloff and her family left the farthest southeastern edge of France to escape to America. Her decision to leave was extraordinarily difficult. The subsequent rupture she experienced—physically and emotionally—from France colors her work from that time.

She lived in exile in so many senses of the word. In a letter to her sister-in-law Fanny Ettinger in August 1942, Bespaloff writes that she lives like an "amputation" and that "here the war has no reality."[5] At the Pontigny gatherings, Bespaloff gave a talk on existentialism.[6] In analyzing Sartre's work she says: "I am present to the world and at the same instant, I am tearing myself away from it, toward the world that isn't yet. As you can see, we have come back to that pair Being and Nothingness—Being, the presence to, Nothingness, the flight from."[7] She never returned to France, even though her closest colleagues and friends started returning after the war. Obligation to her family kept her in America.

She writes to Jean Wahl in 1945: "Do you know that I have a difficult time realizing you are leaving? Will we see each other one day in Paris? Try not to forget about me too quickly. Write to me. Think what your letters will bring to me in this sort of chronic exile I live in. (But please, remember to write the address legibly)."[8]

More themes that weave themselves through Bespaloff's work are like those of many existentialists: freedom, death, and a search for meaning in life. She analyzes Heidegger, Camus, van Gogh, Péguy, Julien Green, Leon Shestov, Homer, and countless others to try to make sense of their work in response to this question: What is this existence? And, more particularly, What is this existence in times of war?

Perhaps it is not surprising that her last formal analysis, an article on Camus titled "The World of the Man Condemned to Death," was published posthumously in 1950. In it she writes about *The Plague:* "It may seem strange that Camus should have deliberately left aside torture and the demonic attempt to reduce man to the state of a superfluous puppet. But we should not forget that the sentence of death is the central theme of his work. It matters little here whether it is nature, fate, justice, or human cruelty which pronounces the sentence. We know that in his most diabolic inventions man only imitates the tortures of life."[9] Even less surprising is that her last work, left unfinished and unpublished, was a study on the formation of the myth of freedom, using the work of Milton and Blake as a departure point.[10] Rachel Bespaloff, from all accounts, was a beautiful woman inside and out. Her beauty was a deep intellectual beauty and sophistication of thought. Here was a woman for whom students would relinquish their Saturdays. Here was a woman whose native country had changed many times over. Here was a woman haunted by tragedy.

I hope that our remembrance of her will bring us all one step closer to her, especially those of us who never had the pleasure of meeting this extraordinarily complex woman.

NOTES

1. Emily Dickinson to Austin Dickinson, February 17, 1848, in *The Letters of Emily Dickinson,* ed. Thomas H. Johnson and Theodora Ward (Cambridge: Harvard University Press, 1958), 62.

2. Simone Weil and Rachel Bespaloff, *War and the Iliad* (New York: New York Review Books, 2005), 60–61.

3. Bespaloff, "The Twofold Relationship," 249–50.

4. Ibid., 253.

5. *Rachel Bespaloff: lettres à Jean Wahl 1937–1947* (Paris: Éditions Claire Paulhan, 2003), 31.

6. A conversation with Laurent Jeanpierre after I presented this essay helped illuminate why this was improbable. Naomi Levinson, Rachel Bespaloff's daughter, showed me what was clearly a typed speech given by Bespaloff, complete with slight changes in her distinctive handwriting. Bespaloff was slated to talk on other subjects at Pontigny, so it is not likely that she would have been asked to change her talk to an analysis of existentialism. The question now is not whether she presented the talk but when she did. On some reflection, I'd argue that she gave the presentation either during or shortly after Sartre's visit to Mount Holyoke College in 1946.

7. This quotation is taken from the unpublished manuscript (see note 6); the page number is unknown.

8. Bespaloff, *Lettres,* 109.

9. Bespaloff, "The World of the Man Condemned to Death," in *Camus: A Collection of Critical Essays,* ed. Germaine Brée (Englewood Cliffs, N.J.: Prentice-Hall, 1962), 99.

10. Bespaloff, *Lettres,* 112–13.

Blend and Belong

RENEE SCIALOM CARY

FIRST, I WOULD like to set the scene. Mount Holyoke during World War II. Visualize two wars going on and very slight communication from the outside. The only news that we had about the war was through the newspapers or through the newsreels. We were told only what they wanted us to hear. We were not on the battlefield.

My own journey to Mount Holyoke was a very long one. I left Turkey at the age of seven. My family moved to Prague because my mother, who had been educated at Barnard and at the Sorbonne, felt she needed more cultural nourishment than she could get in Turkey. Prague at that time was the cultural center of Europe, and there was plenty to entertain all of us. But we were there on a very limited basis. We lived in a hotel for three years. We were in Paris, visiting my grandmother, when the first invasion of Czechoslovakia by the Nazis started, and we were not able to return to Prague. I went to school in Paris for two years, and during the summer of 1939, while we were vacationing in St. Malo, the war broke out. The war between Germany and France was supposed to last only three weeks, they told us, so we went back to Paris, checked into a hotel, and waited for the three weeks to be over; I don't have to tell you what happened.

The next move was as far south as possible for protection. We chose a city called Pau because it had an English school and I was able to continue my schooling in English. I was bilingual because my father spoke French but not English and my mother spoke English and French. So my first language was actually French. I didn't learn English until I was six.

We waited for the war to be over and lived during that time in hotels or furnished apartments. Then came the Armistice. Luckily, our town was in unoccupied territory. Unfortunately, when we decided that we had better leave the country, our passports were tied up in Bordeaux. Bordeaux was occupied, so we didn't think that we would be able to leave. In those days, when you left a country you had to have an exit visa. So we had sent the passports to Bordeaux. But, lo and behold, one day a miracle happened and the passports arrived. Within one hour we were in a taxi to the border with Spain. And after about five hours of paperwork and having to wait at the border—you've seen all this in movies, so you know what that looks like—with one suitcase, my family crossed the border at 11:30 at night. It was dark, and in a group of thirty people or so we walked to the nearest town. Spain was in a terrible state at that time, and most cities were in rubble. We eventually went on to Barcelona because that was one city that had been saved during the civil war. And we waited for a boat. You've heard that expression many times: waiting for the boat.

We had missed the last boat from Marseilles to the United States. It was the SS *Washington,* and we had missed it because our passports had been held up in Bordeaux. So we waited for a boat, then finally, two months later, sailed from Lisbon to Brazil in a converted freighter dating from World War I. You can imagine what that was like. There were probably twenty-five or thirty refugees on board, and it took us twenty-four days to cross the ocean. We ran out of food on the way, but we finally arrived in Rio. There again we had to wait for a boat to sail to New York, where we arrived at last in March 1941. And everywhere we had traveled and stopped, my parents put me in school. By the time I got to Mount Holyoke in 1944, I had been to nine schools. And I think I had become a master in something we called "blend and belong." Blend and belong. The proof is that when I got to Mount Holyoke, the Speech Department called me in and said that I had to take corrective speech classes because I had a New York accent! For four years we weren't able to get rid of that accent, which I still have, although I haven't lived in New York since 1951.

My first impression of Mount Holyoke was walking through the college gates when I arrived in the fall of 1944. To this day, those gates have a special meaning for me. I had never been on the campus and I didn't know a soul. When I came to Mount Holyoke, I suddenly realized that I was finally going to be in a place of my own, and I was finally going to have an opportunity to be myself—and find out who I *really* was. I was obviously not the only refugee student here. We did not have many international students at Mount Holyoke in those days because there were two wars going on. We did have a few refugee students, however, for one reason or another. Interestingly, we did not seek one another out. We found one another in various ways, but we never talked about the past. The curtain had gone down...the curtain, when you reach the safe haven, just goes down, and you don't want to talk about it. And to be honest, I very seldom have talked about it. I would say that probably I didn't even tell anyone that I was born in Turkey because that was just too complicated. I would have had to start explaining. There were a lot of things that you had to do just to "blend and belong." And, of course, there were also the refugee professors. I'm sure that we were drawn to them, although we didn't know much about them because they also didn't talk about their background. They didn't identify themselves. We could probably tell by the accent or by other means that they came from elsewhere. We felt so privileged to have these wonderful minds on our campus.

In closing, I would like to say a few words about Rachel Bespaloff because she had such an impact on me. She was just the most incredible teacher. She was tough, and she was hard, and you didn't sign up for her classes until you thought you were really ready for it. But once you were there, I remember, you took a deep breath before you went in the classroom, you sat on the edge of your seat during the classes, and you floated out. This is the effect that she had on us. She stretched our minds, and she lifted our perceptions way beyond the material that we were studying. She challenged us all continually, and she expected the most from us. She made us believe that we could be more than students and that we could be scholars. Perhaps we started believing that ourselves. I just felt terribly fortunate to have had that intellectual experience; it turned me around in so many ways. Rachel Bespaloff was definitely the icon in the French Department. We knew this, even though we knew so very little about her. We knew she was special, but we didn't quite know why or perhaps even how. She taught us on a Sorbonne level because she believed in us. I suppose everyone has special professors or teachers throughout their lives that they remember. For me, Rachel Bespaloff is someone whom I have never forgotten.

Memories of Rachel Bespaloff

Barbara Levin Amster

As a brand-new freshman in Pearsons Hall, I crossed College Street, walked through the gates, and fell in love with Mount Holyoke College. It is a love affair that has lasted more than fifty years. Little did I know in those early days that Mount Holyoke would change my life forever. Rachel Bespaloff was the architect of that change. Indeed, the most significant part of my college and lifetime experience was my relationship with her.

For weeks I have been searching for the appropriate words to do justice to her brilliance and magnetism. Lo and behold, I heard those word in Chris Benfey's superb description of Stanley Cavell as teacher. What Madame Bespaloff generated was "intellectual excitement in a classroom." It was breathtaking, especially since I was holding my breath hoping not to be called on.

Upon arriving at Mount Holyoke, I viewed the world and my studies with a hopelessly uncritical eye. Madame made short shrift of my apathy. Early in her course an essay, the first of many, was assigned. Madame returned my sorry excuse for an essay with more critical comments than my paper itself contained. Therein began my intellectual relationship with this extraordinary woman and great teacher, a relationship that is as vivid today as it was more than fifty years ago.

Paramount among her criticisms was that I translated English into French. "Think in French," she said. I could hardly think in English let alone French. Furthermore, I was to get into the hearts and souls of the main characters in the books and plays that we were reading. Perhaps this could be done with Emma Bovary, but I challenge you to get into the heart and soul of an existentialist.

The result of her ability to be a great teacher at last bore fruit. My papers at long last contained more of my writing than hers. Her great gift to me was to make me better than I ever thought I could be. I soared under her tutelage. (There are sixteen years of my own students who indirectly benefited from Madame B. I tried to make my classrooms as challenging and exciting as hers. I tried to treat my students' work as carefully as she had treated mine.)

By the end of the year I was bold enough to use comparisons from works other than French. I had the temerity to compare Julien Sorel with a character in the *Iliad*. Now I had piqued her curiosity. She peppered me with questions seeking to ascertain how I had arrived at that comparison. I explained that I was reading the *Iliad*. Again she asked why I would be doing that, as if I didn't have enough reading to do for her. I explained that I was a second-year Greek student. "Aha," she said. "Are you reading it in Greek?" A "yes" answer changed our relationship.

Prior to spring break of my junior year in 1949, I submitted a hurriedly prepared paper which suffered from the effect of my desire to get home. How I have subsequently wished that last paper had been my best, but it was not. Madame called me to her modest apartment quite disappointed with my regression. She was frowning because of the many inadequacies of my paper. Among the things she said was that one would think that I was in love. Suddenly she smiled and said, "Mademoiselle Levin, are you in love?" I said yes. She crumpled my paper and said, "Now, Barbara"—calling me Barbara for the first and only time—"you must learn about life. There are some things in life more important than writing papers, and the most enchanting of these is falling in love."

I never saw her again.

Pauvre Rachel

NAOMI BESPALOFF LEVINSON

MY MOTHER, Rachel Bespaloff, looked at a photograph of herself taken at the age of eighteen and said: "*Pauvre* Rachel." [1] In her voice, I heard a world of sadness tinged with longing. She did not explain why she felt sorry for the lovely young woman in the picture, who, being only eighteen years old, appeared to have "her whole life ahead of her." She was fifty-five when she committed suicide. I am almost seventy-six, and I don't think I will kill myself. I, too, know a deep and abiding sadness below the surface of my everyday life, no doubt akin to what I imagine my mother found in her everyday life as a writer and teacher at Mount Holyoke College.

MY MOTHER was a woman of tenacity and strength. I, too, am strong and tenacious. For ten years she held at bay her impulse to commit suicide. In 1939, on a night train, speaking with my father, she announced her death ten years hence. They thought I was asleep, but I wasn't. I heard, and I remembered.

My mother used to tell me there were three kinds of people: those who say God does not exist; those who have found Him; and those who are looking for Him. She said she belonged to the third group, those who search for but fail to find God.

Both of us were gifted with the dual vocations of teaching and writing. Both of us became the parent of an only child. I am a good teacher but was not a good parent. My mother was not a reachable parent except in brief flashes; but she was a superb, encouraging teacher. I took and enjoyed her French literature classes at Mount Holyoke. She treated her students as equals, on "adult-to-adult" terms. You found yourself in the presence of a thinker who invited you to partake of her thinking process. One of her courses followed a Tuesday-Thursday-Saturday schedule. Weekends at Mount Holyoke, in those days, were dedicated to hunting future husbands. Girls who signed up for my mother's course were making a sacrifice. This speaks to the loyalty she inspired.

In the recently published correspondence between my mother and Jean Wahl, I read that she (in her own estimation) was having a nervous breakdown in 1939. I do not recall any family talk about a breakdown. That year, however, I spent a few months with her in a sanatorium in Switzerland, in Montana-Vermala. First, she and I stayed in Paris for two or three weeks. Nor-

Rachel Bespaloff as a child. Photograph provided by Naomi Bespaloff Levinson.

Rachel Bespaloff, about eleven years old. Photograph provided by Naomi Bespaloff Levinson.

mally, she went there by herself. I met some of the members of her circle of intellectual friends. About the civil war in Spain at the time I remember her
saying, "This is the beginning of the end." She was right in her assessment. She
knew that Jews were in danger, yet she did not want to leave France. She said,
"There will be no trees in America."

After Paris, we went to Geneva. There, we saw the treasures of the Prado, an
experience I never forgot. At the recent Picasso-Matisse show in New York,
I learned that Picasso had been put in charge of these masterpieces; to safe-
guard them, he had them shipped to Geneva. My mother and I discovered
Velásquez, El Greco, and Goya. (Born in 1927, I was twelve years old at the
time.)

Through the years I shared with her, we had many moments of enjoying
landscapes, books, music, and art. She taught me the piano—my message to

Rachel Bespaloff, age eighteen. Photograph
provided by Naomi Bespaloff Levinson.

Rachel Bespaloff, when she was teaching at Mount
Holyoke College in the 1940s. Photograph provided
by Naomi Bespaloff Levinson.

anybody with children is, do not teach your own children; it will probably be a disaster! Yet we did play Mozart's "Eine Kleine Nachtmusik" four-handed—a happy memory. She also taught me Dalcroze eurythmics; to this I owe the fact that I am flexible; I can fall without hurting myself seriously.

My mother was educated at the Geneva Conservatory. She never attended public high school. She ended up teaching at Mount Holyoke College because of her books and a recommendation from Jean Wahl, who had preceded her there. Before her marriage, she taught at the Paris Opéra. But, in my opinion, she foolishly gave up her career when she married my father. Like her own mother, who had founded a girls' boarding school in Geneva, my mother was a feminist in advance of modern feminism. I think giving up her professional life was a mistake. I believe it made her feel dependent, and probably angry; it must have exacerbated the depression that was already in her.

Let me go back to my opening words. My mother looks at the photograph and says, "Poor Rachel." A world of intractable sadness tinged with longing is in her voice. What she saw in that picture was her death-to-come. She had decided to die, most likely long before the "nervous breakdown." And she did die within ten years, as she promised my father on that train ride: 1939 to 1949 is ten years.

People feel guilty when a suicide occurs. They think, "If only I had…" There is no "if only…" This is my personal belief; you can't cause another person's suicide, nor can you prevent it. I believe the impulse to commit suicide to be an internal process; external factors may delay, not arrest, that process. We have all known people who, seen from the outside, appeared to "have their life before them." We can't understand why they wanted to die. My mother was a recognized thinker and writer; she remained so, in a low-key way, through the long years that intervened between her death and the recent resurgence of interest in her work. She killed herself while she was working on a new book for which she had been awarded a Bollingen Foundation fellowship.

As I look back on the past of my mother and me, I see some sadness, and I see some gladness too.

NOTE

1. This text is an excerpt from a transcript of Levinson's remarks during the roundtable held in memory of her mother at the Pontigny symposium on November 8, 2003. She and the other roundtable speakers, Danigelis, Cary, and Amster, kindly took time to edit their remarks and granted us permission to publish them here.

First of all, the few who exist in all nations have to try to communicate with each other. If they are to do that, it is important that they not cling desperately to their own national pasts, pasts that can't explain anything anyhow (for Auschwitz cannot be explained by German history any more than it can by Jewish history); that they know that the Flood is upon us and that we are all like Noah in his ark; and that they are still able to summon up gratitude for the fact that there are still, relatively, so many Noahs who are floating about on the seas of the world and trying to steer their arks as close to one another as they can.

Hannah Arendt, *Hannah Arendt–Karl Jaspers Correspondence, 1926–1969*

Conclusion

Encounters of Hope

KAREN REMMLER

THE FOUR photographs of Rachel Bespaloff—as a girl, as a young woman, and as an adult marked by the experience of exile—haunt us. The ghostly images are silent, even as the presence of this elusive and driven thinker is all around us, transported by the words of those who knew her and those who study her writing. Even as Bespaloff and many of the other Pontigny participants past and present wrote again and again of violence, I am struck by the ferment of creativity that emerged out of the encounters of Masson and Chagall, Stevens and Moore, and many others in 1942–1944, and the more recent 2003 symposium to which we have dedicated this volume. Do hardship, pain, and violence produce memorable art, art that mesmerizes as much as it shocks? Why the stagnation in plentiful times? What is it that stirs creativity, if not violence? Stevens notes that a violence from within protects us from a violence without. Is it this violence within imagination and energy that brings forth poetry instead of physical hurt? Is this the force that Christopher Benfey finds in the essays by Weil and Bespaloff, or the glimpses of secular redemption and resistance that many of the essays in this volume have left us with? Or is this the force that Arendt alludes to, the force in the political realm that is always bound to cause death, or, at the very least, alienation? Are the realms connected? Where do we find the hope that the past pushing us forward and the future pushing us back will not destroy the precious moments of the present?

One way out of the impasse may be conversation and its prose form, correspondence. Holger Teschke tells us of the encounter between Brecht and Benjamin, in the midst of the Nazi deluge. They are in Denmark, sitting at a wooden table, talking about difficult things, yet surrounded by simplicity. I am reminded of Bespaloff's reading of the *Iliad* and of Benfey's reading of her essay.[1] Recall the scene of supplication when Priam comes to claim the corpse of his son Hector from Achilles, who has not only slain Hector but also desecrated his body. This is perhaps one of the most poignant and unforgettable encounters in world literature. It provides not only a brief reprieve from battle, but also a coming together of enemies in grief—an encounter that is otherwise unfathomable. Two enemies engage in a conversation amid destruction:

"Revere the gods. Achilles! Pity me in my own right,
remember your own father! I deserve more pity...
I have endured what no one on earth has ever done before—
I put to my lips the hands of the man who killed my son."

Those words stirred within Achilles a deep desire
to grieve for his own father. Taking the old man's hand
he gently moved him back. And overpowered by memory
both men gave way to grief. Priam wept freely
for man-killing Hector, throbbing, crouching
before Achilles' feet as Achilles wept himself,
now for his father, now for Patroclus once again,
and their sobbing rose and fell throughout the house.[2]

In this "exceptional deviation from the laws of the mechanism of violence," Bespaloff finds "one of the most beautiful silences in the *Iliad*—one of those absolute silences in which the din of the Trojan War, the vociferations of men and gods, and the rumblings of the Cosmos, are engulfed. The Becoming of the universe hangs suspended in this impalpable element whose duration is an instant and forever."[3] How does this beautiful silence come to be? First, the person who has come to claim the corpse (this is no innocent corpse) supplicates the warrior Achilles. He comes to retrieve the corpse of his son so that he can perform the proper funerary rites. Achilles and Priam are bound by codes established by the gods. Yet they step out of their roles by acknowledging the humanity of the other—in the form of beauty and noble appearance. The sound of their mourning and weeping is the sound heard in the silence during the cessation of the war. Second, Achilles, who killed Hector, enraged by Hector's killing of his friend Patroclus, does not rebuke him and even "gently" touches him, an extraordinary moment as Benfey shows us in his essay in this volume on the Iliads. Achilles will give the corpse to Priam and not attack Troy during the funeral rites. And finally, both men share a moment of mourning, even as they remain utterly separate. The sound of their weeping is what Bespaloff has called the silence in the vociferous din of war. Perhaps the brief interlude of quiet mourning is the flickering glimpse of possible reconciliation despite ongoing genocide and warfare. Yet, we know that war will soon recommence and that Troy will be destroyed, both men killed, and the Greeks thrown into the disastrous aftermath of war. What these two enemies achieve, however, is the semblance of a possible break in the continuum of war and slaughter. Each acknowledges the pain of the other, even as their status or power is not called into question.

It is this silence that allows for compassion to be stirred among enemies and for the dead to be properly mourned. Again, Bespaloff:

During this strange pause arranged for him by destiny on the extreme edge of suffering, Priam delights in Achilles' beauty—the beauty of force. The soul, delivered from the bondage of events, substitutes the order of contemplation for the order of passion; it is a moment of sacred truce. Under the influence of grief, the atrocious reality had hardened into something stony; now it melts, becomes fluid and fleeting. Hatred is disconcerted and relents. The two adversaries can exchange looks without seeing each other as targets, as objects which there is merit in destroying. Thanks to this detachment, private life, the love of the gods and of earthly beauty, the frail and obstinate will of whatever defies death to flower and bear fruit—all those things that rage had trampled down—are reborn and breathe again.[4]

Achilles, though not remorseful for his deeds, can say to Priam, "Chill grief is profitless," and they can sit together at the same table once Hector's corpse has been prepared and placed upon the bier. The experience of acknowledging the sensation of grief has not inherently changed the warrior and the king. A moment of silence may be all we can ask for.

The brilliance of Bespaloff's thinking is encapsulated most beautifully, I think, in her essay *On the Iliad*. In the midst of war she experienced firsthand, Bespaloff seeks the rare moments of silence that create a space for true human relationships based on deep mutual respect and the recognition that violence can be stopped. This is possible for Helen for no more than a fleeting moment as she stands with Priam on the ramparts of Troy overlooking the battlefield. Priam listens as Helen tells him about the warriors: "Here, at the very peak of the *Iliad,* is one of those pauses, those moments of contemplation, when the spell of Becoming is broken, and the world of action, with all its fury, dips into peace" (62). The battlefield, on which Helen and Priam gaze, "where the warrior herd was raging is no more than a tranquil mirage to Helen and the old king" (62).

This sense of futility in the space of brief respite has its place, too. For the humanity of the Other to be recognized, so too must the humanity of the Other's descendants be acknowledged. As Emmanuel Levinas has written, the "in-difference" of the Other is preserved. It is not through identification, but through the recognition of difference, even in death, that a semblance of responsibility can be borne for the Other.

We sometimes look back with something bordering on nostalgia even to those dark and uncertain times of war. Perhaps the fascination with the Pontigny gatherings in 1942–44, and "the incalculable, improvisational, and unpredictable" encounters, to quote Derrida, that took place then and in the correspondences and meetings that they engendered, may be best expressed by Mary Goodwin, a 1938 graduate of Mount Holyoke. She wrote in 1944,

"Unquestionably the spirit of Pontigny was one of anxious hope that the cultural individuality of nations would be preserved while the national selfishness leading to wars and the destructions of culture would be somehow put down."[5] While war was raging, students at Mount Holyoke caught a glimpse of a cosmopolitan world, a world brought to them by artists, writers, and intellectuals seeking refuge in the United States. Most of all, these sojourners sought a chance to do what they loved most: teach, write, make art, and embody a more liberal, open, and international Europe than the one either embracing Hitler or under siege by him. Similarly, one of the participants at the gatherings in the 1940s, the journalist Elizabeth Wallace, wrote of hope:

> The last day came and we felt a sadness. We had come to this Pontigny at Holyoke cautiously. We had begun gropingly. We had feared that we should not have enough to say, and when the day of parting came we had said too much. We had made friendships, there were friendships that we should have liked to make, we had glimpses of possibilities…and now it was over…no, not altogether over, for we had helped to add to the continuous pattern of life. We had realized again that thought must be forever in motion and that only in its "restless iteration" as Wallace Stevens puts it, is there hope of progress and revelation.[6]

We may have a more skeptical stance today in light of the result of so many misguided actions in the name of progress. Yet perhaps the record of so many "counter-institutional" encounters and memorable exchanges across disciplines and ideologies represented in this volume might reveal the essential necessity of trusting the "violence from within." Perhaps imagination, creativity, and conversation in dark times are not enough to carry the Noahs through the storms and toward one another. But it may create a space to hear the cries of others stranded without recourse to beauty or action, and to respond.

NOTES

1. Simone Weil and Rachel Bespaloff, *War and the Iliad* (New York: New York Review Books, 2005).

2. Homer, *The Iliad,* trans. Robert Fagles, introduction and notes by Bernard Knox (New York: Penguin, 1990), 604–5.

3. Weil and Bespaloff, *War and the Iliad,* 79, 80.

4. Ibid., 81; subsequently cited in the text.

5. *Hartford Courant,* August 17, 1944.

6. Elizabeth Wallace, *The Unending Journey* (Minneapolis: University of Minnesota Press, 1952), 270.

Contributors

BARBARA LEVIN AMSTER graduated from Mount Holyoke College in 1950 cum laude and Phi Beta Kappa. She took advanced courses at Seton Hall University and taught elementary school from 1949 to 1952 and 1970 to 1986. Her daughter, Dr. Jeanne H. Amster, is also a graduate of Mount Holyoke College and a former trustee.

CHRISTOPHER BENFEY, Mellon Professor of English at Mount Holyoke, served for four years as co-director of the Weissman Center for Leadership and the Liberal Arts. A contributor to *The New Republic*, the *New York Times Book Review*, and the *New York Review of Books*, he is the author of three books on American culture during the Gilded Age: *The Double Life of Stephen Crane, Degas in New Orleans*, and *The Great Wave*. With Karen Remmler, Benfey planned the sixtieth-anniversary celebration of Pontigny-en-Amérique, the basis for this volume.

RENEE SCIALOM CARY was born in Istanbul. Her mother was American; her father was born in Greece. From the age of seven she moved with her family across Europe, ahead of advancing Nazi occupations and the threat and spread of World War II, finally arriving in New York City (via Brazil) in early 1941, at the age of fifteen. She attended Mount Holyoke College, graduating cum laude in 1948, and served as a trustee of the college from 1993 to 1998.

STANLEY CAVELL is professor emeritus of philosophy at Harvard University, where he was the Walter M. Cabot Professor of Aesthetics in the General Theory of Value. He is the author of numerous books, including *The World Viewed, Pursuits of Happiness*, and *Cities of Words: Pedagogical Letters on the Register of the Moral Life*. In 1992 Cavell received the MacArthur Foundation "Genius Award."

MARY ANN CAWS is Distinguished Professor of Comparative Literature, English, and French at the Graduate School of the City University of New York. Her many areas of interest in twentieth-century avant-garde literature and art include Surrealism, the poets René Char and André Breton, Virginia Woolf and the Bloomsbury group, and the artists Robert Motherwell and Joseph Cornell.

ALYSSA DANIGELIS is a journalist whose feature writing has appeared in the *Burlington (Vermont) Free Press*, the *Valley Advocate*, and MIT's alumni magazine, *Technology Review*. She graduated from Mount Holyoke College in 2001 and has a master of science degree from Columbia University's Graduate School of Journalism.

JACQUES DERRIDA, the author of over fifty books on philosophy, literature, the arts, Marxism, human rights, and many other subjects, died in 2004. At the time of his death he held a distinguished professorship at the University of California, Irvine, and had served as professor of philosophy and directeur d'études at the École des hautes études en sciences sociales in Paris.

ELISSA GELFAND is professor of French at Mount Holyoke College. She is the author of *Imagination in Confinement: Women's Writings from French Prisons* and *French Feminist Criticism: Women, Language, and Literature* (with Virginia Thorndike Hules). She is working on representations of aging women in French fiction.

ROMY GOLAN is associate professor of twentieth-century European art and theory at the Graduate Center, City University of New York. She is the author of *Modernity and Nostalgia: Art and Politics in France between the Wars* and co-author of *The Circle of Montparnasse: Jewish Artists in Paris, 1905–1945.* Her forthcoming book is titled "Muralnomad: The Mural Effect in European Art, 1927–57."

LEAH D. HEWITT is professor of French at Amherst College. She is the author of *Autobiographical Tightropes* and is currently finishing a book titled "Marianne on Screen: Ambiguous Representations of World War II France."

LAURENT JEANPIERRE is a sociologist and historian at the Centre d'étude des discours, images, textes, écrits, communications at the Université Paris XII Val de Marne, France. He works on intellectual migrations in the twentieth century and has written a dissertation on French intellectual exiles in the United States. His article "Occult Encounters and 'Structural Misunderstanding' in the United States" appeared in *Exile, Science, and Bildung: The Contested Legacies of German Intellectual Émigrés.*

MONIQUE JUTRIN teaches French literature at Tel Aviv University and is the founder of the Benjamin Fondane Society. She is the editor of the correspondence between Jean Wahl and Rachel Bespaloff and is currently editing Rachel Bespaloff's works in France.

JEROME KOHN is the director of the Hannah Arendt Center in New York City and a trustee of the Hannah Arendt Bluecher Literary Trust. His edition of *Responsibility and Judgment* was published in 2003; his edition of *The Promise of Politics,* and a new edition of his *Essays in Understanding,* appeared in 2005. All of these volumes comprise unpublished and uncollected essays and lectures by Hannah Arendt. Kohn writes frequently on other topics for *Raritan* magazine.

ANDREW LASS, who divides his time between western Massachusetts and the Czech and Slovak Republics, teaches courses on contemporary anthropological theory, linguistics, science and technology, and the culture of memory. His research interests include the social construction of historical consciousness, print culture, and the cross-overs between linguistics, anthropology, and avant-garde art.

Naomi Bespaloff Levinson graduated from Mount Holyoke College in 1948 and from Radcliffe in 1949 with an M.A. in comparative literature. She taught English in the New York City school system from 1960 to 2003 with a focus on the teaching of writing. Excerpts from her novel *Les chevaux de bois d'Amérique,* with an introduction by Jean Wahl in 1955, appeared in English translation in *New Directions* in 1957.

Nadia Margolis, an independent scholar, received her training in French and medieval studies at Stanford and the universities of Dijon and Paris. Her scholarly publications focus primarily on Christine de Pizan and Joan of Arc. She co-edited and co-authored *Women in the Middle Ages: An Encyclopedia* and is preparing a new edition and a translation of Christine de Pizan's biography of King Charles.

Jeffrey Mehlman is University Professor and Professor of French and Comparative Literature at Boston University. He is the author of *Walter Benjamin for Children: An Essay on His Radio Years, Genealogies of the Text,* and *Émigré New York: French Intellectuals in Wartime Manhattan, 1940–1944.*

Donal O'Shea is a mathematician who has taught at Mount Holyoke since 1980, where he has served as the dean of faculty since 1998. Much of his scholarly work has centered on the geometry of complex singularities, work that mixes differential, hyperbolic, and algebraic geometry. He is currently working on papers on polynomial knots, detection of colon tumors, and the history of the Poincaré conjecture. He maintains a strong interest in mathematical physics and is considered an authority on computational methods in algebraic geometry.

Claire Paulhan, granddaughter of the writer and editor Jean Paulhan, is herself an editor specializing in twentieth-century autobiographical literature. With Edith Heurgon, she co-directed the colloquium on the century-long history of Pontigny and Cerisy, held at the Centre culturel international de Cerisy in August 2002.

Jed Perl has been covering the contemporary art scene for *The New Republic* since 1994. His work has appeared in *Salmagundi,* the *Partisan Review,* the *Threepenny Review,* the *Yale Review,* the *New York Times Book Review,* and *Elle.* He is the author of *Eyewitness: Reports from an Art World in Crisis, Paris without End: On French Art since World War I, Gallery Going: Four Seasons in the Art World,* and *New Art City.*

Karen Remmler, professor of German studies at Mount Holyoke College, served for five years as the co-director of the Weissman Center for Leadership and the Liberal Arts. She has published on Jewish culture and writing in Germany, on sites of memory, on remembrance in the work of Ingeborg Bachmann and Walter Benjamin, and on the culture of memory in post-Wall Berlin and Germany in the work of W. G. Sebald and Ruth Beckermann. With Christopher Benfey, she planned the sixtieth-anniversary celebration of Pontigny-en-Amérique, the basis for this volume.

OLIVIER SALAZAR-FERRER is professor of French literature at the Alliance Française in Glasgow. He is the author of *Benjamin Fondane* and *Le temps: la perception, l'espace, la mémoire* and is a contributor to numerous collections and journals. His focus is on the poetry of the avant-garde of the 1930s and on such poets as Emily Dickinson, Joseph Brodsky, and Louis Calaferte.

HELEN SOLTERER is professor of French at Duke University with a teaching focus on medieval and early modern vernacular culture. She has published *The Master and Minerva: Disputing Women in French Medieval Culture,* which won the MLA Scaglione Prize. She continues to write on questions of verbal violence in "Flaming Words" *(Romanic Review,* 1995) and "States of Siege" *(New Medieval Literatures,* 1998). Her current book project, *Playing the Dead,* explores the question of revivalism.

HOLGER TESCHKE is a writer, freelance journalist, and former director and dramaturge at the Berliner Ensemble in Germany. His directs productions and teaches theater workshops and courses in North America and has been a guest artist at Mount Holyoke College, Notre Dame University, New York University, and other universities in Australia, Hong Kong, and Germany.

ELISABETH YOUNG-BRUEHL, a practicing psychoanalyst in New York City, is on the faculty of the Columbia Center for Psychoanalytic Training and Research. She is the author of a biography of Hannah Arendt, reissued in 2004 with a new preface. She has also written a biography of Anna Freud and a number of other books, including *Creative Characters, The Anatomy of Prejudices, Cherishment* (with Faith Bethelard), and three collections of essays.

Index

Page numbers in italics refer to illustrations.